When I heard that Giles was writing a book on a shared  chance to read it and further fire up my passion for Busin

T0248455

In many respects, Agile and Business Agility are often m still, misused. This often leads to a poor representation of a mindset that could serve businesses and their people in so many ways. In this context, I love that Giles has written this informative book for those curious about Business Agility.

This quote from the book resonated with me and hopefully inspires someone to pick up the book and start their journey into the rewarding world of Business Agility through the lens of Giles' CLEAR Model®:

> Just as the world constantly evolves, so must the Agile Manifesto. We must look at it not as an unchanging scripture but as a living document that adapts to modern business needs. The future of business agility lies in its ability to evolve and grow with the ever-changing business world.

Amen to that!

T. C. Gill,
Transformation Lead and People Development Coach

Clearly Agile is the definitive guide for leaders navigating the ever-evolving business landscape. With deep insights and actionable advice, it demystifies the principles of business agility, providing a clear roadmap for those seeking to drive innovation and adaptability in their organizations. Giles, a seasoned tech executive and eminent business agility coach, has authored a must-read for anyone committed to future-proofing their leadership skills.

Neil A. Walker, Business Agility Specialist,
BJSS Consulting, with 32 years of championing agile and agility

Giles is well known as an excellent executive and agile coach. I am very pleased that he has shared his comprehensive knowledge in this excellent book. It covers a wide spectrum of guidance on business agility and is definitely worth a read.

Mark Lines,
Co-creator of Disciplined Agile

In *Clearly Agile*, Giles connects the dots of agility, guiding readers from the importance of leadership and mindset to team and enterprise agility. This book serves as a crucial bridge, guiding organizations from current Agile practices to future-ready business agility. Filled with case studies, actionable insights and thought-provoking questions, this book will leave you with actionable strategies to improve how your organization works – no matter what the future brings.

Laura M. Powers,
Chief Executive Officer, Business Agility Institute

Giles' deep experience, and ability to share that wisdom, shines throughout *Clearly Agile*. Any leader who is hoping to evolve their organization into an agile enterprise will discover actionable and impactful insights in this book.

Scott Ambler, Co-creator, PMI's Disciplined Agile Toolkit;
Thought Leader, Agile Data and Agile Modeling Methods

Embark on a transformative journey with *Clearly Agile* as Giles blends reflection and practical insights. As a seasoned leader in digital transformation, Giles delves into the dynamics of change, demonstrating empathy for all within the business. Beyond the mechanics of processes and methodologies, *Clearly Agile* underlines the truth – it's about the people. Giles describes creating an environment where colleagues not only deliver value but also feel valued. This book guides agile leaders to foster collaboration, navigate transformational conflict, and create a workplace where cooperation becomes the norm.

A compelling read that invites you to explore the heart of agile leadership and discover the impact it can have on both your team and the entire system of work.

Anneke Panman,
Director of Coaching, Agile Delta Consulting

Business Agility is well evidenced as a major business trend which Giles clearly demonstrates with the value to be gained thoroughly exampled. Not surprisingly there are increasing sources of material on the subject, and the better ones not only get business agility right but explain what it comprises and how to achieve it. This book does so with completeness and clarity while being very accessible. What makes this book stand out for me are three things. Firstly, the clarity Giles brings to the nature of business agility and what it looks like. Secondly, the move to business agility is far from trivial. It is not and cannot be a modification of business operations but a Transformation. While this second idea is enough to scare the life out of any Board member. Giles makes it clear not just what the risks of Transformation are but also the risks to the future of a business that fails to adopt business agility. Then provides a thorough picture of the transformation journey with an excellent focus on leadership. One truly key point made is that the leadership towards business agility starts at the top, which I concur with as I have never seen organizational business agility achieved, let alone sustained, when built from the bottom-up, as some suggest. Thirdly, there are useful tools embedded along the way, such as learning aids and reflection prompts. In addition, any really good business book must have broad applicability. As an author on project agility, I understand the need for examples and case studies from various sectors, and so does Giles. I heartily recommend this book and know it will become key reference material for my own work on Business Agility.

Adrian Pyne, Author of Agile Beyond IT

CLEARLY AGILE

A LEADERSHIP GUIDE TO BUSINESS AGILITY

GILES LINDSAY

First published in Great Britain by Practical Inspiration Publishing, 2024

© Giles Lindsay – Agile Delta Consulting Limited, 2024

The moral rights of the author have been asserted

ISBN   9781788605472   (hardcover)
        9781788605489   (paperback)
        9781788605502   (epub)
        9781788605496   (mobi)

Want to bulk-buy copies of this book for your team and colleagues? We can customize the content and co-brand *Clearly Agile* to suit your business's needs.

Please email info@practicalinspiration.com for more details.

To my wife, Anneke, who has always been my source of inspiration and support. Thank you for believing in me and encouraging me every step of the way. This book is dedicated to you with all my love and gratitude.

In our fast-changing world, business agility is the compass that guides organizations through uncharted territory, transforming challenges into opportunities for growth and innovation.

Table of Contents

Foreword

Outside of international events, not many meetings make a difference to the world. Only one British person and zero women signed the Agile Manifesto in 2001, so it was far from diverse, yet thousands worldwide celebrated its twentieth anniversary in February 2021. We celebrated because the Agile Manifesto transformed how software is developed, and firms now see Agile as a way to transform their organizational effectiveness.

The Manifesto for Software Development can be seen as an engineering solution to an engineer's problem, or at least to a problem that exists from the engineer's perspective. The clue is in the opening words, "We are uncovering better ways of developing software by doing it and helping others do it." Agile was a reaction to how software projects were managed in large companies. It represented the collective experience of many people involved with software and software development methods, distilled into four values and 12 principles.

How did the Agile Manifesto transform software development and overall business agility? Did it take control away from project managers, replace Waterfall methodology, or eradicate bureaucracy from the Unified Process? No, it did none of those things. It asserted that technology was an engineering discipline and that engineers were most effective when they self-organized to understand problems and develop solutions. Despite the questionable name, it was a manifesto for software development. Development teams that organized themselves around its principles, including those that adopted XP and Scrum methods, impressed stakeholders by quickly delivering valuable and usable features.

But with no equivalent management update to explain the difference between managing traditional activities and Agile work, leaders and managers have been left to work things out for themselves. This lack of guidance has created new conflicts as some managers "have an Agile mindset", and others are seen to "not get it". Agile methods amplify problems in firms' operating models, such as treating technology departments as internal suppliers rather than business colleagues. Senior managers must lead the organization through these newly exposed tensions. Leaders must find the balance between continuing to get value from existing processes whilst exploring the uncertain world of Agile work.

In this book, Giles uses his extensive executive and technical experience to directly address everything executives and senior managers need to know about business agility. He does so in appropriate language, not the tech talk that often clouds the answer to a simple question. Summing up Agile execution, for instance, "Agile requires a different discipline, one centred on adaptability and iterative progress."

My most memorable "a-ha" moment in this book came when reading about scaling Agile. Whilst it is usually easy to adopt Agile practices and massively improve the performance of single teams, it is much more challenging to coordinate teams across a whole organization because Agile is appropriate in places but not everywhere. Thus, team managers must understand when teams need to be self-organizing and use Agile planning methods and when teams need a project plan. Portfolio managers must understand how and when different pieces of work will come together, and executives must keep everyone focused on short- and medium-term priorities. In other words, Agile at Scale is complex, with many people adapting to many new and moving parts.

In the chapter on scaling Agile, Giles says structure, customer involvement, technical and business agility metrics, portfolio and risk management, and culture are all needed to scale Agile because each one is an obstacle to agility. This is certainly true and made me think: if it could address these points so that the organization was flatter, more collaborative, made evidence-based decisions, and practised "inspect and adapt" process improvement at all levels, then surely it would be an Agile organization? It would operate more like Google or Amazon, and nobody would be talking about adopting or scaling Agile. If that were the case, a transformation would have already occurred. This is the outcome of Agile transformation, a leadership vision for the organization.

I also really liked his idea of "descaling the organization". Not removing limescale build-up but "simplifying structures and processes, eliminating bureaucratic obstacles, and promoting lean principles". These seem to me to be commendable objectives for a leader to set, perhaps supported by specific measures (or key results if using Objectives and Key Results) such as reducing onboarding time, limiting work in progress, or working towards zero defects.

Giles is bold, with whole chapters on "Embracing an Agile Mindset" and "Building an Agile Culture". I try to avoid these phrases when I encounter them because they are so subjective, but not Giles. His book dares to go where others fear to tread. While I agree with most things, it offers so many viewpoints that there is always something new for me to discover.

I sincerely hope it offers you insights and food for thought, and I wish you a CLEAR and Agile journey.

Russ Lewis
Digital transformation specialist and author of
An Operating Model for Business Agility

Preface

In this book, I examine how your organization can evolve to meet the demands of our fast-changing business world, with a specific focus on navigating the technological and industry transformations characterizing the current Fourth Industrial Revolution. This era is marked by disruptive technologies and trends, such as the Internet of Things (IoT), robotics, Machine Learning (ML) and Artificial Intelligence (AI). These advancements are reshaping how we live, work, and conduct business. Throughout the book, I offer strategies to deliver value to your customers more effectively, ensuring you remain a front-runner in this evolving domain. I passionately believe in the transformative power of Agile, and I want to share that passion with you so your organization can truly excel.

Unlike its predecessors, this revolution is unfolding exponentially, blurring the lines between the physical, digital and biological spheres. It's not just an extension of the digital revolution but a distinct, sweeping transformation affecting nearly every industry globally. As it disrupts production, management, and governance systems, the Fourth Industrial Revolution calls for an integrated and comprehensive response, something that business agility is perfectly suited to provide.

I wrote this book specifically for business leaders seeking ways to navigate the complexities of this revolution, focusing on adopting an Agile mindset and attitude, implementing Agile approaches, leading teams effectively, planning and executing strategies, and scaling operations successfully. I offer these approaches not just because I believe in them but because I have seen the remarkable changes they can ignite. I want you to be armed with these powerful tools to lead your organization toward a future of unbounded potential.

This book explains how to build an Agile culture that values and supports business agility in its truest form, which spans far beyond mere Agile transformation. It's about taking a holistic approach to your organization's evolution, ensuring you're equipped to navigate both the nuances of Agile practices and the broader challenges of modern business adaptability. I guide you in developing and managing Agile teams and in planning and executing Agile methodologies. The book also sheds light on the common challenges organizations face when adopting business agility and provides insights on overcoming them. I want you to feel empowered, not overwhelmed, by these challenges.

But this book is not just about theory; it includes practical tips, real-world examples, and case studies to help you apply Agile practices to your organization. It explores emerging trends and technologies that will impact business agility in the future so that you can stay ahead of the competition. I want to equip you with the knowledge and foresight to confidently navigate the uncharted waters of the future.

By the time you finish reading my book, you will be equipped with the essential tools and strategies to lead the Agile transformation within your organization and embrace the wider scope of business agility. You will know how to deliver value to your customers more effectively and build an organization that is agile in the truest sense, one that can adapt and thrive in a changing business environment. My aim for you, the reader, is to gain a sense of mastery over these Agile practices and a readiness to face and shape the future, along with the thrill of leading a vibrant, agile organization.

So why should you choose my book over others? Because it is written specifically for business leaders who want to improve their organization's agility and responsiveness, with a deep understanding of the difference between "Agile" and "Agile Business". It is easy to read, practical and full of real-world examples. I want this for you because you can lead, innovate and inspire. This is not just a book; it is a catalyst for change.

Start building a more agile and responsive organization grounded in both Agile practices and a comprehensive understanding of business agility in the modern world. Your journey towards business agility begins here, and I am excited to join you on this transformative journey. Let's create an unstoppable momentum together!

Giles Lindsay FIAP FBCS FCMI
CEO, Agile Delta Consulting Limited

Mastering Agility with the CLEAR Model®

A Comprehensive Framework for Agile Excellence

The CLEAR Model®, used throughout the book, represents a comprehensive framework guiding organizations' Agile transformation journey. It stands for **Culture, Leadership, Execution, Adaptability, and Responsiveness**. These five principles intertwine to create a robust framework that empowers organizations to excel in dynamic business environments.

Historical Context and Evolution

The CLEAR Model® was developed in response to a growing need for a holistic approach to Agile transformation. Born out of years of Agile practice and refinement, it addresses gaps in traditional Agile methodologies and frameworks by providing a more comprehensive approach that aligns with broader business objectives.

Purpose and Relevance of the CLEAR Model®

The CLEAR Model® is our answer to the complexities of modern business operations. It offers a structured yet flexible framework that helps organizations navigate and thrive amid constant change. This model is particularly pertinent for businesses integrating agility into their core operations and strategy.

Adaptability and Integration with Existing Practices

Today's business world is dynamic, requiring organizations to be highly adaptable. The CLEAR Model® enhances this by fitting smoothly with current practices. This approach empowers organizations to swiftly adjust to new market demands and customer insights while preserving the essential stability of their core operations.

Application within an Organization

1. Culture

- **Definition** – Establishing a workplace environment that embraces Agile values, fostering collaboration, innovation, and continuous improvement.
- **Application** – Develop an organizational culture that supports Agile ways of working. This development involves creating policies, practices, and an environment conducive to open communication, collaboration, and flexibility. Encourage a mindset of continuous learning and improvement among all employees.

2. Leadership

- **Definition** – Agile leaders are not just managers but visionaries who guide, inspire, and nurture an Agile mindset throughout the organization.
- **Application** – Train leaders and managers in Agile principles and leadership styles that promote autonomy, empowerment, and collaboration. Leaders should act as role models in embracing Agile practices and driving the Agile transformation process.

3. Execution

- **Definition** – The practical application of Agile ways of working in day-to-day operations, ensuring effective and efficient task completion.
- **Application** – Implement Agile frameworks in project management and operational processes. Focus on delivering value through iterative development, regular feedback, and continuous improvement.

4. Adaptability

- **Definition** – The ability of an organization to quickly adjust to changes in the external and internal environment.
- **Application** – Foster a culture of adaptability where teams are encouraged to experiment and learn from their experiences. Implement processes that allow for quick pivots and adjustments in strategies or operations in response to changing market conditions or customer feedback.

5. Responsiveness

- **Definition** – The capacity to react swiftly and effectively to customer needs, market changes, and internal demands.
- **Application** – Develop mechanisms to gather customer feedback and market intelligence rapidly. Ensure that the organization's structure and processes allow quick decision-making and implementation.

Using the CLEAR Model®

1. **Assessment** – Begin by assessing the current state of your organization in relation to the five CLEAR principles. Identify areas of strength and those that can be improved.

2. **Strategy Development** – Based on the assessment, develop a strategic plan addressing gaps and leveraging strengths. The plan should include specific goals and actions related to each CLEAR principle.

3. **Implementation** – Roll out the strategy across the organization. The implementation process may involve training, restructuring teams, implementing new processes, and changing leadership practices.

4. **Monitoring and Adjustment** – Continuously monitor the effectiveness of the implementation and make adjustments as needed. Such monitoring should include regular feedback loops and retrospectives, which are essential to ensure that the organization remains aligned with the CLEAR principles.

5. **Integration** – Make the CLEAR Model® an integral part of the organizational DNA. It should not be a one-time project but an ongoing approach that permeates all aspects of the organization.

Looking Forward

In summary, the CLEAR Model® offers a holistic approach to adopting and sustaining Agile ways of working in an organization. By focusing on Culture, Leadership, Execution, Adaptability, and Responsiveness, organizations can ensure a successful Agile transformation that is sustainable and effective in the long term.

Adopting the CLEAR Model® in an organization goes beyond mere methodology; it is about embedding a culture of agility, responsiveness, and continuous improvement. Each model principle aligns closely with the challenges and needs of modern businesses, providing a comprehensive roadmap for Agile transformation.

As we explore each principle in depth throughout this book, readers will gain a clearer understanding of how to navigate their organizations' journey towards true business agility.

Introduction

Simply put, businesses that don't adapt are destined to fail.

Picture a global brand, a leader in its field for years, but with time it becomes complacent. Suddenly, an unexpected rival emerges, delivering unique value by tapping into the very pulse of today's consumer. This isn't a plotline from a business thriller but a reality many organizations confront today.

Moving to a distinct example, Wilko has graced British high streets for over nine decades, establishing itself as a beloved, family-run business. Yet, even such long-standing institutions are not immune to the relentless currents of change. On a fateful Thursday in August 2023, the firm faced the bleak reality of going into administration, putting approximately 12,500 jobs in jeopardy. The immediate causes? Inflationary pressures, supply-chain challenges and the omnipresent burden of evolving consumer behaviours.

But was this demise inevitable? Nadine Houghton, a national officer at the GMB union, presented a different narrative. She poignantly remarked that the unfortunate fate of Wilko was, in truth, "entirely avoidable". The tragedy lay not in the company's external challenges but in its complacency and lack of adaptability. Despite repeated warnings, Wilko, nestled comfortably in its established business model, missed the golden chance to harness the burgeoning bargain retailer market. A glaring example of a company's inability to evolve with the times, the downfall is a potent reminder: adaptability isn't just an asset in business. It's a necessity.

Internal complacency and a failure to recognize and adapt to evolving market conditions can harm organizations. Rapid adaptation to shifting market dynamics and customer expectations is essential for sustained success. However, beyond these internal challenges, organizations must also become agile to ensure their rivals do not overtake them, given the ever-present external competition they face.

Initially created for software development, Agile practices have become a cornerstone for business adaptability across many global sectors, proving their worth in fostering resilience against both external threats and internal stagnation.

Reflect for a moment on your business journey so far. Think of a scenario in which market fluctuations aren't threats but exciting challenges, invitations to innovate and outshine. With a foundation rooted in agility, this can be more than imagination – it can be your business reality.

Clearly Agile is more than a book; it's a guide for leaders who have never led Agile change before but who are ready to embrace it and lead with agility. If you want to set the pace in the marketplace and adapt confidently, this book is for you.

In this book, we discuss methods for evaluating and expanding business agility, addressing common challenges and preparing for the future of Agile business. This book provides practical insights and actionable strategies to support leaders in driving organizational transformation and achieving enduring success.

It is important to note what this book does not encompass. It does not aim to be a comprehensive guide on implementing a specific Agile approach, nor must it replace professional Agile consulting services. This book includes valuable insights and real-life examples but is not a one-size-fits-all solution or framework to follow for every organization.

Instead, this book offers a step-by-step approach to understanding business agility along with the supporting "CLEAR Model®" and its principles of Culture, Leadership, Execution, Adaptability and Responsiveness, which are introduced in Chapter 1. This will equip readers with the skills and knowledge they need to adapt and thrive in our modern business environment.

What is This Book Trying to Solve?

The business world is fraught with relentless challenges, such as rapid technological innovations, unstable market conditions and growing customer expectations. Traditional frameworks, techniques and management approaches often need help to address these challenges.

Understanding the Complexities of Modern Business

This book addresses the pivotal challenge of equipping organizations to be agile, enabling them to overcome obstacles and thrive in their fiercely competitive market. The book dissects today's organizational challenges, from rapid decision-making and global market dynamics to digital transformation and evolving consumer needs.

Recognizing the Limitations of Traditional Management Approaches

Many organizations rely on traditional, top-down management structures and linear processes that need help to adapt to change. This book highlights the limitations of conventional management approaches and illustrates the need for increased adaptability, responsiveness and agility.

Transitioning from Traditional to Agile Approaches

Traditional management structures are not without value. They have proven their effectiveness repeatedly in more stable circumstances. Yet, faced with modern Volatility, Uncertainty, Complexity and Ambiguity (VUCA), these established structures may find themselves hard-pressed to respond with the requisite agility. While they need to keep certain functional aspects, there is room for improvement and a pressing need to upgrade and adapt these traditional frameworks to thrive in our modern, evolving business world.

This book introduces Agile approaches, demonstrating how they can offer a more flexible, customer-centric and collaborative approach to problem-solving. The book aims to facilitate the shift from conventional management approaches to increased adaptability by exploring the advantages of Agile processes and practices.

Creating a Foundation for Agile Transformation

To successfully transition to Agile, organizations must internalize their core tenets – teamwork, flexibility, openness and ongoing refinement. The book guides readers on creating an Agile mindset and fostering a conducive environment within their organizations by emphasizing the importance of these principles.

What Solution is the Book Offering?

The book offers a holistic solution: fortifying business resilience through Agile ways of working. Organizations can become increasingly adaptive, responsive and agile, ensuring their continued success when they adopt Agile principles. The following highlights the book's specific solutions to help organizations achieve business agility.

Embracing an Agile Mindset

The first step towards business agility involves appreciating the emergence of an Agile mindset as an individual's emerging worldview, shaped by outside events and experiences. While mindset remains individualistic, the book also delves into cultivating an attitude, a collective feeling or opinion that values adaptability, collaboration, customer-centricity and continuous improvement. Recognizing the nuances between an evolving mindset and a shared attitude allows organizations to transition from rigid, hierarchical structures to more agile and responsive models, better equipped to address today's business challenges.

Adopting Agile Approaches

By adopting Agile, organizations can refine operational processes and pivot more effortlessly to customer needs. This book delves into specific frameworks and methodologies, such as Scrum, Kanban and Lean, summarizing their principles and practices. While Scrum provides a framework focusing on iterative progress through team collaboration, Kanban emphasizes continuous flow and efficiency and Lean prioritizes eliminating waste to improve overall value. For a more detailed explanation of these approaches, please see Chapter 3. Understanding these frameworks and methodologies empowers organizations to select the most suitable approach for their needs and challenges.

Creating High-Performing Agile Teams

A critical component of business agility is the formation of high-performing Agile teams. The book offers practical recommendations on assembling cross-functional, self-organizing teams capable of swiftly adapting to new challenges and opportunities. This includes advice on team composition, roles, responsibilities and techniques for promoting a collaborative and transparent working environment.

Efficient Agile Planning

Efficient planning is indispensable for the success of Agile organizations. The book imparts insights into Agile planning techniques, such as iterative and incremental planning, and strategies for managing work in progress and prioritizing tasks based on customer value. Organizations can remain focused on delivering value to their customers while preserving the flexibility to respond to fluctuating market conditions when they adopt these practices.

Developing Agile Leadership

Agile leadership is crucial in driving organizational transformation and fostering a culture of agility. The book investigates the characteristics of successful Agile leaders, emphasizing the importance of servant leadership, continuous learning and adaptability. Servant Leadership is a leadership philosophy where the leader's main goal is to serve. It focuses on the growth and well-being of people and the communities to which they belong rather than the leaders' accumulation of power and authority by the leaders themselves. In an Agile context, this means facilitating team collaboration and enabling others to perform their roles effectively. The book enables readers to instigate change within their organizations and champion adopting Agile practices by offering guidance on nurturing Agile leadership skills.

Assessing and Scaling Agile Practices

Organizations must evaluate their impact and effectiveness to ensure the ongoing success of Agile endeavours. The book introduces various metrics and tools for assessing business agility and shares strategies for scaling Agile practices across the organization, ensuring that organizations consistently enhance their performance and adaptability by providing readers with the knowledge and tools to measure and scale their Agile efforts.

Preparing for Emerging Trends and Technologies

The book also sheds light on emerging trends and technologies that could influence business agility in the future. The book equips readers to stay ahead of the curve and prepare their organizations for the challenges and opportunities these advancements may present by examining cutting-edge developments, such as Artificial Intelligence, Machine Learning and automation.

The book offers a comprehensive solution for organizations aiming to achieve business agility by adopting Agile approaches and practices. Organizations can evolve into nimble, responsive powerhouses capable of flourishing in our rapidly changing business environment when they cultivate an Agile mindset, implement Agile approaches, form high-performing teams, ensure effective planning and execution, develop Agile leadership and continuously measure and scale Agile practices.

What is the Urgency?

With swift technological advancements, shifting customer preferences and escalating global competition characterizing the current business world, the demand for business agility has reached unprecedented urgency. The following underscores the pressing need for organizations to embrace Agile approaches and practices. It's essential to learn from the past. Historically, firms that haven't adapted proactively no longer exist. They were overtaken by challenger businesses, often initially viewed as no threat, that evolved more rapidly than anticipated. Think of Blockbuster, of Kodak; such examples highlight the peril of complacency. Now, it's a matter of thinking: who is next? This stark reality illustrates why transformation is vital for survival and expansion in an increasingly complex and competitive commercial world.

Accelerating Pace of Change

The pace at which technological advancements and market conditions evolve is faster than ever. Companies that do not keep up risk falling behind their competition, which can lead to a loss of market share and the possibility of becoming obsolete. Embracing Agile practices allows organizations to navigate the complexities of constant change more adeptly and seize new opportunities while tackling challenges with greater agility.

Rising Customer Expectations

Today's customers, equipped with a wealth of information and options, demand higher standards for product quality, personalization and speed of delivery. Organizations must meet these expectations to retain customers to more agile rivals. Embracing Agile approaches empowers organizations to become more customer-centric, ensuring efficient delivery of value to their customers.

Increased Global Competition

As the world becomes increasingly interconnected, organizations face competition from businesses worldwide. To remain competitive, companies must adapt to new market realities, including shifting regulations, volatile exchange rates and emerging competitors. Implementing Agile practices helps organizations become more flexible, allowing them to better compete in the global marketplace.

Growing Complexity of Products and Services

As technology progresses, products and services grow more complex. Organizations must manage and support increasingly intricate processes and systems. Agile approaches enable organizations to break down complex projects into manageable iterations by promoting collaboration and empowering teams to address problems more effectively.

The Need for Innovation

Innovation is a crucial driver of growth and success. Organizations that cannot innovate risk stagnation and decline. Agile practices encourage experimentation and continuous improvement, allowing organizations to test new ideas and adapt to market changes.

Talent Attraction and Retention

With the growing demand for skilled professionals, attracting and keeping top talent has become increasingly important for organizations. An agile, collaborative and empowered culture appeals to high-performing individuals seeking personal and professional growth opportunities. Organizations can cultivate an environment that promotes learning, development and engagement, making them more attractive to top talent when they adopt Agile practices.

Evolving Workplace Dynamics

The rise of remote work, flexible schedules and geographically dispersed teams require organizations to adapt to new ways of working. Agile approaches support these modern workplace dynamics by emphasizing effective communication, collaboration and adaptability, ensuring organizations thrive in changing work environments.

In summary, organizations must implement Agile practices to address rapid changes, rising customer expectations, increased global competition, complex products and services, the drive for innovation, personnel recruitment and retention, and shifting work dynamics. Through adopting Agile transformation, organizations can become more adaptable, responsive and resilient, positioning themselves for long-term success.

How is This Book Organized?

Across 12 comprehensive chapters divided into five parts, the text offers insights into various facets of building an Agile organization. Each chapter is aligned with one or more principles of the CLEAR Model®, allowing you to delve deeper into specific aspects of the principles.

> Whether diving into the book from the beginning or selecting specific chapters, *Clearly Agile* offers a unique structure where each chapter stands on its own yet seamlessly connects with the others, ensuring you receive comprehensive guidance on the path to business agility, tailored to your immediate needs.

Part 1: Understanding Business Agility

Embark on your Agile journey by exploring the basics of Responsiveness and Adaptability. This section unveils why businesses must be agile today and introduces you to the mindset that fuels Agile transformations. It guides you through popular Agile approaches, helping you select the right fit for your organization.

Chapter 1: The Need for Business Agility (Responsiveness, Adaptability)

In this chapter, we introduce the concept of business agility, unravelling its importance for organizations navigating the intricacies of an ever-evolving market. We explore how the ability to respond swiftly and adapt effectively to change is a compelling reason for embracing business agility. This agility enables organizations to deliver value to customers more effectively and maintain a competitive edge.

Chapter 2: Embracing an Agile Mindset (Culture, Adaptability)

This chapter delves into the Agile mindset, explaining why fostering an Agile culture encourages adaptability and resilience in the face of change. It is critical to building an Agile organization. We explore the principles and values underpinning Agile thinking and discuss how to nurture an environment conducive to Agile transformation.

Chapter 3: Agile Approaches (Execution, Responsiveness)

In this chapter, we introduce various Agile frameworks and methodologies, such as Scrum, Kanban and Lean. We provide an overview of their roles in effective execution and prompt responses to shifting circumstances, demonstrating how these approaches can suit your organization's specific needs and requirements.

Part 2: Leadership and Culture in Agile Business

Witness the Agile revolution in Leadership and Culture. This section illustrates how the right leadership approach and a conducive cultural environment form the backbone of business agility, guiding your organization to thrive in an ever-evolving market.

Chapter 4: Leadership in Business Agility (Leadership)

This chapter underscores the pivotal role of Agile leaders in driving Agile transformation. It discusses the importance of Agile leadership and the qualities that define an effective leader. Also, we provide strategies for cultivating Agile leaders within your organization, leaders who can guide the successful transformation of your business.

Chapter 5: Building an Agile Culture (Culture)

In this chapter, we explore the role of a supportive, Agile-centric culture in ensuring the success of Agile business adoption. We delve into the importance of establishing a culture that values and supports business agility. We discuss key aspects, such as communication, transparency, empowerment and strategies for nurturing an Agile culture within your organization.

Part 3: Building and Managing Agile Teams

Dive into the dynamics of Agile teams. This part unravels the secrets of building and managing effective Agile teams, drawing on the CLEAR principles of Culture and Leadership, equipping you with the knowledge to create collaborative, innovative, high-performing units that drive success.

Chapter 6: Building and Managing Agile Teams (Culture, Leadership)

In this chapter, we explore how a robust Agile culture and effective leadership serve as catalysts in forming exceptional Agile teams. We delve into the dynamics of building and managing Agile teams, exploring team composition, structure and performance. We also provide strategies for creating high-performing Agile teams within your organization.

Part 4: The Agile Process

Navigate the day-to-day intricacies of Agile operations through the lens of Execution and Responsiveness. This section details the journey from planning to execution and measurement in an Agile environment, culminating with insights on how to scale Agile practices across your organization for maximum impact.

Chapter 7: Agile Planning (Leadership, Execution)

In this chapter, we discuss the role of Agile leaders in aligning planning with Agile objectives. Agile planning enables the efficient transformation of strategic goals into actionable tasks, and we summarize this process. We explore essential concepts like product backlogs, sprint planning, release planning and strategies for effective Agile planning within your organization.

Chapter 8: Agile Execution (Execution, Responsiveness)

This chapter illuminates the essence of Agile execution in achieving efficient work delivery. We discuss executing Agile approaches effectively and how a rapid response to change fortifies this execution. Fundamental practices, such as sprint planning, daily stand-ups, sprint reviews and retrospectives, are covered. Also, we provide strategies for achieving effective Agile execution within your organization.

Chapter 9: Measuring Business Agility (Execution, Responsiveness)

This chapter delves into how effective execution is essential for accurately measuring agility and how responsive adjustments keep the business on track with Agile transformation. We explore how to measure the effectiveness of business agility in your organization, discussing critical metrics like cycle time, lead time and customer satisfaction. Strategies for measuring and improving business agility within your organization are also provided.

Chapter 10: Scaling Business Agility (Leadership, Execution)

In this chapter, we explore the importance of Leadership in driving Agile at Scale and how execution comes into play to ensure a consistent approach. We discuss how to scale business agility across the entire organization, exploring vital aspects such as portfolio management, programme management and organizational structure. Strategies for effectively scaling business agility within your organization are offered.

Part 5: Overcoming Challenges and Looking Forward

Prepare to conquer Agile challenges and anticipate the future of Agile. This section presents a candid discussion on potential hurdles in Agile adoption and equips you with strategies to overcome them, reflecting all CLEAR principles in a balanced manner. It concludes with a forward-looking perspective on the changing world of business agility.

Chapter 11: Overcoming Challenges in Agile Adoption (Culture, Leadership, Execution, Adaptability, Responsiveness)

In this chapter, we reflect upon all CLEAR principles, specifically how each principle helps address and surmount the various obstacles encountered during the Agile transformation journey. We explore the common challenges organizations face when adopting business agility and provide strategies for overcoming these obstacles to ensure a successful transformation.

Chapter 12: The Future of Business Agility (Culture, Leadership, Execution, Adaptability, Responsiveness)

In this chapter, we articulate how the principles of the CLEAR Model® will continue to shape and influence the future landscape of business agility. We discuss the future of business agility, exploring emerging trends and technologies that will impact business agility in the years to come. Strategies for staying ahead of the curve and preparing your organization for challenges and opportunities are provided.

Key Features of the Book

1. **Step-by-step guidance** – The book provides a structured approach to understanding and implementing Agile principles and practices in organizations, making it accessible and practical for readers.

2. **Comprehensive coverage** – The book covers a wide range of topics related to business agility, including Agile mindset, leadership, culture, project management, collaboration, scaling Agile and emerging trends and technologies.

3. **Real-world case studies** – The book includes many case studies from various industries and organizations, demonstrating the successful application of Agile principles in real-world situations and offering valuable insights for readers.

4. **Learning aids** – Each chapter features learning aids such as key takeaways, summaries and self-assessment exercises to help readers consolidate their understanding of the concepts and apply them to their organizations.

5. **Practical examples and exercises** – The book offers practical examples and exercises to help readers apply Agile principles and practices to their organizations and teams, fostering a deeper understanding of the subject.

6. **Expert advice and insights** – Drawing on the author's extensive experience as a technology executive, Agile consultant and coach, the book offers expert advice and insights into adopting Agile practices in an organization.

7. **Reflection prompts** – Integrated within each chapter, reflection prompts engage readers in their learning journey, encouraging critical thinking and self-assessment while connecting Agile principles to their experiences and organizations.

8. **Further readings and resources** – At the end of each chapter, readers are provided with a list of further readings and resources to explore the topic in greater depth and enhance their learning.

9. **Glossary** – The book includes a glossary of key Agile business terms and concepts to help readers become familiar with the terminology used throughout the book.

Part 1

Understanding Business Agility

1

The Need for Business Agility

In a world where the only constant is change, businesses must act quickly or risk being left behind. Consider the story of Blockbuster, a once-dominant player in the video rental industry that failed to adapt to the rise of digital streaming and ultimately filed for bankruptcy. Organizations must embrace business agility as their primary competitive advantage to avoid a similar fate.

At its core, business agility is an organization's capacity for rapid, effective and sustainable adaptation to change within both the internal and external business environment.

Business agility isn't just about streamlining processes and improving workflow; it's also about the human elements that make an organization truly agile. This includes emotional intelligence, mature leadership and an aligned culture. An organization that excels in both the operational and human aspects of business is far more likely to achieve true business agility.

Consider this scenario: you're leading a thriving mid-sized technology company with a reputation for timely project delivery, content stakeholders and robust business performance. All is well until a competitor releases a game-changing product, transforming customer expectations overnight and claiming a significant market share…

Your team scrambles to respond, but traditional project management approaches can't keep up with this abrupt shift. It's not just about speed and adaptability in the business processes but also about your organization's ability to manage change on a human level. The once smooth-running operation now struggles under the pressure of uncertainty and the ticking clock. This is the challenge that a comprehensive approach to business agility, encompassing both operational and human systems aspects, seeks to address.

Business agility offers a radical paradigm shift, inviting us to embrace change rather than dread it. It allows your organization to pivot rapidly, responding to market changes and customer needs quickly and efficiently. It's no longer about merely surviving in the face of change but thriving in it, turning potential threats into fresh opportunities for growth and innovation. It's about fostering an environment that values adaptability, responsiveness and resilience.

Business agility is not a single event but an ongoing, pervasive process throughout your organization. It involves constantly changing and improving products and services, addressing customer needs and manoeuvring through fluctuating market conditions. Gaining insight into the core principles of agility and understanding how they contribute to your organization's success is crucial in a modern business environment.

Imagine a world where your organization not only survives change but thrives in it, converting potential threats into new opportunities for growth and innovation. Are you prepared to harness the disruptive power of agility for the long-term success of your business?

This chapter sets the stage for the book by introducing the concept of business agility and illustrating its importance for organizations seeking to thrive in an ever-transforming commercial environment. Understanding the necessity for business agility helps to explain its vital role in maintaining a competitive edge and ensuring the long-term success of your organization.

Before we delve into the subject, it's crucial to note that business agility cannot be achieved through a one-size-fits-all approach. No universal playbook or Agile-in-a-Box solution guarantees success in all contexts. Implementing business agility requires a customized strategy addressing each organization's needs and challenges. **An organization will only ever be as Agile as its least Agile part.**

Restricting agility to software teams alone does not suffice. Let me paint you a picture: a software team efficiently employs Agile methods but is embedded in a wider business framework that does not embrace agility. It's like a speedboat tied to a docked ship. Without overall business agility, we can't fully leverage the benefits of Agile.

With many years of experience in leading both failed and successful Agile transformations and mentoring teams of varying sizes, I realized that leadership adoption and backing are indispensable to the success of business agility. These elements are necessary for attempts to embrace Agile practices to continue; otherwise the organization will be ill-equipped to adapt to an increasingly competitive and fast-changing business world.

Swift technological progress, ongoing shifts in customer demands and a perpetually changing competitive marketplaces render traditional models outdated. Organizations must embrace a new mindset and work style to thrive in such conditions – they must become Agile.

However, it's critical not to regard Agile as a panacea for all organizational challenges. Over-expectations of Agile can obscure our judgement by overestimating its transformational power. Agile certainly streamlines processes and bolsters adaptability, but we may confront disappointment and disillusionment if we expect it to tackle deep-rooted organizational problems like cultural resistance or communication bottlenecks.

Alistair Cockburn, one of the original signatories of the Agile Manifesto, expressed this best when he said: *"Agile is an attitude, not a technique with boundaries. An attitude has no boundaries, so we wouldn't ask 'can I use agile here', but rather 'how would I act in the agile way here?' or 'how agile can we be, here?'"*

What is Business Agility?

Business agility refers to an organization's capability to adapt swiftly and efficiently to changing market conditions, customer preferences and technological advancements. It encompasses flexibility, adaptability and responsiveness in decision-making, operations and management. Agile organizations foster a culture of continuous learning and improvement, enabling them to navigate uncertainties and disruptions while staying ahead of the competition.

The notion of "agility" itself became prominent in the 1990s with the rise of Agile software development practices. As businesses saw the benefits of Agile principles – such as adaptability, quick responses to change and customer-centricity – they explored how these principles might be applied beyond just software development.

Business agility emerged from a blend of lean manufacturing principles and Agile software development practices. As organizations recognized the broader applicability of these principles, the concept expanded to encompass agility across all facets of a business. Today, business agility is more critical than ever as companies strive to adapt, innovate and meet customer needs more quickly.

The first use of business agility is not clearly pinpointed in a single document or publication. It's more of an evolving term that gained traction as businesses sought to describe a holistic approach to agility encompassing the entire organization.

It is a people-centric, pervasive attribute that empowers a company to deliver value in a world marked by escalating Volatility, Uncertainty, Complexity and Ambiguity (VUCA). Agile organizations inspire and harness the collaborative, inventive work methods of the people within the organization, causing a different attitude and approach to work. Adapting to changing circumstances and seizing new opportunities is at the heart of business agility.

While sometimes wrongly perceived as a capability exclusive to sectors outside software development, business agility seamlessly integrates Agile principles both within software development arenas and across the entirety of an organizational structure, fostering adaptability at every nexus.

Several factors drive the need for Business Agility, including:

1. **Increased competition** – Globalization and digital transformation has increased competition in nearly every industry. This compels organizations to adapt and innovate to maintain a competitive edge.
2. **Changing customer expectations** – Customers today demand personalized experiences, instant information access and seamless business interactions. Agile organizations can rapidly respond to these expectations, increasing customer satisfaction and loyalty.
3. **Disruptive technologies** – Technological advancements like Artificial Intelligence, automation and big data are transforming the business environment. These require organizations to adapt their strategies, processes and workforce capabilities to stay relevant.
4. **Accelerated product delivery** – The iterative nature of Agile practices significantly speeds up product development. The constant alignment with customer feedback allows for quicker adaptations, leading to faster and more effective market launches.
5. **Evolving team dynamics** – Agile processes foster enhanced collaboration between diverse teams. This synergy increases problem-solving capacity and sparks innovation, making the organization more adaptable and responsive.

Mastering business agility is no small feat, but it is an endeavour made tangible by understanding and effectively leveraging five key components. These components provide a comprehensive framework to guide your organization towards business agility. Table 01 offers a succinct snapshot of these crucial components of business agility.

Table 01: Five Key Components of Business Agility – the CLEAR Model®

Component	Description
Culture	The shared values, beliefs, behaviours and practices within an organization that underpin its approach to change and enable agility
Leadership	The capacity to inspire, empower and guide teams towards shared Agile objectives while maintaining a vision for the future
Execution	The art of transforming strategic Agile plans into action, focusing on doing things not just quickly but correctly and maintaining iterative cycles of planning, implementing, reviewing and improving

| Adaptability | The capacity to alter organizational structures, operations and decision-making to thrive in a changing environment |
| Responsiveness | The ability to quickly react and respond to market shifts, customer needs and emerging opportunities |

Five Key Components of Business Agility – The CLEAR Model®

It is essential to comprehend the underpinning components contributing to an organization's Agile transformation. This section introduces the five pivotal principles of the CLEAR Model® – Culture, Leadership, Execution, Adaptability and Responsiveness.

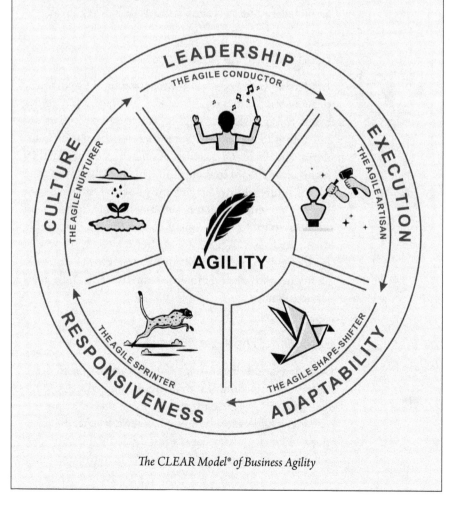

The CLEAR Model® of Business Agility

Culture: "The Agile Nurturer"

Culture is the fertile soil from which agile organizations grow and flourish. It defines the shared values, beliefs, behaviours and practices that underpin an organization's response to change. A culture supportive of agility encourages open communication, values diversity and promotes a learning mindset. It empowers teams to experiment and learn from failures, fostering resilience and the capacity to bounce back stronger. The key component of Culture will permeate our discussions in Chapter 5 on Building an Agile Culture and will serve as the foundation for our conversation on Embracing an Agile Mindset in Chapter 2. Culture is the crucible within which agility is fostered and sustained, setting the tone for the Agile journey ahead.

Leadership: "The Agile Conductor"

Leadership is the conductor orchestrating the symphony of Agile transformation. It inspires, empowers and guides teams towards shared Agile objectives. Agile leaders are not authoritative but collaborative, prioritizing team autonomy and fostering a sense of shared ownership. They maintain a forward-looking vision, planning and preparing for the future while managing the present. Leadership as a key component will feature prominently in Chapter 4 on Leadership in Business Agility and will play a crucial role in our analysis of Agile Planning in Chapter 7. The role of leaders in driving Agile transformation is crucial, and their ability to motivate and mobilize teams towards Agile goals is paramount.

Execution: "The Agile Artisan"

Execution is the hands-on, masterful artistry behind the Agile transformation. It's about translating strategic Agile plans into action, efficiently transforming goals into tangible outcomes. Agile execution emphasizes a balance between speed and quality, focusing not just on doing things quickly but on doing them right. It involves iterative planning, implementing, reviewing and improving cycles, propelling the organization forward one Agile sprint at a time. In the Agile context, a "sprint" is a fixed time period, usually two to four weeks, during which a specific set of tasks is planned and completed. It's a foundational building block of many Agile approaches, allowing teams to break down complex projects into manageable chunks. The role of Execution will be explored in Chapter 8 on Agile Execution and will underpin our insights shared in Chapter 9 on Measuring Business Agility. Execution is the motor that drives the Agile transformation journey, turning the wheels of progress with each meticulously planned and executed step.

Adaptability: "The Agile Shape-Shifter"

Adaptability is the shape-shifting ability of an Agile organization, the capacity to transform structures, operations and decision-making processes to thrive amidst evolving circumstances. It's not just about reacting to changes; it's about anticipating them, preparing for them and capitalizing on them. Adaptability ensures that the organizational structures we'll discuss in Chapter 5 on Building an Agile Culture and the leadership strategies we'll delve into in Chapter 4 are malleable and capable of morphing to accommodate new demands or directions. It fosters an environment where innovation flourishes and teams can experiment, learn and grow. It's a key component that will echo through our conversations about Managing Agile Teams in Chapter 6 and Scaling Business Agility in Chapter 10.

Responsiveness: "The Agile Sprinter"

Responsiveness is the Agile organization's sprinting capability. It's about moving swiftly, not aimlessly, but with clear purpose and direction. Responsiveness involves reacting to shifts in the market, evolving customer needs and emerging opportunities with velocity and precision. An Agile organization listens to its customers, monitors market trends and keeps an eye on its competition to respond in real time.

This is not about hasty decisions; it's about informed, efficient action. The techniques we'll discuss for Measuring Business Agility in Chapter 9 and the insights we'll share on Overcoming Challenges in Agile Adoption in Chapter 11 will be underpinned by the key component of responsiveness.

These CLEAR principles provide a comprehensive, nuanced perspective on business agility and the outcomes we want to achieve. From the nurturing ground of Culture to the robust sprint of Responsiveness, each element plays a crucial role in steering the Agile journey. They encapsulate the essence of Agile, combining to form a synergistic whole that empowers businesses to thrive amidst change and uncertainty. As we delve into each chapter, these principles will serve as our faithful compass, providing context and clarity to our exploration of business agility.

The Benefits of Business Agility

Being agile is not just a competitive advantage but a necessity.

Adopting business agility can yield many advantages for organizations, such as heightened innovation, increased customer satisfaction and high employee engagement. Agile organizations often display heightened responsiveness to market shifts and customer needs, enabling them to preserve a competitive edge and capitalize on new opportunities.

Examples of successful business agility include companies like Amazon, which continuously adapts and expands its product and service offerings based on customer needs and market opportunities. Netflix shifted from its initial DVD rental business model to become a global streaming giant. Another example is Airbnb, which started as a home-sharing platform and expanded into a comprehensive travel marketplace, offering unique experiences and stays. Consider also Slack, a communication platform that started as a gaming company before pivoting to address the growing need for team collaboration tools. Tesla has successfully disrupted the automotive industry through its continuous innovation and agility.

Table 02: Key Benefits of Business Agility

Benefits	Description
Increased Customer Satisfaction	Agile organizations can better respond to customer needs and expectations, increasing satisfaction
Shorter Time-to-Market	Agile practices enable faster delivery of products and services, allowing companies to seize market opportunities quickly

Improved Employee Engagement	Agile work environments encourage collaboration, empowerment and continuous learning, increasing employee engagement and satisfaction
Enhanced Innovation	Agile organizations foster a culture of experimentation and learning, promoting the development of innovative solutions
Greater Flexibility	Agile companies can adapt quickly to changing market conditions and customer demands, maintaining a competitive advantage
Better Risk Management	Agile approaches support iterative development, which helps identify and mitigate risks early in the project life cycle
Improved Quality	Continuous feedback and iterative improvements in Agile processes lead to higher-quality products and services
Cost Savings	Agile practices often result in more efficient use of resources and reduced waste, leading to cost savings

Pause for a moment and think about your own organization. How swiftly does it adapt to change? What challenges have you faced while trying to introduce new strategies or ideas? Keep these thoughts in mind as we delve into the factors that drive the need for business agility.

Factors Driving the Need for Business Agility

Rapid technological advancements are a significant aspect driving business agility. The unprecedented emergence of new technologies disrupts conventional industries and generates new ones. Organizations that cannot keep up with this relentless pace risk becoming obsolete, underscoring the critical importance of agility in the prevailing business environment.

Customer demands are also transforming. They seek more personalized, accessible and exceptional experiences. Organizations that cater to these needs can avoid losing customers to competitors who can fulfil them.

The competitive landscape experiences continuous shifts as new contenders enter the market and established ones reinvent themselves. Organizations that cannot adapt to such changes risk declining market share and profitability.

Adopting a way of working that highlights swiftness, flexibility and adaptability is crucial. Embracing change, uncertainty, risk-taking and experimentation is essential.

An Agile mindset centres on adaptability and ongoing improvement. Business leaders must cultivate a culture promoting experimentation, risk-taking and learning from setbacks. Empowering employees to make decisions and take responsibility for their work is vital.

Business agility incorporates core Agile principles and practices throughout the enterprise, increasing responsiveness to change, accelerating time-to-market and cutting costs without compromising quality.

Agile approaches foster collaboration, transparency and continuous enhancement. Agile teams operate in short cycles, regularly reviewing progress and adjusting direction. This enables organizations to react swiftly to market fluctuations, customer needs and emerging technologies.

To adopt a business-wide Agile approach, organizations need leaders who offer vision and guidance while empowering their teams to decide and assume responsibility. This calls for a diverse leadership style centred on collaboration, communication and trust.

Here are practical tips and tactics for adopting an Agile approach to work:

Start Small

Begin with a small pilot project to test Agile ways of working and determine what works best for your organization.

Invest in Training

Provide training to help employees understand Agile ways of working, what is in it for them and how to work effectively in an Agile environment.

Embrace Technology

Leverage technological advancements to bolster Agile approaches, employing tools like project management software and collaborative platforms.

Celebrate Success

Recognize and reward success to build momentum and reinforce the importance of agility.

Celebrate Failure

Embrace and appreciate failures as invaluable learning opportunities, fostering a culture that views setbacks as stepping stones towards agility and innovation.

Measure Success

Develop key performance indicators (KPIs) to assess the influence of agile methods on factors like productivity, customer happiness and employee commitment.

Encourage Regular Reflection and Feedback

Establish a culture where teams regularly reflect on their work, share feedback and adjust their processes and strategies based on their learnings. This iterative approach helps ensure continuous improvement and adaptability.

Fostering a diverse and inclusive workforce is a vital aspect of business agility. A diverse workforce encompassing different backgrounds, experiences and perspectives can enhance creative problem-solving and innovation. This is essential for organizations to adapt quickly to changing market conditions and customer needs.

Research has shown that diverse teams are more likely to develop innovative solutions and identify new market opportunities. Nurturing an inclusive atmosphere and actively promoting diversity and inclusion initiatives allows company leaders to tap into their teams' full potential and propagate agility throughout the organization. Such initiatives may include unconscious bias training, mentorship programmes and diversity hiring practices. All these contribute to a more agile and adaptable organization.

Statistical Evidence for Business Agility

Let's better understand the importance of business agility using real data. It's not just theory; the figures show how important being agile is for businesses dealing with a fast-changing marketplace.

According to Digital.ai's 14th State of Agile Report (2020), 95% of respondents affirmed that their organizations practised Agile development methods. This overwhelming number exhibits the broad acceptance and implementation of Agile techniques globally, reflecting their value in managing business operations effectively.

In the same report, they identified the top three benefits realized from adopting Agile as the "ability to manage to change priorities" (71%), "project visibility" (66%) and "business alignment" (65%). This data clearly illustrates the benefits of business agility in dynamic environments, allowing businesses to pivot swiftly and ensuring projects align with overarching business objectives.

What's more, the Business Agility Report (2020) by the Business Agility Institute underscores that organizations that rank high in business agility outperform their lower-ranking counterparts. They reported 60% higher revenue growth and 235% higher customer satisfaction, underscoring the clear relationship between business agility and organizational performance.

Picture an organization shackled by traditional practices, viewing Agile as a mere software development tool, stuck in a loop of "doing Agile" without ever truly "being Agile". As we delve deeper into the world of business agility, we need to clear this misconception. Agile is not a magic wand that you wave at your projects to make them successful overnight. It's a philosophy, a mindset, an attitude, even an ethos that requires a deep-seated transformation from within.

Challenges in Implementing Business Agility

While adopting business agility can bring many benefits, organizations may face challenges during their organizational transformation. Some common challenges include resistance to change, lack of leadership support, inadequate training and difficulty measuring progress.

To effectively navigate these challenges, it is crucial for organizations to not only be aware of these potential obstacles but also to develop targeted strategies for addressing and overcoming them.

For instance, managing resistance to change might involve open communication with employees, promoting transparency and providing support during the transition. Similarly, overcoming a lack of leadership support could cultivate a solid case for agility that highlights its benefits and aligns with the organization's strategic objectives.

Ego, fear and overconfidence can impede business agility, presenting obstacles at all hierarchical levels. Adopting agile tactics often requires a significant shift in mindset, which can prove difficult for some employees.

Even adhering to inflexible, top-down management is unlikely to yield long-term success in the modern business world. To prosper, organizations must welcome agility and enhance adaptability. As organizations implement Agile practices, they may face challenges maintaining momentum and ensuring the changes are embedded in the company culture.

Embarking on the journey toward business agility can occur at different rates, and some may leap in, while others may slowly incorporate agile elements while retaining traditional practices elsewhere. Regardless of the chosen path, any steps taken toward agility can notably improve a business' capacity to adapt to changing environments and emerging technologies.

For hesitant companies, merely recognizing areas of inflexibility and limited adaptability offers value. However, it is vital to understand that business agility is not trivial; overlooking its benefits could harm organizations clinging to outdated practices.

For instance, Kodak, once a leader in the photography industry, struggled to adapt to the digital age and eventually filed for bankruptcy. On the other hand, Adobe successfully transitioned from selling boxed software to offering cloud-based subscription services by embracing Agile principles and overcoming resistance to change. Companies must adopt a fresh approach centred on speed, flexibility and resilience to increase agility. This entails embracing Agile principles, fostering a new mindset, developing leadership skills and encouraging collaboration, open discussion and self-assurance.

CLEAR Lens for "The Need for Business Agility"

We can apply two CLEAR Model® principles to The Need for Business Agility:

Responsiveness: Business environments today are typified by their volatility and constant flux. Being nimble and reactive to such change isn't just helpful, it's essential for survival. In this challenging environment, Responsiveness comes to the fore, encouraging organizations to act swiftly and decisively to the ever-evolving market trends, customer needs and other dynamic external factors. This principle is integral to the CLEAR Model® and highlights how essential it is for an agile organization to survive and thrive.

Adaptability: Successful organizations aren't merely reactive but proactive and forward-thinking. They can expect market shifts and adjust their strategic direction accordingly. The Adaptability principle, central to the CLEAR Model®, emphasizes the need for an anticipatory mindset to outpace the competition and stay ahead of the curve.

Reflection Prompts

1. Reflect on a time when your organization faced a significant challenge or change. How did it respond? Would a more agile approach have led to better outcomes?

2. Consider your current business environment. What external factors are driving the need for increased agility in your organization?

Case Study: Spotify – A Model for Agile Transformation and Adaptability

One of the most successful implementations of business agility comes from Spotify, the Swedish music streaming and media services provider. The company's Agile journey started in 2008 with the goal of developing a learning organization that continually improves and innovates.

Spotify initially embraced Agile principles, learning and adapting from their first experiments. They moved beyond just implementing Scrum, evolving a framework that worked optimally for their dynamic context. As a result, they successfully cultivated a culture of adaptability, leading to increased innovation, customer satisfaction and overall business success. Examining Spotify's approach can provide organizations with insights into the unique strategies and tactics that have enabled Spotify to respond swiftly to changes, outpace rivals and thrive in various situations.

Agile Culture and Structure at Spotify

Spotify is known for its unique Agile team structure, called "squads". These small, cross-functional teams are granted the autonomy to work independently, make decisions about their work and take risks. They collaborate with other squads when necessary, allowing for greater adaptability and innovation. This structure enables Spotify to respond to changes in the market quickly and continuously deliver value to its customers.

However, as highlighted in Henrik Kniberg's "Spotify Engineering Culture (Part 1)", it's important to note that this model resulted from experimentation when the teams found no further improvement after adopting Scrum. The "Spotify Model" was a temporary solution that served the company better. Once the benefits plateaued, Spotify did not hesitate to change it again to a newer model, showcasing the genuine spirit of Agile – continuous adaptation to maximize efficiency and value delivery. Therefore, while the model that Spotify briefly used was a significant milestone in its Agile journey, it was not a permanent or one-size-fits-all solution but an example of how organizations can and should change Agile practices to suit their evolving needs best.

Innovative Tools and Processes at Spotify

Another key factor contributing to Spotify's Agile success was the company's adoption of innovative tools and processes that support collaboration and continuous improvement. For instance, Spotify utilizes Jira, a project management tool designed for Agile teams, GitHub for version control and code sharing and Slack for real-time team communication. These tools streamline workflows, facilitate collaboration and enhance the overall Agile experience.

Spotify also embraces practices such as regular retrospectives, where teams reflect on their work and identify areas for improvement. These processes help teams continuously refine their methods, improve productivity and ultimately deliver better products to their customers. Embracing innovative tools and processes that align with their Agile principles has fostered a culture of adaptability, innovation and collaboration at Spotify. However, it's important to underline that the Agile mindset goes beyond adopting such software tools. While they play a significant role in fostering agility, Agile's principles and practices – like continuous improvement, adaptability and customer-centricity – truly drive Agile transformation across many teams and organizations, not just in software development.

Spotify's Unique Agile Model, Commonly Called the "Spotify Model"

The "Spotify Model" revolves around creating a structure that encourages autonomy, collaboration, and adaptability, ultimately contributing to Spotify's success in the music streaming industry. This model emphasizes the importance of people, culture, and a network within the organization, focusing on how businesses can structure an organization to enable agility. By leveraging their culture and network, the Spotify team has been able to scale agility successfully across their organization, moving beyond specific practices or ceremonies to a more holistic approach to organizing around work.

Table 03: Key Components of Spotify's Agile Model

Component	Description
Squads	Small, cross-functional teams that work independently and make decisions about their work, fostering innovation and adaptability
Tribes	Groups of squads with related objectives work together to facilitate knowledge-sharing and collaboration

Chapters	Functional teams within a tribe focus on specific areas of expertise, such as software development, design or testing
Guilds	Informal, organization-wide groups where members share knowledge, tools and best practices related to their area of expertise

Key Takeaways from Spotify's Agile Success

1. **Autonomy and decision-making** – Spotify empowers its Agile teams by granting them the autonomy to make decisions and take risks. This approach encourages innovation and allows teams to adapt to industry changes quickly.
2. **Cross-functional collaboration** – Spotify's Agile teams comprise members with diverse skill sets, enabling them to collaborate effectively and develop innovative solutions to complex problems.
3. **Emphasis on continuous improvement** – Spotify is committed to continuous learning and improvement, which helps them stay ahead of their competition and deliver value to their customers.
4. **Supportive culture** – Spotify has cultivated an environment encouraging experimentation, learning from failure and open communication. This type of culture enables Agile teams to thrive and adapt to changes in the market.

Challenges and Strategies for Overcoming Resistance

While specific details about the challenges Spotify faced during its Agile transformation are not widely available, it is reasonable to assume that, like any organization undergoing significant change, it would have had to address resistance to change, invest in employee training, and develop new leadership styles aligned with their Agile approach. Acknowledging potential obstacles and committing to continuous improvement enables Spotify to maintain its position as a model of agility.

Key Strategies for Overcoming Resistance (General Recommendations)

1. **Clear communication of Agile benefits** – Articulating the benefits of Agile approaches and their positive impact on the organization can help gain employee buy-in.

2. **Targeted training and support** – Providing employees with the necessary training and resources can ease the transition to Agile and empower teams to succeed in their new roles.

3. **Leading by example** – Embracing Agile leadership styles and demonstrating adaptability can inspire employees to adopt Agile principles and embrace change.

Business Outcomes and Competitive Advantage

Spotify's Agile approach has led to concrete business outcomes such as increased revenue, reaching over 345 million monthly active users and maintaining a competitive edge against rivals like Apple Music and Amazon Music. Constant innovation and adaptation to user preferences have kept Spotify at the forefront of the music streaming industry.

Leaders can learn from Spotify's example and apply strategies and tactics to transform their organizations. Key elements to consider include:

1. **Building a culture of adaptability** – Encourage a mindset of continuous learning and improvement, enabling employees to adapt and respond to changes in the business environment.

2. **Empowering teams** – Grant autonomy to cross-functional teams, allowing them to make decisions and take risks, fostering innovation and adaptability.

3. **Investing in training** – Provide targeted training to help employees understand Agile principles and how to work in an Agile environment effectively.

4. **Encouraging collaboration** – Promote cross-functional collaboration among teams to drive innovative solutions and effectively address complex challenges.

5. **Overcoming resistance to change** – Address employee concerns and resistance to change by clearly communicating the benefits of Agile approaches and providing necessary support.

6. **Measuring success** – Develop key performance indicators (KPIs) to assess the impact of Agile methods on productivity, customer satisfaction and employee commitment.

7. **Leading by example** – Adopt Agile leadership styles that encourage adaptability, innovation and continuous improvement, inspiring employees to embrace change and contribute to the organization's success.

Applying these principles allows business leaders to drive Agile transformation in their organizations, harnessing the power of adaptability to stay ahead of the competition and thrive in the changing business environment. However, it's essential to consider that there's no one-size-fits-all approach. Numerous organizations inspired by the "Spotify Model" have encountered challenges in meeting their expectations. The intricacies of, for instance, a 100-year-old finance organization can significantly differ from a music streaming service, and as such, its application of Agile principles might require a more tailored strategy.

Exercise: Assessing Your Organization's Agile Readiness

To effectively evaluate your organization's readiness for Agile transformation, it's crucial to consider key aspects that impact adopting Agile practices. Examining these factors can help identify areas for improvement and better prepare your organization for a smooth Agile transformation.

Consider examining the following aspects:

1. **Culture** – Assess your organization's culture to encourage flexibility, collaboration and learning from failure. Determine the willingness to embrace change, adapt to new ways of working and reflect on the values that drive decision-making and behaviour.
2. **Leadership support** – Evaluate leaders' commitment to Agile principles and willingness to empower teams. Strong leadership support is essential for a successful Agile transformation and sets the tone and direction for the entire organization.
3. **Existing processes** – Analyse your current working processes to determine if they can be adapted to Agile ways of working or if a complete overhaul is necessary. Consider whether your organization's practices facilitate rapid feedback and continuous improvement or whether they create barriers to Agile adoption.
4. **Abilities** – Assess the level of Agile knowledge and experience within your organization, evaluating whether teams possess the necessary skills to adopt Agile practices effectively. Identify skill gaps that need to be addressed through training or coaching.
5. **Resources** – Examine the availability of resources, such as time, budget and personnel, to support the Agile transformation. Determine your organization's willingness to invest in the necessary tools and training for successful Agile adoption.

Reflect on these questions and identify areas for improvement to ensure a smooth Agile transformation. Keep these aspects in mind as you progress through the book, and leverage the concepts and case studies to address your organization's unique context and challenges. Continuously reassess your readiness and refine your approach to maximize your Agile transformation's success.

Chapter Summary

This chapter emphasized the importance of business agility amidst constant change and rapid developments. It explored the key drivers behind the need for agility, such as increased competition, changing customer expectations and disruptive technologies. The chapter also highlighted the benefits of business agility, including shorter time-to-market, increased customer satisfaction and improved innovation. Finally, the chapter overviewed business agility's key principles: flexibility, adaptability and responsiveness.

Further Readings and Resources

1. Book: *Accelerate: The Science of Lean Software and DevOps*, by Nicole Forsgren, Jez Humble and Gene Kim, 2018, IT Revolution Press.

2. Book: *Business Agility: Sustainable Prosperity in a Relentlessly Competitive World*, by Michael H. Hugos, 2009, Wiley.

3. Website: Agile Business Consortium – www.agilebusiness.org

4. Article: "Embracing Agile", by Darrell K. Rigby, Jeff Sutherland and Hirotaka Takeuchi, *Harvard Business Review*, May 2016.

2

Embracing an Agile Mindset

Let's imagine a familiar setting: a once-productive boardroom discussion now stuck in a stalemate. Leaders arguing about priorities and metrics, each rooted in their departmental concerns, seemingly resistant to adapt and evolve. In one corner of the room, a member advocates for adopting an Agile approach, suggesting it's the key to unravelling the gridlock. But there's scepticism. "Isn't Agile just a tech thing?" someone retorts. Believe me, this is a misconception many hold.

Imagine, for a moment, you are steering a large ship in treacherous waters. Agile is your compass, directing you through unpredictable currents and fierce storms. The key? A transformative mindset that emerges as an individual's evolving worldview, shaped by outside events and experiences that not only reads the compass but embraces its guidance wholeheartedly.

Cultivating an Agile mindset is not about imposing a specific way of thinking but about recognizing and nurturing this evolving worldview. It's an ongoing process involving incorporating various methods and tactics throughout an organization's lifespan. Grasping the essence of Agile principles and customizing them to align with each organization's distinct objectives, priorities and market context allows business leaders to foster a more flexible and resilient organization. However, translating this mindset into practice involves cultivating the right attitude – a proactive approach to change. This allows the organization to navigate fluctuating market conditions better, consistently offer value to customers and flourish in a demanding business climate.

Adopting Agile involves more than just implementing a new set of practices; it represents a profound shift in mindset and attitude. Employees steeped in traditional methods may resist this change, becoming a major challenge. The move from long, static meetings to Agile's dynamic, brief daily stand-ups, short, typically 15-minute meetings held each day by the Agile team to discuss progress and plan the day's work, for example, can shock the system. The real test lies in transforming this resistance into acceptance, forging a path for a smoother Agile transition.

To cultivate genuine agility, it's also important to grasp that Agile is not just a collection of frameworks branded by different companies. Instead, it's an underlying philosophy that can transform how we approach work. Embracing the Agile mindset and fostering the accompanying attitude means moving beyond these brand names and recognizing Agile's true essence as a unique and powerful way of thinking.

Are you prepared to champion the seismic cultural shift that an Agile mindset necessitates, turning resistance into the fuel for transformative change?

This chapter explores the benefits business leaders can reap by embracing an Agile mindset. This approach provides a unique edge in the highly competitive world of business. While you may be familiar with the idea of a "Change mindset", a general disposition towards change, you may still need to become familiar with the "Agile mindset" and the attitudes it can foster. This specific approach deals with change distinctly. Both mindsets share essential characteristics, such as an openness to new concepts, flexibility in adapting to evolving circumstances and resilience in the face of unpredictability.

N.B. The term mindset used throughout this book pertains to individuals, their beliefs, attitudes, experiences and approaches towards work and challenges.

Table 04: Agile Mindset Characteristics

Characteristic	Description
Adaptability	The ability to adjust to changing conditions and respond quickly to new challenges and opportunities
Collaboration	Working together across teams and departments to share knowledge, ideas and resources
Continuous Improvement	Constantly seeking ways to refine processes, enhance performance and increase efficiency and innovation
Customer-centricity	Placing the customer's needs and feedback at the centre of decision-making and product development
Empowerment	Encouraging autonomy and self-management among team members, fostering ownership and accountability
Flexibility	Being open to new ideas, methods and approaches and willing to adjust plans as needed
Learning Orientation	Emphasizing learning and growth and nurturing a culture that values curiosity and innovation
Transparency	Maintaining open communication, sharing information and fostering trust within the organization

What is an Agile Mindset?

Underpinning all Agile principles and practices, an Agile mindset comprises beliefs championing collaboration, fostering experimentation and promoting continuous improvement. It represents a way of individualistic thinking that is both transformational and forward-looking.

The origins of the Agile mindset are rooted in software development, with its genesis tracing back to the turn of the millennium. Discontent with traditional project management approaches, a collective of industry thought leaders (a term used to describe influential experts and visionaries in the field of software development who are known for their innovative ideas and leadership in shaping industry trends) convened in February 2001 to plan an alternative methodology to address software development's dynamic nature. This gathering culminated in creating the Agile Manifesto – a declaration of key values and principles designed to foster flexibility, collaboration and customer focus. This pivotal moment set the stage for the Agile mindset we recognize today.

Imagine a fully agile and efficient software team surrounded by traditional, rigid business units. They are like a well-tuned orchestra trying to perform in the middle of a bustling market. Expanding the principles throughout the organization is crucial to truly embracing an Agile mindset.

The Agile mindset has since transcended the confines of software development, proving its relevance and utility across diverse industries and disciplines. It is not just a methodology but a philosophical shift, reshaping how organizations view and manage their projects, people and overall business strategy.

Let us inspect each of these values:

Individuals and Interactions Over Processes and Tools

In an Agile organization, people are more important than processes or tools, meaning communication and collaboration are essential for success. Instead of following rigid processes and procedures, people work together in self-organizing teams. They are empowered to make decisions and take ownership of their work, fostering a sense of ownership and accountability, which motivates people, leading to high-performing teams.

Working Software (or Products) Over Comprehensive Documentation

Delivering value to customers is more important than dotting the i's and crossing the t's of what you are mandated to deliver. Getting feedback from customers early often means delivering small increments of value quickly rather than waiting for a large, complex deliverable. This allows you to adjust your approach as you learn more about the problem you are looking to solve.

Customer Collaboration Over Contract Negotiation

Another key aspect of the Agile mindset is the importance of customer collaboration. This means involving your customers in the development process and seeking their feedback and input. Doing this increases our confidence in delivering value.

Responding to Change Over Following a Plan

Finally, the Agile mindset values responding to change over following a plan. This means you embrace change and uncertainty and will adjust your plans and priorities as needed. This requires a willingness to take risks, experiment and learn from successes and failures.

Besides the four central values, the Agile Manifesto presents 12 guiding principles offering more detailed instructions on applying the Agile mindset. These principles range from prioritizing customer satisfaction to maintaining a sustainable work pace. Familiarity with these principles can facilitate better comprehension and implementation of an Agile mindset within your organization.

Let us imagine you walk into a new organization, a fresh setting with unique strengths and challenges. Where do you begin? I always start with a checklist, a handful of questions that unveil whether the organization is merely "doing Agile" or "being Agile", having adopted this Agile mindset fully. These questions are as follows:

1. Is the organization open to change?
2. Is collaboration valued over individual performance?
3. Are teams empowered to make decisions?
4. Is learning from failure celebrated?

Use this as your compass when you start embracing an Agile mindset.

Table 05: Traditional vs. Agile Mindset

Aspect	Traditional Mindset	Agile Mindset
Decision-making	Top-down, with decisions primarily made by management	Decentralized, empowering teams to make decisions
Communication	Often formal and hierarchical, potentially slowing down information flow	Open, continuous and collaborative, enhancing information flow and transparency

Planning	Detailed, long-term plans that can be rigid and slow to adapt	Iterative and flexible, with short-term goals set for each iteration
Team Structure	Often siloed with a focus on individual tasks and roles	Cross-functional teams with shared responsibilities and focus on collective achievement
Response to Change	Typically resistant to change; changes often result in delays and cost overruns	Welcomes change; the methodology's inherent flexibility allows for quick adaptation
Customer Focus	Customer feedback is generally collected at set intervals and may not always result in immediate changes	Customer feedback is integral and continuous, leading to immediate improvements and high customer satisfaction

Why is the Agile Mindset Important?

The Agile mindset holds significance for business leaders, as it helps them establish an organization well suited to adapting to the swift and dynamic business environment. Traditional business models hinge on hierarchical structures, inflexible processes and an emphasis on predictability and control. This hierarchical command and control approach must change.

Contrastingly, the Agile mindset is rooted in collaboration, experimentation and continuous enhancement. It highlights the necessity of team collaboration, swift delivery of value to customers and adjusting to change. This method enables organizations to respond rapidly to new opportunities and challenges and adapt their strategies and processes accordingly. At its core, the Agile mindset challenges leaders with the "Why Not?" attitude, emphasizing the "art of the possible" rather than remaining restrained by established norms.

Business leaders who adopt the Agile mindset can cultivate a culture that appreciates innovation, risk-taking and learning from setbacks. This perspective ensures that the journey of learning and discovery is always prioritized. Furthermore, it fosters an environment where failure isn't frowned upon but is seen as an invaluable avenue for growth. This can empower teams and enhance engagement, resulting in elevated productivity and superior output quality.

Aligning organizational structures and processes with the Agile mindset is crucial for nurturing agility. Traditional hierarchical structures require re-evaluation, and decision-making authority must be delegated to self-organizing teams. Flexible work set-ups, efficient communication channels and an emphasis on results over strict adherence to processes contribute to a more Agile work environment.

The Agile mindset is vital for business leaders because it offers a blueprint for an adaptable organization that can quickly adjust to changing situations. Embracing the Agile approach empowers leaders' teams, fosters an innovative culture and positions their organizations for long-term prosperity.

Real-Life Examples of an Agile Mindset

Understanding theoretical frameworks is a good start as we delve into Agile mindsets. However, examining real-life examples can solidify these concepts, providing a practical lens to appreciate their application.

As noted in Chapter 1, Spotify is a prominent example of a company that has embraced an Agile mindset. Spotify's Agile framework, the "Spotify Model", incorporates squads, tribes, chapters and guilds to drive efficiency and innovation. This model fosters autonomy, facilitating teams to make decisions quickly without getting mired in layers of management. The way Spotify frequently changes its Agile organization model epitomizes an Agile mindset, valuing responsiveness and flexibility over rigid hierarchical structures.

Another company that embodies an Agile mindset is ING. The Dutch bank adopted an Agile transformation to navigate the rapid digitalization in the banking sector. ING moved from a traditional, siloed structure to Agile squads to drive customer-centric operations. The transition witnessed a remarkable enhancement in efficiency and customer satisfaction, demonstrating the power of an Agile mindset in catalysing organizational change and customer focus.

Finally, Bosch, the engineering and technology company, has adopted an Agile mindset to drive innovation in its product development process. By adopting Agile practices such as Scrum, Bosch has responded swiftly to changing customer demands and market conditions, underlining the Agile mindset's role in bolstering business resilience.

These real-life examples underscore the power of embracing an Agile mindset. It's clear that such a shift doesn't just contribute to business efficiency; it is the bedrock for an organization's adaptability and resilience in the face of change.

Common Misconceptions About the Agile Mindset

Several misconceptions about the Agile mindset often lead to confusion or misguided implementation. Addressing these misconceptions can help clarify the true nature of Agile thinking:

1. **Agile is only for software development** – While Agile was initially created for software development, its values and principles can be effectively applied to any industry or project. The Agile mindset is adaptable and can bring value to various organizations.

2. **Agile means no planning or documentation** – Agile does not eliminate planning or documentation but prioritizes delivering value to customers. Planning and documentation are still essential but are continuously refined and updated based on customer feedback and changing needs.
3. **Agile teams do not have any structure or discipline** – Agile teams have structures and disciplines but are more flexible and adaptive than traditional hierarchical structures. Agile teams are self-organizing and empowered to make decisions, which fosters a sense of ownership and accountability.
4. **Agile teams work without deadlines** – Agile teams use time-boxed periods, called sprints or iterations, to work towards specific goals within a set time frame. This approach ensures that progress is continuously monitored and adjustments can be made as needed.

How to Adopt an Agile Mindset

Adopting an Agile mindset means collaborating and perceiving work differently. Competent business leaders must encourage and support their teams to communicate transparently and collaborate while fostering a culture that values continuous growth and development.

Here are some steps to assist your organization in adopting the Agile mindset:

Start with Leadership

Business leaders, including those beyond the top echelons, must exemplify Agile mindset behaviours and values. Everyone who influences others is a leader, whether in the boardroom or on the ground. They must stress the importance of collaboration, experimentation and continuous progress, inspiring their teams to adopt these principles.

Just focusing on organizational top leaders is a mistake. Addressing this across all leadership levels ensures a holistic embrace of Agile.

Encourage Collaboration

In Agile organizations, cross-functional teams collaborate to attain shared objectives. Leaders must facilitate this cooperation, design a workspace that encourages interaction and communication and give team members the autonomy to make decisions and resolve issues collectively.

Build Self-Organizing Teams

Business leaders must endorse self-organizing teams and empower individuals to make decisions and take responsibility for their work. This fosters a sense of accountability and ownership, which is crucial for an Agile work style.

Foster Psychological Safety

Psychological safety is pivotal in Agile environments where team members must feel secure in expressing their ideas, asking questions and admitting mistakes without fear of retribution. This is crucial for fostering collaboration, innovation and continuous improvement. Below are some suggestions for promoting psychological safety within your organization:

1. **Encourage open communication** – Create an environment where team members feel comfortable sharing their thoughts, ideas and concerns without fear of negative consequences.
2. **Acknowledge the value of diverse perspectives** – Encourage the expression of different viewpoints and emphasize that every team member's input is valuable and can lead to better solutions and innovations.
3. **Create a blame-free culture** – Promote a culture that focuses on learning from mistakes and failures rather than assigning blame. This will encourage team members to take risks, experiment and learn from their experiences.

Embrace Experimentation

Business leaders must embrace risk-taking and experimentation. Inspire teams to explore new ideas without fearing failure. Instead, view it as a learning opportunity. Celebrate successes and failures equally, using them as learning experiences to facilitate continuous improvement.

Foster a Culture of Continuous Improvement

Agile organizations constantly seek ways to enhance processes and deliver greater value to customers. Encourage teams to reflect on their work, question assumptions and identify areas for improvement routinely. Implement feedback loops, such as regular team retrospectives and iterative development cycles, enabling teams to learn from their experiences, recognize areas for improvement and swiftly adapt to changing conditions.

Prioritize Delivering Value to Customers

In an Agile environment, the goal is to consistently deliver value instead of waiting until the project's end to present a complex outcome. Doing so lets you get customer feedback early and frequently, ensuring that the value you deliver aligns with their needs and expectations.

Involve Your Customers

A key component of the Agile approach is customer collaboration. Engage your customers in the development process, actively seeking their feedback and insights. This fosters robust customer relationships.

Respond to Change

Business leaders must be prepared to adapt to change and ambiguity. This requires embracing new ideas, shifting priorities and modifying plans as necessary. Empower your teams to be versatile and resilient, providing them with the resources and support required to implement changes efficiently and effectively.

Address Potential Challenges

Embracing an Agile mindset might bring up specific challenges, such as resistance to change or dismantling silos, or overcoming ingrained habits. To navigate these issues, business leaders must:

1. Emphasize the advantages of integrating Agile principles and provide real-life examples of organizations that have successfully navigated these challenges.
2. Provide ongoing training and support customized to meet employee needs and concerns.
3. Celebrate incremental achievements and progress, highlighting the benefits of Agile transformation at each stage.
4. Encourage open discussions about concerns and challenges and actively involve employees in the change process, giving them a sense of ownership and control over the transition.
5. Provide training and support to help middle managers transition into new roles as servant leaders, coaches and mentors. This will enable them to support their teams better and understand the benefits of an Agile mindset.
6. Communicate the benefits of a more decentralized decision-making process and involve employees in the change process. This can help ease concerns and demonstrate how Agile principles can increase efficiency, innovation and adaptability.

The Dilution of Agile

Additionally, over the years, the term "Agile" has permeated beyond software development into various aspects of business operations. However, this saturation has led to a devaluation of what Agile truly stands for. It's crucial for organizations to understand that Agile is not a buzzword but a set of principles that require thoughtful implementation. Guard against "Agile fatigue" by constantly revisiting the Agile manifesto and aligning your strategies accordingly.

Monitor Progress with Metrics

Measure progress to keep your organization focused and ensure continuous customer value delivery. Agile organizations frequently use cycle time, lead time and outcome based metrics to monitor progress and performance. Tracking these metrics allows business leaders to pinpoint areas for improvement, make data-informed decisions and ensure their teams consistently deliver value. Additionally, communicating these metrics to employees is encouraged to incentivize them. Sharing progress and performance insights fosters transparency and motivates teams by providing clear goals and tangible benchmarks for success.

Business leaders who comprehend and champion Agile principles and can exemplify them for the rest of the organization are invaluable. Team structures must be flexible, supporting self-organizing teams that can adapt to evolving requirements. Communication must be open and transparent, fostering collaboration and feedback. Prioritizing customer focus, with consistent customer engagement and feedback sessions, is essential. Lastly, continuous improvement must be ongoing, with regular retrospectives and adjustments based on feedback and outcomes.

Implementing this Agile mindset enables business leaders to cultivate a culture that values collaboration, innovation and continuous growth. This leads to an agile organization capable of swiftly adapting to change and outperforming competitors. Are you willing to change your thoughts and adopt that Agile mindset?

CLEAR Lens for "Embracing an Agile Mindset"

We can apply two CLEAR Model® principles to Embracing an Agile Mindset:

Culture: A successful Agile transformation is anchored on a supportive, Agile-oriented culture. This culture fosters an environment that is not resistant but welcoming of change, promotes continuous learning and growth, and always maintains a relentless focus on delivering customer value. Embodying such a culture is the starting point of any successful Agile journey, which is firmly rooted in the principles of the CLEAR Model®.

Adaptability: Adaptability sits at the very heart of an Agile mindset. It signifies an organization's capacity for continuous learning and proactive response to changes in the business environment. It emphasizes the importance of remaining agile and adaptable in the face of changing market conditions, underlining the role of the CLEAR principles in navigating an uncertain business world.

Reflection Prompts

1. Assess your own mindset. To what extent do you exhibit the characteristics of an Agile mindset?

2. Think about the communication and decision-making processes in your organization. How could these be improved to better align with an Agile mindset?

Case Study: Netflix's Agile Mindset and Ethos

Let us examine how Netflix's Agile mindset, often referred to as its organizational ethos, has been instrumental in its business agility success.

Netflix's Agile mindset, or its intrinsic ethos, has played a pivotal role in its business agility success. Its unique culture of freedom and responsibility, a manifestation of this ethos, has inspired many companies to adopt Agile transformations. At Netflix, employees are granted decision-making autonomy and encouraged to take risks while being held accountable for the outcomes. This approach creates an innovative and experimental environment that fosters creativity and adaptability. For example, their decision to greenlight "House of Cards" based on data analytics is a testament to their commitment to integrating testing into every step of the software development lifecycle.

Netflix's journey to becoming an Agile organization began with a strong vision and a commitment to embracing change. The company started as a DVD rental service but quickly pivoted to an online streaming platform, foreseeing the potential of the internet to revolutionize the entertainment industry. This strategic move laid the foundation for Netflix's collective Agile mindset or ethos, which has continued to evolve and mature. The company's emphasis on Agile principles and practices, reflective of its characteristic spirit and culture, is clear in its operations, including its organizational structure, employee culture, decision-making processes and innovative product development strategies.

Netflix's Agile mindset and ethos rest upon several core principles: autonomy, risk-taking, collaboration and data-driven decision-making. The company's emphasis on teamwork and collaboration enables it to rapidly adapt to change and outperform competitors. Additionally, their strategy to support a diverse range of devices emphasizes their commitment to customer satisfaction and continual improvement.

What's more, Netflix is known for its microservices architecture, a design approach where an application is created as a collection of small, independent and loosely coupled software services, enabling it to develop and deploy features more flexibly. This architecture is a fundamental aspect of their Agile approach to product development. Leveraging data to inform decisions allows Netflix to spot patterns quickly and make well-informed choices, enhancing its platform and content. Their frequent release of new movies and shows demonstrates their commitment to continuous integration and delivery, keeping their content fresh and engaging for customers.

Table 06 highlights key Agile mindset principles and practices contributing to Netflix's Agile mindset and organizational ethos, making it a shining example of business agility success.

Table 06: Agile Mindset and Ethos Principles and Practices

Principle	Practice
Decision-making Autonomy	Empower employees by giving them the authority to make decisions, fostering an environment that values individual creativity and critical thinking
Encouragement of Risk-taking	Allow employees to take risks, promoting innovation and encouraging them to push boundaries, ultimately driving the organization forward
Accountability and Responsibility	With freedom comes responsibility; hold employees accountable for their decisions and actions, ensuring a strong sense of ownership and commitment to the organization's goals
Emphasis on Collaboration and Innovation	Focus on teamwork and innovation to build an agile organization that can rapidly adapt to change and outperform competitors
Data-driven Decision-making	Employ data to shape decisions, allowing the organization to spot patterns swiftly and make well-informed choices that enhance products and services
A/B testing	Conduct thorough A/B tests on various aspects of the business, such as features and user interfaces, to refine user experiences and make rapid adjustments based on genuine user input
Innovative Content Strategies	Be open to exploring diverse content styles, formats and release strategies to break new ground and cater to evolving customer preferences

Netflix thrives on experimentation, a trait that shines through in product development and content production. Using data to inform their choices, they can rapidly test new features, interfaces and algorithms, enhancing the user experience through continuous iteration. Similarly, Netflix's content creation team has experimented with different storytelling formats, episode lengths and release strategies, underlining their readiness to challenge conventional media norms and embrace risk-taking.

Key Takeaways from the Case Study

1. **Boost autonomy in decision-making** – Empowering employees to make decisions can foster a climate that values creativity and critical thinking.
2. **Encourage a culture of risk-taking** – Nurturing an environment where employees can take risks can stimulate innovation and inspire them to stretch their boundaries, thus propelling the organization forward.
3. **Cultivate a sense of accountability and ownership** – Ensuring that employees take responsibility for their actions and decisions instils a profound sense of commitment and alignment with the organization's objectives.
4. **Promote a spirit of collaboration and innovation** – Concentrating on teamwork and ingenuity can shape an agile organization that is well equipped to adapt to changes and swiftly gain a competitive advantage.
5. **Capitalize on data-driven decision-making** – Utilizing data to guide decisions can empower the organization to promptly identify trends and make well-grounded decisions that enhance its offerings. Netflix's use of advanced personalization in content recommendations is a prime example of this strategy in action, making it highly successful in engaging its user base.
6. **Utilize A/B testing** – Conducting comprehensive A/B tests on different business elements, such as features and user interfaces, can enhance user experiences and allow for rapid adjustments based on real-time user feedback.
7. **Explore innovative content strategies** – Being receptive to diverse content styles, formats and release strategies can pave the way for new opportunities and cater to changing customer preferences.

Absorbing these insights from Netflix's Agile mindset equips business leaders to cultivate a more adaptable and resilient organization. An Agile mindset can offer organizations the competitive advantage they require to thrive in business. Incorporating Agile practices and principles can cultivate a culture of innovation, teamwork and customer-centricity that empowers teams to consistently deliver high-quality products and services.

Exercise: Cultivating an Agile Mindset in Your Organization

To foster an Agile mindset within your organization and ensure sustainable Agile implementation, it's essential to embed Agile values and principles into your organization's culture. Promoting these values empowers your teams and leadership to embrace change, drive innovation and deliver value to customers.

Consider implementing the following strategies to cultivate an Agile mindset:

1. **Promote a learning culture** – Encourage continuous learning, experimentation and innovation by providing training, resources and personal and professional development support. Create opportunities for employees to gain new skills and broaden their understanding of Agile principles and practices.

2. **Embrace failure as a learning opportunity** – Foster an environment where teams can take calculated risks and learn from failures. Encourage sharing lessons learned from setbacks, iterating and improving based on feedback, and adopting a growth mindset.

3. **Focus on customer value** – Prioritize initiatives that deliver the most value to customers and make customer feedback a central part of your decision-making process. Establish processes to gather, analyse and act on customer insights, ensuring your organization remains responsive and customer-centric.

4. **Encourage collaboration** – Foster cross-functional collaboration by breaking down silos, promoting open communication channels and creating opportunities for teams to work together on shared goals. Empower employees to contribute their ideas and expertise, fostering a sense of ownership and commitment to the Agile journey.

5. **Celebrate successes and progress** – Recognize and reward teams and individuals demonstrating Agile values and contributing to the organization's Agile transformation. Celebrate milestones and achievements, both big and small, to reinforce the positive impact of Agile practices and maintain momentum.

As you delve deeper into Agile, consider these strategies and how they can apply to your organization. Reflect on your progress, continuously cultivating an Agile mindset within your teams and leadership, as it serves as the foundation for a successful Agile implementation and long-term success.

Chapter Summary

This chapter delved into an Agile mindset to achieve business agility. It explored the core principles of the Agile mindset, including a focus on customer value, collaboration and continuous improvement. The chapter also discussed the importance of embracing a culture of experimentation and learning and showed how to cultivate this mindset within your organization, as well as covering common misconceptions about the Agile mindset and providing strategies for overcoming resistance to change.

Further Readings and Resources

1. Book: *Agile Estimating and Planning,* by Mike Cohn, 2005, Prentice Hall.

2. Book: *Mindset: The New Psychology of Success,* by Carol S. Dweck, 2006, Random House.

3. Website: Agile Alliance – www.agilealliance.org

3

Agile Approaches

Picture a traditional manufacturing line where each worker has a specific, unchanging task. It's efficient but rigid. Then, imagine a scenario where the market suddenly demands a different product. In a traditional system, this change can cause chaos. Now, imagine a different manufacturing line where teams are cross-functional and can swiftly adapt to new tasks as market demands change. This flexibility is the essence of Agile approaches in the business world.

Though the terms "framework" and "methodology" are often used interchangeably in less formal contexts, they have distinct meanings, particularly among professionals in fields like software development and project management. Methodologies are more prescriptive, providing defined steps to take, the rationale behind these steps and specific guidelines for accomplishing each step. In contrast, a framework offers a more flexible, skeletal structure designed to be adapted to fit the problem at hand. Both frameworks and methodologies aim for systematic problem-solving, but methodologies offer more comprehensive instructions, while frameworks provide the flexibility for adaptation.

Agile approaches encompass diverse frameworks and methodologies that promote teamwork, expedite the delivery of value to customers and bolster adaptability to change. Although these frameworks and methodologies differ in approaches, principles and practices, they aim to generate valuable products that cater to client needs while optimizing efficiency, speed and quality throughout the software development process.

Imagine leading a team where every member is aligned with the company's objectives, collaborating seamlessly and delivering value consistently. When you create the right Agile approach tailored to your organizational needs, this can be your reality.

Choosing the appropriate Agile approach for your organization is critical as a leader. Embracing suitable Agile ways of working will enhance your organization's flexibility and responsiveness, improving its capacity to navigate our modern business world's complex and dynamic market conditions.

As a leader, you have the power to shift your organization from a rigid, traditional way of working to an agile, adaptable one. Are you ready to be the catalyst that transforms not only workflows but also the very culture of your organization?

This chapter uncovers some of the most popular Agile approaches, presenting a road map for building an Agile, responsive and highly adaptable organization. It provides insights into how these approaches can help teams work more efficiently, deliver customer value more effectively and respond swiftly to shifting market demands. This chapter is a must-read for leaders seeking to enhance their organization's competitive edge.

While there are well over 40 variants and 70 practices within the Agile landscape, it's essential not to lose sight of the fact that these approaches stem from the same underlying Agile values and principles. Rather than becoming fixated on any single approach as the definitive answer, appreciate Agile as a dynamic and adaptable way of working.

However, as we embark on the Agile journey, we must be conscious of the ghosts of methodologies and frameworks past. Traces of legacy work habits can prove tenacious, with employees striving to fit these square pegs into Agile's round holes. This merging of old and new can dampen Agile's spirit, hampering progress and diluting the intended benefits of Agile ways of working.

A Brief History of Agile Approaches

Agile approaches trace their roots to the 1990s, an era marked by challenges and failures in software development. Conceived as an alternative approach to work, Agile emphasizes adaptability, flexibility and customer satisfaction. Fast forward to 2001, and the Agile Manifesto, published by a group of 17 software visionaries (Beck et al., 2001), heralded a new era, catalysing the Agile movement and establishing the principles that underlie the diverse Agile frameworks and methodologies we see today.

Before diving into these Agile approaches, it's crucial to understand how they differ from the traditional Waterfall method. Waterfall is a linear project management approach, where each phase is completed before moving on to the next. In contrast, Agile approaches focus on iterative progress and frequent feedback and are well suited for navigating the complexities of the modern business environment. Their adaptability often results in quicker delivery and higher customer satisfaction.

Table 07: Traditional vs. Agile Approaches

Aspect	Traditional Methodologies (e.g. Waterfall)	Agile Approaches (e.g. Scrum, Kanban)
Planning	Detailed upfront planning	Iterative, adaptive planning
Requirements	Fixed requirements	Flexible, evolving requirements
Scope Management	Strict scope control	Emphasis on prioritization and flexibility to deliver value
Communication	Formal, structured	Informal, collaborative
Documentation	Heavy emphasis on documentation	Lightweight, "just enough" documentation
Adaptability	Limited ability to adapt to change	High adaptability to changing needs
Team Structure	Hierarchical, functional roles	Cross-functional, self-organizing teams
Decision-making	Centralized	Decentralized, team based
Delivery Approach	Sequential phases	Incremental, iterative delivery
Progress Measurement	Stage-based, focus on deliverables	Time-boxed, focus on working product
Risk Management	Reactive	Proactive, continuous risk assessment

Benefits of Adopting Agile Approaches

Incorporating Agile approaches into your organization can bring many benefits that aid you in maintaining a competitive edge. These advantages include:

1. **Improved collaboration** – Agile frameworks nurture improved communication and collaboration among team members, resulting in heightened productivity and more effective problem-solving.
2. **Shorter time-to-market** – Agile practices enable organizations to launch products quicker and utilize feedback to adjust to evolving customer needs.
3. **Increased customer satisfaction** – Focusing on continuous improvement and customer feedback, Agile processes help ensure that developed products align with customer expectations and deliver value.
4. **Better adaptability** – Agile organizations are better prepared to adapt to shifting market conditions and evolving customer demands. This gives them a competitive edge over slower-moving, traditional companies.

Agile approaches support businesses in crafting and refining software by fragmenting projects into smaller, manageable increments that can be delivered routinely. This empowers businesses to acclimate to evolving market conditions and customer expectations promptly.

Fostering collaboration, communication and flexibility throughout the software development life cycle ensures Agile practices align development efforts with business objectives. This approach enables businesses to deliver superior software swiftly while mitigating risks and costs associated with traditional, large-scale development projects.

Agile teams collaborate closely with customers or end-users to get feedback, comprehend their needs, prioritize work based on business value and continually refine and improve the product to ensure customer delight.

Agile Manifesto and Agile Principles

As discussed in Chapter 2, the Agile Manifesto is a set of four values and 12 principles that guide Agile ways of working. As a reminder, the four values are:

1. Individuals and interactions over processes and tools
2. Working software over comprehensive documentation
3. Customer collaboration over contract negotiation
4. Responding to change over following a plan.

The 12 Agile principles emphasize customer satisfaction, early and continuous delivery of valuable software, collaboration, self-organization, simplicity and regular reflection for improvement. These values and principles form the foundation of all Agile methodologies and frameworks.

While the Agile Manifesto was initially created for software development, we need a version of agility that's universally applicable. As a seed needs the right conditions to grow into a tree, so the Agile principles need to be adapted and evolved for organizational usage.

To establish an Agile enterprise, it is vital to understand the various Agile approaches and how they can help you attain your objectives. Let us examine some of the most prevalent Agile frameworks and methodologies:

Scrum

Scrum, a widely used framework, aids teams in organizing and managing their tasks by embodying a set of values, principles and practices. It emphasizes teamwork, collaboration and iterative development to deliver high-quality products rapidly.

Scrum breaks work into small, manageable segments, called sprints, with a fixed duration. It relies on frequent meetings, including daily stand-ups, to collaborate, assess progress, assist one another as needed and adapt to change. Although Scrum is often associated with IT projects, it has also been effectively used in non-IT contexts such as marketing and people teams.

Table 08 compares the similarities and differences between Scrum in IT and non-IT contexts.

Table 08: Comparing Scrum in IT and Non-IT Organizations

Aspect	IT Organizations	Non-IT Organizations
Practices	– Software development – Continuous integration – Automated testing	– Product development – Marketing campaigns – Business process improvement
Key Roles	– Scrum Master – Product Owner – Developers	– Scrum Master – Product Owner – Cross-functional team
Common Challenges	– Technical debt – Integrating with legacy systems – Managing dependencies	– Adopting an Agile mindset – Cross-team collaboration – Adapting Scrum to non-IT context
Benefits	– Faster delivery – Improved quality – Enhanced collaboration	– Enhanced adaptability – Improved customer satisfaction – Increased innovation
Success Factors	– Commitment to Agile principles – Skilled Scrum Master – Clear product backlog	– Leadership buy-in – Effective communication – Continuous learning and improvement
Potential Modifications	– Tailoring Scrum events to team needs – Adapting to distributed teams	– Adjusting Scrum artefacts for non-IT projects – Integrating Scrum with other frameworks

Lean

Lean, a philosophy that emphasizes waste elimination and continuous process improvement, creates efficient, streamlined processes in an Agile context. This delivers customer value more swiftly. By focusing on optimizing the workflow and removing non-value-added activities, Lean principles enhance the agility and responsiveness of teams. This approach not only accelerates the delivery of products and services but also ensures that every step in the process adds meaningful value, aligning closely with customer needs and expectations.

Kanban

Kanban, a Lean workflow management method, helps teams operate more efficiently by visualizing work in progress and simultaneously limiting the work being done. Teams using Kanban typically employ a board to visualize their flow of work, with cards representing work items and columns signifying different stages of the process. This method enhances transparency and accountability, as team members can easily identify bottlenecks and balance workloads. It also facilitates continuous improvement and adaptability, as teams can quickly respond to changes and refine their processes in real-time, ensuring a more dynamic and responsive approach to project management.

XP (Extreme Programming)

XP, an Agile methodology, accentuates superior software development practices. It encompasses ongoing testing, integration, pair programming and regular releases. It deals with managing requirements and prioritizing work. Central to XP's philosophy is its emphasis on customer satisfaction and adaptability. This is achieved through short development cycles and a willingness to embrace changes in requirements, even late in the project. Furthermore, XP advocates for a sustainable work pace and a high level of communication within development teams, fostering a collaborative and efficient software development environment.

Disciplined Agile

Blending elements of Agile and Lean practices, Disciplined Agile presents a flexible toolkit for software development. The process is tailored to each team and each project's unique needs, offering various practices and tools to support this approach. This method fosters a culture of continuous learning and improvement, encouraging teams to experiment and evolve their practices over time. By embracing adaptability and iterative progress, Disciplined Agile effectively addresses complex project challenges, ensuring both efficiency and quality in the delivery of software solutions. Its versatility makes it particularly suitable for hybrid environments, where it can harmoniously integrate diverse methodologies and operational approaches.

SAFe (Scaled Agile Framework)

SAFe provides a comprehensive framework for scaling Agile practices across large organizations, offering a structured approach for coordinating multiple teams engaged in substantial projects. It incorporates various practices such as Agile Release Trains, PI Planning, and Value Streams, which are instrumental in ensuring synchronized progress and cohesive goal alignment. Additionally, SAFe emphasizes continuous learning and improvement cycles, fostering an environment of constant evolution and adaptation.

LeSS (Large Scale Scrum)

LeSS is a framework for applying Scrum principles to broader enterprises. Similar to SAFe, it involves practices for coordinating multiple teams on a sizeable project. However, it concentrates more on Scrum principles and values than developing a formal framework. This focus ensures that while scaling up, the core tenets of Scrum – transparency, inspection, and adaptation – are not lost but rather amplified across larger teams. LeSS aims to simplify complexity by empowering teams with Scrum's agile practices, encouraging them to collaborate efficiently and effectively in large-scale project environments.

Scrum at Scale

Scrum at Scale is another framework designed to broaden the application of Scrum methodologies within larger organizations. It incorporates practices for effectively coordinating multiple teams, such as modular work organization and regular synchronization events. This framework facilitates seamless collaboration and alignment among teams, ensuring that the combined efforts are geared towards common organizational goals. Moreover, Scrum at Scale emphasizes scalable decision-making processes and streamlined communication channels, enabling organizations to adapt swiftly to changing demands while maintaining a cohesive and agile operational structure.

Table 09: Comparison of Agile Frameworks and Methodologies

Framework/ Methodology	Key Principles	Roles	Practices
Scrum	– Iterative and incremental development – Time-boxed sprints – Empirical process control – Self-organizing teams – Continuous improvement	– Product Owner – Scrum Master – Developers	– Sprint Planning – Daily Scrum – Sprint Review – Sprint Retrospective – Product Backlog – Sprint Backlog – Definition of Done

Kanban	– Visualize work – Limit work in progress – Manage flow – Make process policies explicit – Improve collaboratively, evolve experimentally	– No specific roles defined, but can have roles like: * Manager * Team Member * Product Owner	– Kanban Board – Work in Progress (WIP) Limits – Continuous Delivery – Pull System – Metrics (e.g. Lead Time, Cycle Time) (Roles and practices can vary based on specific implementation)
XP (Extreme Programming)	– Embrace change – High-quality software – Frequent communication – Rapid feedback – Simplicity – Continuous integration – Sustainable pace – Shared code ownership	– Coach – Tracker – Developer – Tester – Customer	– Pair Programming – Test-Driven Development – Continuous Integration – Refactoring – Planning Game – Small Releases – Simple Design – Collective Code Ownership – System Metaphor
SAFe (Scaled Agile Framework)	– Business alignment – Transparency – Programme execution – Built-in quality – Continuous improvement – Lean Agile mindset – Decentralized decision-making	– Release Train Engineer – Product Manager – System Architect – Business Owner – Agile Teams	– Agile Release Train – Programme Increment – Innovation and Planning Iteration – DevOps – Continuous Exploration – Continuous Integration

			– Continuous Deployment – Lean Portfolio Management – Team and Technical Agility
Disciplined Agile	– Context-sensitive – People-first – Learning-oriented – Hybrid approach – Process improvement – Agile governance – Scalable	– Team Lead – Product Owner – Team Member – Architecture Owner – Stakeholder	– Goal-Driven Process – Inception Phase – Construction Phase – Transition Phase – Continuous Improvement Process – Context-specific practices from Scrum, Kanban, Lean, etc.
LeSS (Large Scale Scrum)	– Whole-product focus – Customer-centric – Empirical process control – Continuous improvement – Lean thinking – Systems Thinking – Decentralized decision-making	– Product Owner – Scrum Master – Feature Team – Area Product Owner – Area Scrum Master	– Overall Backlog – Overall Sprint – Coordination Practices (e.g. Overall Sprint Planning, Overall Retrospective) – Multi-team Product Backlog Refinement – Shared Definition of Done – Feature Teams – LeSS huge for larger organizations

Scrum at Scale	– Scalable Scrum – Synchronize teams – Continuous improvement – Inspect and adapt – Empirical process control – Decentralized decision-making	– Executive Action Team – Executive MetaScrum – Scrum Master – Product Owner – Development Team	– Cycles (Scaled Cycles) – MetaScrum – Scrum of Scrums – Cross-Teamleaders
Lean	– Eliminate waste – Build quality in – Create knowledge – Defer commitment – Deliver fast – Respect people – Optimize the whole	– No specific roles defined, but can have roles like: * Manager * Team member * Product Owner	– Value Stream Mapping – Continuous Improvement (Kaizen) – Just-in-Time (JIT) Production – Pull System–Standardized Work – Gemba Walk – Andon – Heijunka (Load Levelling) – Poka-Yoke (Error-Proofing) (Roles and practices can vary based on specific implementation)

While many Agile approaches exist, the common thread binding them all is a flexible, adaptable framework focusing on delivering value. It is essential to remember that Agile isn't about rigidly adhering to a particular system or methodology; it's about embracing an organizational ethos that emphasizes continuous improvement, collaboration and customer-centricity.

Consider factors such as team size, project complexity and organizational culture when comparing Agile frameworks and methodologies. For instance:

- Scrum is well suited for small to medium-sized projects with high uncertainty.
- SAFe (Scaled Agile Framework) is designed to scale Agile practices across large organizations with complex solutions and multiple teams.

- Large-Scale Scrum (LeSS) focuses on simplicity and flexibility to scale Scrum in large organizations.
- Kanban focuses on visualizing and optimizing the flow of work and can be easily combined with other Agile approaches.

Hybrid Agile Approaches

Some organizations not only achieve better outcomes through adopting a hybrid approach but also unlock unparalleled agility by essentially building their own custom framework. Whether that's by combining elements of different Agile methodologies or frameworks or creating something entirely new, what matters most is that it meticulously suits their specific needs and context. Hybrid Agile approaches often lead to unprecedented levels of flexibility and adaptability, serving as the catalyst for organizational transformation. These custom approaches allow organizations to tailor their processes in such a way that they are in perfect harmony with their goals and objectives. Importantly, no matter the level of customization, it remains crucial to anchor your strategy with the Agile mindset and principles at its core, ensuring a future-ready, resilient organization. For this very reason, embracing a hybrid Agile approach could very well be the ultimate competitive edge for businesses today.

Choosing the Right Agile Approach for Your Organization

Each Agile approach has unique nuances and advantages. The primary goal is to create a way of working that best aligns with your organization's needs and objectives. However, avoiding the pitfall of assuming that leadership always knows best is essential. Empowering teams to be part of this decision may be more effective, leveraging their insights and on-the-ground experiences.

Remember, it's not just about selecting an Agile approach; it's about determining whether Agile is the right fit for the problem or solution space. Drawing from complexity theory, your chosen approach should address the specific nature of the challenge – be it simple or chaotic. As with hybrid approaches, your approach must underpin the Agile mindset and principles discussed earlier.

Consider creating a decision-making framework or flowchart to help you choose the most suitable Agile approach for your project. This can include project size, complexity, team size and available resources. Incorporate feedback loops that allow your teams to provide insights, as this bottom-up input can be invaluable. Evaluating each option based on these criteria equips you to make more informed decisions.

Picture this – you can work in a structured manner with your team, deliver value to your customers on time, and quickly and effectively adapt to changes. Sounds like a dream, right? Well, that's the reality when you adopt an Agile approach. However, ensure that the approach you adopt aligns with the problem's nature and the solution space, allowing your organization to navigate complexity effectively.

Assess Your Organization's Readiness

Before implementing Agile approaches, assess your organization's readiness by examining its current processes, culture and structure to determine whether they are compatible with an Agile approach. Key questions include:

1. Do your teams have decision-making power and ownership of their work?
2. Is there a culture of collaboration and open communication?
3. Can your processes adapt to change and remain flexible?
4. Is there a willingness to experiment and learn from failures?
5. Are business leaders open to embracing an Agile mindset and supporting necessary changes?

If your organization needs to prepare for Agile approaches, you may need to implement changes to facilitate the transition.

Addressing Potential Drawbacks of Agile Approaches

While Agile methodologies and frameworks offer many benefits, there are potential drawbacks and challenges associated with their implementation. Some of these include the risk of scope creep due to frequent changes, potential difficulties in accurately estimating time and resources and the need for a high level of discipline and commitment from team members. To mitigate these drawbacks, it is crucial to establish clear project goals, maintain effective communication and regularly review and adjust your Agile processes as needed.

Agile Theatre

Imagine a theatre stage, actors following a script, playing their parts but missing the essence of the story – this is "Agile Theatre", a production where Agile approaches are enacted but not truly lived. It serves as a haunting reminder of what could go wrong if we treat Agile approaches as just another set of procedures.

Common Obstacles and Potential Solutions

As organizations adopt Agile approaches, they might encounter certain obstacles. Awareness of these challenges enables proactive measures to address them, leading to a more seamless transition.

Common issues and potential solutions are:

1. **Resistance to change** – Change can unsettle team members. Promote open discussions about worries and apprehensions, addressing them empathetically and supportively. Emphasize Agile's advantages and share

success stories to facilitate the transition. Make sure that team members understand the why of Agile.

2. **Lack of vision** – Vision provides direction, inspiring your team to align with the organization's objectives. Ensure a clear vision statement resonates with your team's aspirations and paves the way for adopting Agile approaches.

3. **Lack of clarity** – Teams may feel lost, leading to inefficiencies and missed opportunities. Clearly define roles, responsibilities and expectations in your Agile transition, ensuring each member understands their contribution to the overall objective.

4. **Lack of understanding** – Agile approaches can be intricate, causing a change in perspective. Offer comprehensive training and resources to help your team grasp Agile's principles and practices. Engage Agile coaches or consultants for guidance and support.

5. **Difficulty scaling Agile practices** – Expanding Agile approaches throughout a large organization can be tough. First, descale and assess processes for fitness. Only then, as scaling challenges arise, consider scaling frameworks for managing sizeable Agile projects.

Executing Agile Approaches in Your Organization

Incorporating Agile approaches into your organization can be daunting but is ultimately rewarding. Adopting Agile demands alterations to your organization's culture, processes and structure. Here are some tips for getting this done:

Start Small

Agile approaches thrive when teams can quickly iterate and receive customer or stakeholder feedback. Starting with a small project lets you test the waters without excessive risk. Introducing any Agile methodology or framework is an experiment. You may have to modify your approach as you discover more.

Train Your Teams

Training your teams on the selected methodology or framework is crucial. Teach them Agile principles and practices and provide practical training on tools and techniques. This helps teams perceive the benefits, spurring motivation for change.

Engage Agile Coaches

Consider enlisting Agile coaches or consultants if your organization is new to Agile or seeking to refine its practices. These professionals offer support during implementation, help overcome challenges and ensure a smooth transition. They can also pinpoint potential hurdles, deliver tailored training and share best practices from other organizations, securing a successful Agile transformation.

Empower Your Teams

Agile relies on self-organizing teams with decision-making autonomy and ownership of their work. Cultivate a trusting, empowering environment where team members feel secure taking risks and experimenting.

Embrace Change

Agile centres around adapting to change. Stay open to fresh ideas and be ready to adjust. This needs a culture where we always learn and improve. Even difficult feedback is important and can lead to changes.

Measure Progress

Frequent feedback and measurement are vital in Agile approaches to monitor progress and identify improvement areas. Establish metrics and key performance indicators (KPIs) to gauge progress and ensure you and your team deliver value to customers.

Focus on Communication

Agile focuses on teamwork and communication, so create clear communication channels and encourage open dialogue among team members. This helps detect issues early and avert misunderstandings.

Develop Agile Leadership

Agile leaders play a crucial role in fostering an Agile way of working and supporting the successful implementation of Agile methodologies or frameworks. Agile leaders promote a collaborative environment, empower their teams and make decisions based on Agile principles. They also focus on continuous improvement, adaptability and value-driven delivery. To develop Agile leadership, it is essential to invest in leadership training and coaching, helping leaders to embody and promote Agile values and practices throughout the organization.

Continuously Improve

Lastly, refine your Agile approach. Review your chosen methodology or framework and its processes regularly, get feedback from teams and customers and make necessary adjustments. This helps optimize your approach over time and guarantees continuous delivery of value to customers.

Adherence to these guidelines enables business leaders to successfully integrate Agile approaches into their organization, fostering a culture that values collaboration, experimentation and continuous improvement. This enables them to develop an Agile business capable of adapting to change and outpacing competitors.

CLEAR Lens for "Agile Approaches"

We can apply two CLEAR Model® principles to Agile Approaches:

Execution: Agile approaches epitomize the CLEAR principle of Execution. They embody a customer-centric ethos and provide robust frameworks for delivering high value efficiently and rapidly. Agile practices streamline work processes, prioritize value-adding tasks and ensure teams can deliver top-quality results while maintaining a sustainable work pace. The principle of Execution, as depicted in the CLEAR Model®, is a testament to the power of Agile ways of working.

Responsiveness: An Agile approach is characterized by its inherent ability to adapt and respond swiftly to change, underpinning the Responsiveness principle in the CLEAR Model®. It emphasizes the importance of being alert to changes in the external business environment and being prepared to adjust strategic direction as and when needed. This inherent flexibility and readiness to pivot is a key attribute of Agile approaches.

Reflection Prompts

1. Which Agile methodologies or frameworks have you encountered or used before? What were their strengths and weaknesses in relation to your organization's needs?

2. How can you apply the principles of the Agile Manifesto to your current projects or initiatives?

Case Study: Etsy's Agile Success Story

Let us delve into Etsy's Agile success story, which demonstrates the power of effectively implementing Agile practices and their impact on an organization's performance and adaptability.

Adopting Agile approaches is a strategic move for businesses striving to remain agile in a constantly changing environment. Companies like Etsy exemplify the impact of leveraging these approaches effectively. Analysing their approach offers valuable insights into implementing Agile practices and lessons for organizations seeking the advantages of Agile transformation.

Etsy, a renowned e-commerce platform for handmade and vintage items, has adopted Agile approaches that have contributed to its delivery capabilities and customer experience. This adoption has helped with their transition to a cloud-based infrastructure, adoption of DevOps practices and establishment of a collaborative culture. This has accelerated their delivery process, making it more flexible and responsive to customer needs. Dissolving traditional team barriers and encouraging cross-functional collaboration and open communication has helped Etsy cultivate a more Agile organization capable of adapting to market changes and continuously improving its product offerings.

Etsy's leadership has been crucial in driving the Agile transformation. They have embraced the Agile mindset and promoted transparency, trust and collaboration. This top-down support for Agile ways of working has helped the organization benefit from increased business agility.

A strong feedback loop is another essential factor in Etsy's Agile journey. The company incorporates customer feedback and data-driven insights into its product development process. Continuously iterating and refining products based on user needs has enabled Etsy to remain relevant and responsive to customer expectations. This customer-centric approach has been a key driver of Etsy's success and has allowed the company to maintain a competitive edge in the e-commerce market.

Etsy's journey in adopting Agile and DevOps practices began as early as 2009, moving away from traditional software development approaches and adopting practices that facilitated faster delivery and a shorter turnaround time. Initially, Etsy's engineering team was small and segmented into siloed groups, which hindered its software development efforts. In 2008, the company's engineers recognized the limitations of their monolithic architecture and waterfall business model, leading to challenges like frequent file changes, inconsistencies in deployment and increased deployment time.

The company underwent a significant cultural shift to foster collaboration and synchronization among teams. This was in line with the principles of the DevOps movement, emphasizing the importance of a supportive culture for successful DevOps adoption. Etsy experienced substantial growth over five years, particularly during the pandemic, which led to a threefold increase in traffic almost overnight. To manage this, Etsy had to scale up its infrastructure, product delivery, and talent significantly. The company's foundational scaling work started before the pandemic, in 2017, when Mike Fisher joined as CTO.

With the growth and the need for scaling, Etsy faced challenges with its physical hardware in data centers and identified the product delivery process as a potential bottleneck. This led to a strategic move to the Google Cloud Platform and a re-evaluation of their product planning and delivery processes. Etsy partnered with Thoughtworks, a company with a similar approach to Agile – focusing on principles and culture rather than strict rituals. This partnership helped Etsy to improve and tackle pressing initiatives, contributing to the refinement of its product delivery culture.

Table 10: Key Components of Etsy's Agile Success

Component	Description
Cloud-based Infrastructure	A flexible and scalable infrastructure that enables rapid responses to market changes and customer demands, as demonstrated by Etsy's move to a cloud-based infrastructure
DevOps Practices	Streamlining development and operations processes to reduce delivery times and enhance customer experiences, as exemplified by Etsy's adoption of DevOps practices
Cross-functional Collaboration and Communication	Fostering a culture of collaboration and open communication among team members to work effectively and develop innovative solutions, a key element in Etsy's Agile success
Continuous Improvement	Commitment to regularly iterating and refining products and processes based on user needs and data-driven insights, allowing companies like Etsy to stay ahead of competitors and consistently deliver value to customers

The success story of Etsy's Agile transformation offers valuable insights for organizations embarking on their Agile journey. Businesses can steer successful Agile transformations and enhance agility in rapidly evolving markets by focusing on organizational restructuring, fostering a collaborative culture, establishing a robust feedback loop and ensuring top-down support for Agile ways of working.

Key Takeaways from Etsy's Agile Success Story

1. **Leveraging a cloud-based infrastructure** – Transitioning to a cloud-based infrastructure has allowed Etsy to adjust swiftly to fluctuating market conditions and evolving customer needs.

2. **Implementing DevOps practices** – Etsy's incorporation of DevOps practices has simplified and accelerated its development and operations processes, leading to reduced delivery times and better customer experiences.

3. **Promoting cross-functional collaboration and communication** – Etsy's strategy of encouraging teamwork and transparent communication among their staff has facilitated effective cooperation and nurtured the creation of innovative solutions.

4. **Instilling a culture of continuous improvement** – Etsy's dedication to the ongoing refinement of its products and processes has positioned it ahead of its rivals and ensured it consistently delivers value to its customer base.

5. **Learning from successful enterprises** – Examining the strategies of successful companies such as Etsy can offer invaluable knowledge for organizations aiming to effectively integrate Agile methodologies or frameworks, enhancing their business agility and competitive edge.

Exercise: Choosing the Right Agile Approach for Your Organization

Selecting the most suitable methodology or framework for your organization is crucial for ensuring the success of your Agile transformation. To make an informed decision, carefully consider various factors that could influence the effectiveness of different approaches within your specific context.

Consider the following factors when selecting an Agile approach:

1. **Project size and complexity** – Assess whether a framework like Scrum is better suited for smaller projects or whether a more comprehensive framework, is required for larger, more complex projects.

2. **Team size and distribution** – Evaluate your team's size and geographical distribution. Determine whether a methodology like Kanban works well for distributed teams or whether the closer collaboration required by a framework like Scrum is feasible.

3. **Organizational culture** – Examine how well each framework or methodology aligns with your organization's culture, values and goals. Choose an approach that complements and reinforces your organization's unique strengths and challenges.

4. **Industry and domain** – Factor in any industry-specific requirements or constraints that may influence your choice of framework or methodology.

Some industries, like healthcare or finance, may have unique regulatory or compliance requirements to consider.

5. **Adaptability** – Recognize that no single framework or methodology perfectly fits every organization or project. Be open to adapting and evolving your chosen approach based on your organization's needs and feedback.

6. **Implementation support** – Consider the availability of training, coaching and resources for your chosen approach. Ensure your organization will invest in the support to facilitate smooth implementation.

Reflecting on these factors equips you to select the Agile approaches that best suit your organization's needs and context. As you continue your Agile journey, remember that Agile practices must be continuously adapted and refined to meet your evolving goals and challenges, making it essential to remain flexible and open to change.

Chapter Summary

This chapter delved into the various Agile approaches that can be used toward achieving overall business agility. It provided an overview of key methodologies and frameworks such as Scrum, Kanban and Lean and highlighted the benefits and limitations of each. The chapter also discussed choosing the right approach for your organization and project and guided implementing and customizing Agile approaches to fit your needs. The chapter covered best practices for Agile development, including prioritizing customer value, breaking down work into manageable chunks and embracing continuous improvement.

Further Readings and Resources

1. Book: *Scrum: The Art of Doing Twice the Work in Half the Time*, by Jeff Sutherland and J.J. Sutherland, 2014, Crown Business.

2. Book: *Kanban: Successful Evolutionary Change for Your Technology Business*, by David J. Anderson, 2010, Blue Hole Press.

3. Website: Scrum.org – www.scrum.org

4. Website: Kanban – www.kanban.university

5. Website: Extreme Programming – www.extremeprogramming.org

6. Website: Scaled Agile Framework – www.scaledagileframework.com

7. Website: Disciplined Agile – www.pmi.org/disciplined-agile

8. Website: Large-Scale Scrum – www.less.works

9. Website: Scrum at Scale – www.scrumatscale.com

10. Website: Lean – www.lean.org

Part 2

Leadership and Culture in Agile Business

4

Leadership in Business Agility

Consider the plight of a well-established technology firm. Their products are top-notch and their reputation is unblemished. Yet, as the market shifts, they find themselves playing catch-up. Not because they lack innovation but due to leadership that remains tethered to outdated ways of working, resistant to the dynamic currents of the Agile world.

Imagine a different story: a leader at the helm of this tech giant anticipates change, aligns her team with a unified vision, fosters a culture of continuous improvement and encourages swift, decisive action. This leader doesn't merely adapt to change; she's always two steps ahead, making proactive moves.

The importance of agility cannot be overstated as businesses continuously evolve. It is vital to adapt quickly to emerging challenges and capitalize on opportunities to stay ahead of the competition. Crafting a flexible organization equipped to handle change is no easy feat. Leadership founded on Agile principles and approaches, emphasizing iterative advancement, collaboration and swift adaptation, is essential to this effort.

Agile leaders are vital in cultivating the organizational culture, shaping the work atmosphere and guiding their teams. These visionary individuals adeptly convey their objectives to team members, aligning them with the organization's mission. By emphasizing collaboration, Agile leaders forge solid relationships with their colleagues. They create a trusting, respectful environment that encourages effective teamwork. With an Agile mindset, these leaders are devoted to constant learning and self-improvement, rapidly responding to change.

Being an Agile leader isn't about ticking boxes; it's about evolving alongside your organization, armed with a dynamic skill set that transforms challenges into stepping stones for innovation. Are you ready to pivot your leadership style to become the driving force of your organization's Agile transformation?

This chapter delves into the critical subject of leadership in business agility. Discover how pivotal leadership is in building an Agile organization that adapts quickly to changing market demands. You will gain invaluable insight into the qualities and characteristics that make a successful Agile leader and learn practical tips on identifying and developing these traits within your organization. The comprehensive overview of leadership in business agility will give you the knowledge and tools to lead your team towards unparalleled success in the competitive domain.

Beware, however, of those who insist their variant of Agile is the only solution. Agility is a flexible philosophy, not a rigid blueprint. True leaders encourage a diversity of Agile interpretations to foster a culture of genuine agility.

What Is Agile Leadership?

Agile leadership is a diverse style of leadership that emphasizes adaptability, collaboration, continuous learning and improvement. Agile leaders possess a clear organizational vision that they effectively communicate to their teams. They prioritize setting goals that align with the organization's broader mission while valuing teamwork and cultivating robust relationships with colleagues. They enable cohesive team functioning by fostering an environment of trust and respect.

An Agile leader is not just someone who understands Agile ways of working but someone who embodies the Agile mindset and creates an environment where Agile principles can be effectively applied to achieve organizational and team success. This leadership style is crucial in today's modern business, where adaptability, quick learning, and responsiveness are key to success. Leaders in an Agile transformation are like guides in uncharted terrain. They help senior managers comprehend the philosophy and commitments of Agile. They also carry the responsibility of aligning the team's motivation with higher-level objectives.

Agile leadership fosters an environment where teams feel safe to experiment and learn from failures, promotes inter-departmental collaboration and encourages transparent communication between team members and management. Agile leaders also practice servant leadership, a leadership philosophy where the leader's primary goal is to serve their team rather than command them. With this approach, leaders focus on removing obstacles for their teams and providing them with the resources and support to succeed. They flip the traditional leadership pyramid, putting the team's needs before their own, promoting a more inclusive and effective work environment.

These leaders also embrace a growth mindset, demonstrating a commitment to continuous development and enhancement. They remain receptive to feedback, constantly seeking ways to refine their leadership abilities. Agile leaders empower team members to assume responsibility for their tasks and decision-making. They recognize that valuable ideas can arise from any source and encourage creative thinking and risk-taking. With adaptability at their core, Agile leaders must adjust to change, acknowledging the fluid nature of the business world and adapting their strategies as needed.

Agile Leadership Competencies and Responsibilities

Agile leadership is more than just adopting a new set of management practices. It's about embracing a different way of interacting and connecting with your organization and teams. Table 11 highlights the essential soft skills and interpersonal competencies critical for Agile leaders. These competencies aren't just about "what" an Agile leader does; they're about "how" they do it. They reflect the behavioural shifts and attitudes required to guide teams successfully in an Agile environment.

Table 11: Agile Leadership Competencies and Responsibilities

Competencies	Description
Fostering Collaboration	Promote a culture of teamwork and cooperative problem-solving
Promoting Adaptability	Encourage teams to remain flexible and responsive to changes
Encouraging Continuous Learning	Advocate for an iterative, learning-focused approach to projects
Cultivating Trust	Develop an atmosphere of transparency where ideas and concerns can be freely expressed
Demonstrating Servant Leadership	Act as a facilitator, providing resources and support for the team's work
Inspiring Others	Clearly communicate the organization's mission to motivate team members
Implementing Governance	Guide the application of Agile practices in decision-making, resource allocation and risk management

Agile Leadership Roles and Responsibilities

Mastering Agile leadership requires not only interpersonal prowess but also strategic insight. Table 12 highlights this crucial dimension, particularly the strategic duties and managerial responsibilities inherent to an Agile leader's role. This involves the tasks and roles that relate to the broader organizational context and align with strategic objectives.

Table 12: Agile Leadership Roles and Responsibilities

Roles	Description
Vision Setting	Create a compelling vision that aligns with organizational goals and Agile transformation
Team Empowerment	Foster autonomy, self-management and ownership among teams
Learning Culture Development	Cultivate a culture of continuous improvement and knowledge-sharing

Open Communication Promotion	Encourage transparent and timely communication across teams and departments
Obstacle Removal	Identify and address barriers to Agile adoption and team performance
Change Management	Guide the organization through Agile transformation and change
Coaching and Mentoring	Support individuals' and teams' growth and development through guidance and feedback
Modelling Agile Values	Demonstrate an Agile mindset and values through personal behaviour

Why Is Agile Leadership Important?

Agile leadership holds significant importance as it facilitates organizations in nurturing a culture focused on agility. Adaptable leaders who promote constant improvement inspire their team members to do the same. When leaders empower their colleagues to take charge and make decisions, innovation and new ideas are more likely to emerge.

Agile leadership styles foster a supportive, cooperative and empowering atmosphere that attracts and keeps top talent. A strong Agile leadership presence contributes to a positive company culture in which employees feel valued, engaged and motivated to deliver their best work.

Visionary leaders who provide clear organizational direction help maintain focus and alignment among team members, ensuring everyone is working towards the same goals.

Agile leaders must also be adaptable, drawing from different leadership styles and philosophies to meet the varying needs of their people and organizations.

Cultivating Agile Leaders in Your Organization: Tips and Techniques

To develop Agile leaders, it is vital to grasp the qualities required and the steps to nurture such leadership within your organization. Here are a few strategies to consider:

Identify Potential Leaders

Start by identifying team members who show Agile leadership traits and offer them opportunities to hone their skills. Inclusivity and diversity must be central when selecting potential leaders. A diverse leadership team enables new ideas, fosters innovation and results in a more adaptable organization.

Companies like Spotify and Netflix have successfully nurtured diverse Agile leadership teams in the technology sector, enabling them to remain agile and innovative in their fast-changing industries. Search for individuals who are cooperative, innovative and receptive to feedback, as they are likely ideal candidates for leadership roles.

Provide Training

Once you have identified potential leaders, provide training programmes and workshops that emphasize leadership development, communication and collaboration. These sessions help your team members gain the skills to become proficient Agile leaders.

Provide Feedback

Regular feedback is crucial for nurturing Agile leaders. Give your team members frequent feedback and coaching, enabling them to enhance their leadership skills. This will help them recognize areas for improvement and support their growth as leaders. Provide them with opportunities to reflect and identify where they need to improve.

Establish Mentorship and Coaching Programmes

Mentorship and coaching can significantly contribute to developing Agile leaders. Pair potential leaders with experienced Agile leaders who can guide them through real-world challenges and share their knowledge and insights. Encourage open communication between mentors and mentees to facilitate sharing ideas and experiences.

Create a Succession Plan

A continuous supply of Agile leaders is essential for preserving an Agile culture. Create a succession plan that pinpoints potential future leaders and details the steps needed for their development and advancement. This plan must be regularly reviewed and updated to ensure seamless leadership transitions.

Incorporating Agile Leadership Practices in Your Organization

Integrating Agile leadership practices can be challenging, but it is crucial for establishing an Agile culture. To implement these practices:

Start with a Clear Vision

Agile leaders possess a clear organizational vision and effectively communicate it to their teams. They recognize the significance of aligning goals and objectives with the organization's mission. Therefore, leaders must develop a transparent vision encompassing the company's purpose, goals and values. This vision must be conveyed to all team members and serve as the basis for decision-making.

Foster a Culture of Collaboration

Agile leaders appreciate the need for collaboration and excel at fostering strong team relationships. They create an atmosphere of trust and respect, enabling effective teamwork. Leaders must promote collaboration by allowing team members to cooperate and learn from one another, including voicing different views and opinions. This could include forming cross-functional teams or encouraging knowledge-sharing.

Embrace the Agile Mindset

As mentioned in Chapter 2, Agile leaders adopt an Agile mindset, committing to ongoing learning and improvement. They are receptive to feedback and consistently seek ways to refine their leadership skills. Encourage team members to adopt the Agile mindset by offering training and development opportunities. Consider motivating team members to attend conferences or workshops centred around Agile practices.

Empower Team Members

Agile leaders empower their team members to take ownership of their work and make decisions. Trusting teams to pursue agreed-upon goals is key. These leaders provide support and guidance, ensuring team members have the tools and resources to thrive. Micromanagement is avoided, and open-door policies are maintained. Recognizing that great ideas can come from any source, they inspire their teams to think innovatively and take risks, granting decision-making freedom.

Be Adaptive

Adaptable and responsive, Agile leaders swiftly adjust to new situations. They acknowledge the shifting business environment and are open to altering their strategies. Agile leaders assess market shifts and gather customer feedback attentively to identify changes. They foster these qualities within their teams by encouraging flexibility, adaptability and a willingness to change course for the company's benefit.

Lead by Example

Embody the behaviours you expect from your team members, and show dedication to Agile thinking and principles. Integrate Agile practices into your leadership style, offering regular feedback and coaching to improve team members' leadership abilities. Embracing the Agile mindset, share your experiments, particularly those that fail, and discuss the lessons learned. Display vulnerability to encourage psychological safety.

Recognize and Reward Agile Leadership Behaviours

Encourage and reinforce Agile leadership behaviours by recognizing and rewarding team members who exhibit them. This can include providing public recognition, offering opportunities for career advancement or other incentives that align with your organization's values and culture. Rewarding these behaviours signals their importance and motivates others to adopt them.

Measure Progress and Success

To ensure the effectiveness of your Agile leadership practices, it is important to measure progress and success. Monitor key performance indicators (KPIs) like employee engagement, customer satisfaction and project success rates. Use the collected data to make informed decisions, pinpoint areas for improvement and adapt your leadership style as necessary. Continuous improvement is vital for sustaining and enhancing your organization's Agile leadership capabilities.

Besides these practices, there are a few other things to remember when implementing Agile leadership practices in your organization:

1. **Be patient** – Agile leadership implementation requires time and commitment. Be ready to invest the needed resources.
2. **Be flexible** – Adaptability is central to Agile leadership. Stay open to change, and be prepared to adjust your strategy as needed.
3. **Celebrate successes** – Celebrate your team's achievements, recognizing the effort and hard work that led to the outcomes. Foster a positive culture that motivates team members to pursue excellence.

Recent studies (such as the *Harvard Business Review*'s "Embracing Agile" report) have shown that companies that consistently apply Agile leadership practices achieve higher levels of customer satisfaction, employee engagement and overall business performance.

Leading Change in an Agile Organization

As businesses transition to agile models, leaders must understand how to communicate the need for change, engage employees and address resistance.

1. **Communication strategies** – Leaders must communicate the reasons for adopting Agile practices and the expected benefits. This helps employees understand the rationale behind the change and fosters a shared vision.
2. **Employee engagement** – Involve employees in the change process by encouraging participation in decision-making and giving them

opportunities to contribute ideas. This promotes a sense of ownership and commitment to the Agile transformation.

3. **Addressing resistance** – Identify and address potential resistance to change by understanding employee concerns, providing necessary support and demonstrating empathy. Offer training and resources to help employees adapt to new Agile processes and practices.

Common Challenges and Pitfalls in Agile Leadership Transition

Transitioning from traditional management styles to an Agile leadership approach can be challenging for many leaders. Some common challenges include overcoming resistance to change, adapting to a new mindset and managing uncertainty. Table 13 below summarizes potential solutions and strategies to address these challenges.

Table 13: Agile Leadership Challenges, Solutions and Strategies

Challenge	Solution	Strategy
Resistance to Change	Foster a culture of continuous improvement	Communicate the benefits of Agile, involve employees in the transformation process
Lack of Clear Vision and Goals	Define and communicate a clear vision and objectives	Develop a road map for Agile adoption, align goals with the organization's overall mission
Ineffective Communication	Implement open and transparent communication channels	Encourage regular feedback, hold daily stand-ups and promote collaboration
Hierarchical Management Structure	Adopt a more flexible and decentralized management approach	Empower teams, flatten the hierarchy and create cross-functional teams
Limited Employee Engagement	Encourage employee involvement in decision-making	Create a psychologically safe environment, recognize and reward contributions
Inadequate Agile Training	Provide ongoing training and support	Offer tailored Agile training programmes, provide access to resources and coaching

Inconsistent Agile Implementation	Ensure organization-wide alignment and consistency	Establish Agile governance structures, create a dedicated Agile transformation team
Insufficient Measurement and Metrics	Define and track relevant Agile performance indicators	Implement KPIs that align with the organization's objectives, regularly review and adjust
Insufficient Training and Development	Provide necessary training resources and coaching	Offer workshops, coaching and access to Agile resources for team members
Overemphasis on Short-term Results	Focus on long-term objectives while balancing short-term expectations	Prioritize long-term growth and adaptability, manage short-term performance expectations

Transitioning to Agile – Overcoming Resistance to Change

While navigating towards an agile approach, encountering resistance to change is a given. Leaders are central in soothing this resistance and directing the organization towards successful Agile adoption. Their role is essential, not only as a guide but also as a facilitator of the transition process.

Leaders can employ a number of strategies to manage this resistance:

1. **Transparent communication** – Clear and transparent communication about the necessity for change, its benefits and the potential challenges that can alleviate fears and uncertainties. The leaders' role is to ensure that there's no room for misunderstanding or misinformation. They must construct a narrative that paints an inspiring yet realistic picture of the transformation journey.

2. **Inclusive change process** – Involving team members in the decision-making process imbues them with a sense of ownership, reducing resistance. By turning them into active participants in change, you foster a collective responsibility toward successful implementation. This inclusion, coupled with transparent communication, can help deconstruct barriers of resistance.

3. **Support and training** – Leaders must ensure resources, training and emotional support are available to ease the transition process. This could involve tailored Agile training sessions, mentorship programmes or a "door

always open" policy for employees to share their concerns. Providing the necessary tools and assistance can make the shift smoother and less daunting.

4. **Empathy and patience** – Change can be unsettling for many. Leaders must exercise empathy toward employees' concerns and demonstrate patience as they adapt to new ways of working. Remember, Agile transformation is not a sprint; it's a marathon that calls for understanding and resilience.

5. **Celebrate progress** – Recognizing and celebrating small wins along the way can boost morale and reinforce the positive aspects of the change. It's the little victories that eventually add up to a successful transformation.

6. **Balancing act** – Leaders must balance short-term achievements and long-term strategic goals. This involves aligning team efforts toward the organization's long-term vision while understanding that sustained improvement often requires patience and persistence. Remember, it's not about reaching the finish line in record time but ensuring everyone crosses it together.

Although reflective of the strategies tabled above, these points are pivotal in driving home the essence of leadership during the Agile transition. Their significance in ensuring a successful Agile adoption cannot be overstated.

In many cases, people do not resist or fear the change. Instead, people want to understand, avoid anxiety and maintain some level of control/autonomy over the change that is happening. The leader's job is not only to help followers cope with the emotion of change but also to work with followers who become collaborators with the change.

The goal is not to eliminate resistance but to navigate it effectively. As a leader, your approach can significantly impact how change is perceived and adopted within the organization.

Agile Leadership in the Real World

Visualize a world where more than just 3% of organizations achieve a successful sustained Agile transformation. To reach that vision, we need the right leadership, leaders who aren't just implementing Agile but embodying it, ready to embrace change and drive their teams towards a more flexible, resilient future.

Introducing Agile leadership practices across an organization demands a clear vision, a collaborative culture, dedication to Agile principles, team empowerment, adaptability and leading by example. Agile leadership benefits extend beyond mere responsiveness to change. Leaders who adopt these practices cultivate an Agile culture and create a team better prepared to react to change, ultimately delivering value to customers more rapidly.

CLEAR Lens for "Leadership in Business Agility"

We can apply one of the CLEAR Model® principles to Leadership in Business Agility:

 Leadership: Agile leadership isn't just about guiding a team; it's about embodying the CLEAR Model®. Agile leaders support and guide their organization through the Agile transformation and foster an environment that encourages continuous learning, innovation and collaboration. Agile leaders don't merely instruct; they inspire, empowering their teams to embrace the Agile mindset and realize their full potential.

Reflection Prompts

1. How do your organization's leadership practices currently suppose to challenge the principles of Agile? Identify specific examples.

2. What leadership behaviours or strategies could be adopted or enhanced in your organization to better facilitate an Agile transformation?

Case Study: Agile Leadership in Action – Amazon and Zappos

In this chapter, we've emphasized the significance of Agile leadership and its role in achieving business agility. Amazon and Zappos serve as prime examples of this notion. When we examine their leadership strategies and practices, we can gain valuable insights into creating and guiding Agile teams that exhibit greater adaptability, innovation, and a customer-centric approach.

Strong leadership drives business agility success, and companies like Amazon and Zappos exemplify Agile leadership practices. Analysing their strategies provides insights into building and leading Agile teams.

Amazon's "Day 1" philosophy, as discussed in Jeff Bezos' annual shareholder letters, encourages a relentless focus on the customer and long-term growth. This mindset and agile decision-making processes enable Amazon to adapt quickly in a dynamic business environment. Bezos calls this mindset "Day 1", which has become the company's mantra for longevity, keeping Amazon on a continuous cycle of experimentation, innovation, iteration, and even failure. From the very beginning, Jeff Bezos was determined not to repeat the mistakes of companies that failed to adapt to shifting climates. This philosophy is evident in Amazon's leadership principles, such as "Customer Obsession", "Ownership" and "Think Big", promoting a culture of innovation, experimentation, and long-term thinking.

For example, Bezos is known for using the "two-pizza rule" for team sizes, which states that teams should be small enough to be fed by two pizzas. This approach ensures that teams remain agile and efficient. Bezos encourages a "working backwards" approach to product development, starting with the customer experience and working back towards the technology required to deliver it. Amazon maintains its e-commerce industry leadership by empowering employees to own their work and make prompt, effective decisions.

Zappos, a leading online shoe retailer, demonstrates exceptional Agile leadership, as detailed in Hsieh's book, *Delivering Happiness* (2010). Zappos has created a highly adaptable organization that consistently delivers exceptional customer service by fostering a culture of empowerment, collaboration, and continuous learning. Its commitment to a strong company culture, underpinned by core values, has driven its business success. In their pursuit of Agile leadership principles, Zappos experimented with the Holacracy management system, which aimed to decentralize decision-making and empower employees. Although the company eventually moved away from Holacracy, the experiment showed its dedication to exploring new ways of fostering agility and adaptability.

Table 14: Amazon and Zappos Agile Leadership Comparison

Aspect	Amazon	Zappos
Leadership Philosophy	"Day 1" Philosophy – Focus on customer and long-term growth	Culture of empowerment, collaboration and continuous learning
Unique Strategies	Two-pizza rule, working backwards approach	Experimentation with the Holacracy management system
Organizational Culture	Customer-centric, nimble decision-making, innovation	Strong company culture, core values and adaptability

Key Success Factors	Empowering employees, rapid decision-making, and customer focus	Dedication to company culture, learning and collaboration

Amazon and Zappos have distinguished themselves by implementing distinct leadership practices supporting their Agile approaches. For instance, Amazon utilizes the "Leadership Principles", a set of 16 guiding values that inform decision-making and help align employees around a shared vision.

One example of this principle in action is their development of Amazon Web Services, where the principle of "Think Big" spurred the creation of a game-changing cloud service platform. These principles, which include "Customer Obsession", "Bias for Action" and "Think Big", promote a culture of innovation, experimentation and long-term thinking.

Similarly, Zappos emphasizes the importance of "The Zappos Family Core Values", a list of ten values that serve as the foundation for their company culture. Among these values are "Deliver WOW Through Service", "Embrace and Drive Change" and "Pursue Growth and Learning", which reflect Zappos' commitment to agility, adaptability and continuous improvement.

Key Takeaways from the Case Study

1. **Embrace a customer-focused mindset** – Amazon and Zappos prioritize customer needs and work relentlessly to deliver value, enabling them to stay ahead of competitors and maintain customer loyalty.
2. **Foster a culture of empowerment and collaboration** – Amazon and Zappos have created environments that encourage innovation and adaptability by empowering employees to take ownership of their work and make decisions.
3. **Prioritize continuous learning and improvement** – Both companies are committed to learning from their experiences, iterating on their processes and fostering a growth mindset, contributing to their long-term success.
4. **Cultivate a strong company culture** – Amazon and Zappos demonstrate that fostering a company culture aligning with Agile values and principles is crucial for driving innovation and adaptability. Leaders must invest in creating a work environment that promotes collaboration, learning and continuous improvement.

5. **Experiment and adapt** – Zappos' willingness to experiment with Holacracy and later adapt its approach shows the importance of being open to change and learning from it, even when it involves unconventional methods.

While Agile leadership has proven to be highly effective for many organizations, it is essential to recognize that it may not be the best fit for every business or team. Certain organizations or industries may require a more traditional or hybrid leadership approach. For instance, highly regulated industries like pharmaceuticals or aviation may find certain aspects of Agile, such as rapid changes and short-term planning, challenging to implement because of stringent safety and compliance requirements. In such cases, a hybrid approach, which combines Agile's adaptability with traditional approaches' structure and control, could be more suitable.

It's important to remember that Agile leadership is not a one-size-fits-all solution but rather a set of principles that can be adapted to fit a variety of contexts and requirements. It is crucial for leaders to carefully evaluate the unique context of their organization and make informed decisions about adopting Agile leadership principles.

Exercise: Developing Agile Leadership Skills

To cultivate Agile leadership skills within your organization, consider the following practices and assess how effectively they are implemented. Remember that Agile leadership is not a one-time effort but an ongoing journey of growth and adaptation.

Consider focusing on the following leadership practices:

1. **Encourage continuous learning** – Foster a culture where leaders are open to learning and growth, investing in their personal and professional development. Support ongoing skill development through training, mentorship and sharing of best practices.
2. **Model Agile behaviours** – Demonstrate the Agile mindset and values through your actions and decisions, leading by example. Embrace adaptability, resilience and a customer-centric focus, inspiring your teams to follow suit.
3. **Empower teams** – Provide teams with the autonomy and authority to make decisions and take ownership of their work, fostering a sense of responsibility and accountability. Encourage experimentation and learning from failure, driving continuous improvement.

4. **Facilitate collaboration** – Act as a servant leader by supporting and enabling cross-functional collaboration and communication. Remove barriers and obstacles that hinder teamwork, fostering an environment where diverse perspectives and ideas can thrive.
5. **Promote transparency** – Encourage open communication and information sharing within and across teams to build trust and facilitate informed decision-making. Create an environment where feedback is welcomed and acted upon, promoting a culture of accountability and continuous improvement.
6. **Embrace change** – Develop the ability to adapt quickly to changing circumstances and navigate uncertainty with agility. Encourage teams to stay flexible and responsive, fostering an environment where change is an opportunity for growth.
7. **Foster innovation** – Encourage a culture of innovation and creative problem-solving. Support exploring new ideas and technologies and create an environment where calculated risks are embraced and rewarded.

Utilize self-assessments, feedback from peers and juniors and tools such as 360-degree evaluations to gauge your Agile leadership effectiveness. Continuously refine your leadership practices based on these insights, ensuring your approach remains relevant and supports your organization's Agile journey. As you progress through the book, draw inspiration from the leadership practices discussed in case studies and integrate the lessons learned into your leadership style.

Chapter Summary

This chapter explored leadership's critical role in achieving business agility. It highlighted the characteristics of Agile leaders, including a focus on collaboration, empowerment and continuous improvement. The chapter also discussed the importance of developing an Agile leadership style and guided how to do so. It covered common challenges that leaders may face when implementing Agile practices and provided strategies for overcoming them. Ultimately, Agile leadership was presented as a key driver of a company's competitive advantage, enabling organizations to respond swiftly to market changes, capitalize on opportunities and foster a culture of continuous improvement.

Further Readings and Resources

1. Book: *Agile Leadership: A Leader's Guide to Orchestrating Agile Strategy, Product Quality, and IT Governance,* by Tony Adams, 2015, iUniverse.

2. Book: *Turn the Ship Around!: A True Story of Turning Followers into Leaders,* by L. David Marquet, 2015, Penguin.

3. Website: Business Agility Institute – www.businessagility.institute

5

Building an Agile Culture

Imagine a bustling, progressive organization on the brink of launching its next big product. Weeks from the launch, market feedback hints at the need for a slight pivot, a tweak in the product's features. Organizations with a traditional, rigid culture might resist, citing time constraints, set processes or fear of the unknown. In contrast, a company with an Agile culture embraces this feedback, rallies its teams and makes the necessary changes, ensuring the product aligns perfectly with customer needs. Which environment would you want to cultivate?

Organizations that foster an Agile culture are in a stronger position to swiftly adapt to changes and efficiently cater to customer needs. Creating an atmosphere that promotes teamwork, open communication and knowledge-sharing and empowers employees is essential.

Agile culture is like a rich tapestry woven from threads of respect, collaboration, learning cycles, pride in ownership, courage to experiment and adaptability to change. Each strand brings unique value, but together, they form the fabric of a truly Agile culture.

Embracing an Agile culture encourages a heightened focus on delivering customer value by actively involving customers in the development process, continually testing and refining products, and aligning with their needs and expectations. An Agile environment also fosters innovation through endorsing experimentation and informed risk-taking, which paves the way for creating enhanced products and services.

Such a culture also cultivates a sense of responsibility and ownership among team members. Empowered to make knowledgeable decisions, they can act with conviction to pursue their objectives.

An Agile culture isn't merely a set of practices or a one-off initiative; it's the lifeblood of an organization that aspires to adapt, innovate and succeed in an ever-changing market. Is your organization's culture poised to be the linchpin of your Agile transformation?

This chapter uncovers the pivotal role of building an Agile culture within an organization, empowering teams to deliver customer value through collaboration, communication, transparency and empowerment. An environment that inspires innovation, flexibility and creativity can be created when an Agile mindset and culture are instilled. This enables teams to adapt to transforming circumstances, maintaining a competitive edge.

N.B. The term "culture" used throughout this book refers to the organization's collective mindset, attitudes, behaviours and practices.

What Is an Agile Culture?

Agile culture is a set of values, behaviours and capabilities that enable businesses and individuals to be more adaptable and responsive to change. To develop an Agile culture, organizations must operate differently, with leadership, values and norms all reinforcing the culture. Building an Agile culture entails a fundamental shift in mindset, wherein business leaders must empower their team members, welcome feedback and concentrate on outcomes rather than inflexible processes. For instance, leaders can establish an open-door policy that encourages team members to express their opinions and concerns or conduct regular feedback sessions where team members can discuss potential improvements and share ideas.

Shaping an Agile culture entails more than merely adopting Agile ways of working. One of the major challenges is to ensure talent development. Agile thrives on collaboration and interaction; therefore, employee skills become paramount. Failing to invest in nurturing these skills can obstruct the journey towards a truly Agile culture.

Agile frameworks and methodologies, such as Scrum and Kanban, offer structured approaches for incorporating these Agile principles into an organization. Acquainting yourself with these frameworks can help you better comprehend how to establish an Agile culture in your organization and effectively support Agile teams.

Table 15: Elements of an Agile Culture

Element	Description
Trust	Encouraging open communication, transparency and honesty, allowing team members to feel comfortable sharing ideas and concerns
Collaboration	Fostering a collaborative environment where team members work together to solve problems, share knowledge and support one another
Empowerment	Giving team members the autonomy and authority to make decisions and take ownership of their work
Customer Focus	Prioritizing customer needs and expectations, making data-driven decisions and continuously delivering value

Adaptability	Being open to change and embracing the flexibility to pivot when necessary to respond to market demands or customer feedback
Continuous Improvement	Encouraging a growth mindset and a focus on constantly refining processes, products and services through iterative development
Learning and Innovation	Supporting ongoing learning and development opportunities for team members and promoting a culture of experimentation and innovation
Transparency	Providing visibility into the team's progress, decision-making processes and challenges to foster accountability and trust

Why Is an Agile Culture Important?

A significant benefit of an Agile culture is fostering a feeling of responsibility and ownership among team members. Encouraging team members to make choices and take action to reach their objectives sparks innovation, creativity and ongoing improvement. Enhancing collaboration, communication and employee cooperation boosts productivity, morale and overall performance. Also, an Agile culture leads to higher employee satisfaction and retention, fostering an environment where team members feel valued, engaged and empowered to make a difference.

We have seen organizations that are "Agile in name only" and others who live by the Agile principles without flaunting the label. The difference lies in the culture. Being truly Agile is not about flaunting a label. It's about the unyielding will to adapt, learn and grow.

How to Build an Agile Culture

Building an Agile culture is not merely about implementing a set of practices or Agile methodologies. It requires fostering an environment that supports trust, innovation, autonomy and experimentation with minimal bureaucracy. Encourage teams to take ownership of their Agile processes rather than relying on off-the-shelf or generic versions.

To develop an Agile culture, organizations must define their aspirational goals based on their unique culture. They also need to comprehend their culture, including the behavioural pain points that can be addressed through cultural change.

Let us inspect some key aspects of building an Agile culture:

Communication

In an Agile culture, communication remains consistently transparent and open. Team members are urged to exchange thoughts, concerns and suggestions.

Communication transcends verbal interactions and can be facilitated through various Agile practices such as daily stand-ups, retrospectives and Kanban boards.

Daily stand-ups are concise meetings held every day where team members discuss their tasks and seek or offer assistance. These gatherings present an opportunity to pinpoint obstacles or challenges requiring attention.

Retrospectives are meetings conducted after an Agile iteration or project to evaluate successes, shortcomings and potential improvements. Kanban boards visually depict work progress, enabling teams to monitor work in various stages of completion.

Transparency

In an Agile setting, information is disseminated openly, granting everyone equal access. This nurtures trust and fosters collaboration among team members. Transparency is achieved through Agile practices such as user stories, release plans and project status reports.

User stories are succinct descriptions of required user functionalities, clarifying user expectations, motivations and the value provided.

Release plans outline the projected product or feature delivery timeline, specifying what will be delivered and when. Project status reports offer updates on project progress and pinpoint risks or issues needing attention.

Empowerment

Individuals must be granted decision-making authority and responsibility for their work. They must be free to select the most suitable strategy for accomplishing their objectives, promoting innovation, creativity and ongoing enhancement.

Empowering team members requires equipping them with the resources and support to make decisions and assume responsibility for their work. This includes training, coaching, mentoring and cultivating an environment that considers mistakes as growth opportunities.

Continuous Learning

At the heart of continuous learning lies three foundational elements: self-reflection, curiosity and the ongoing pursuit of knowledge. Team members must be motivated to pursue new knowledge, experiment with new techniques and learn from errors. Moreover, self-reflection allows them to understand their strengths and areas for improvement, while curiosity drives them to seek out and embrace innovative solutions. This trinity of attributes cultivates a culture of innovation and constant improvement.

Promoting continuous learning requires providing team members with sufficient resources for growth, potentially involving training programmes, coaching, mentoring and access to industry events and conferences. A culture that embraces failure as an opportunity for learning and progress is also vital. Furthermore, fostering an environment where self-reflection is encouraged can help individuals align their personal growth with the team's broader goals.

Consider implementing a knowledge-sharing platform where employees can share resources, insights and best practices or host internal workshops and training sessions to enhance skill development and foster a learning culture. Encouraging curiosity within these platforms can lead to discovering unexpected solutions and new ways of thinking.

To further facilitate the implementation of an Agile culture, consider providing practical exercises or tools to help teams assess their current practices and identify areas for improvement. For example, an Agile culture self-assessment tool can enable team members to gauge their understanding of Agile principles, reflect on their alignment, identify gaps and develop action improvement plans. Similarly, Agile workshops, imbued with a spirit of curiosity, can be organized within the organization to allow employees to apply Agile approaches and collaborate on real-life projects, fostering a hands-on learning experience.

Agile Ceremonies

As just discussed, Agile ceremonies like daily stand-ups, sprint planning and retrospectives can help reinforce an Agile culture's values. These ceremonies allow team members to communicate, collaborate and reflect on their progress.

But, for these ceremonies to be effective, they must be organized well, conducted efficiently and documented thoroughly. Encouraging all team members to participate and providing them with the resources to immerse themselves in the process fully is key to their success.

It is important to adapt Agile ceremonies to suit the team's and the organization's unique needs, ensuring that the practices employed are efficient and effective in driving progress and fostering collaboration.

Measuring Progress and Evaluating Success

It is essential to track your organization's progress in implementing an Agile culture and evaluate the success of your efforts. Consider using metrics (see Chapter 9) such as team performance, customer satisfaction and product delivery speed to measure the impact of the Agile culture on your organization. Additionally, track metrics like Agile maturity, employee engagement and defect rates to further gauge the effectiveness of your Agile approaches. Regularly review these metrics and use them to guide further improvements and adjustments to your Agile practices.

Leading by Example

Building an Agile culture necessitates leading by example. As a business leader, you must exemplify Agile principles and inspire your team members to follow suit. You can create opportunities for team members to learn and implement Agile practices and values while supplying them with the required support and resources. Leading by example can create a setting that prioritizes adaptability, innovation and cooperation.

Developing an Agile culture requires businesses to invest in their workforce. This encompasses hiring and retaining employees who appreciate agility, arming them with the essential tools and resources for success, and shaping a nurturing work atmosphere that promotes collaboration and experimentation.

Challenges in Building an Agile Culture

Building an Agile culture has its challenges. Potential impediments include resistance to change, inadequate management backing, misunderstandings about Agile methodologies or frameworks and organizational inertia.

To overcome these obstacles, it is crucial to address concerns candidly, offer continuing education and training, and actively engage all stakeholders in the Agile transformation journey. Engaging employees in open discussions about the benefits of Agile methodologies or frameworks and addressing their concerns can help ease resistance.

Obtaining executive sponsorship and demonstrating tangible results can help garner the necessary support to drive cultural change. Organizations can create and maintain a thriving Agile culture by recognizing and tackling these challenges.

CLEAR Lens for "Building an Agile Culture"

We can apply one of the CLEAR Model® principles to Building an Agile Culture:

 Culture: An organization's culture is the foundation upon which everything else is constructed. In the context of agility, establishing an Agile Culture is the cornerstone for the successful implementation and adoption of Agile approaches. Building an Agile Culture involves cultivating a nurturing, inclusive environment that promotes transparency and fosters collaboration. It encourages continuous improvement and learning – elements firmly grounded in the CLEAR Model®.

Reflection Prompts

1. Assess your organization's current culture. What aspects align with an Agile culture, and what areas need improvement?

2. Consider a specific change you could implement in your organization to help build an Agile culture. What would you do to implement this change?

Case Study: Google's Agile Culture

Google is an excellent example of an organization that has cultivated an Agile culture, driving innovation and adaptability at its core. Analysing their strategies offers business leaders valuable insights into developing an Agile culture in their organizations.

Google's journey towards an Agile culture originated from a clear vision to nurture a highly adaptable and innovative organization. As the company grew, its leaders recognized the need for a flexible framework allowing employees to work collaboratively and respond quickly to change. To achieve this, Google has implemented several key strategies aligning with Agile principles, from goal-setting to employee empowerment and continuous learning. These strategies have been instrumental in creating an environment that supports individual and collective growth, ultimately contributing to Google's impressive track record of success.

One of the hallmarks of Google's Agile culture is its commitment to fostering a collaborative and transparent work environment. Google encourages open communication and cross-functional collaboration through initiatives like its flat organizational structure, regular team meetings and shared workspaces. These practices help break down silos and ensure teams can easily access the information and resources they need to work effectively.

A pivotal moment in Google's understanding of team dynamics and collaboration came from their internal initiative, Project Aristotle. This research project highlighted the importance of psychological safety, amongst other factors, as a cornerstone for effective teams. The study, spanning two years and involving 180 teams, identified five key characteristics of successful teams: dependability, structure and clarity, meaning, impact and psychological safety. Recognizing this, Google integrated these insights into its Agile culture, strengthening its commitment to creating an environment where individuals feel safe to take risks, voice their opinions and ask questions.

What's more, Google's Agile culture places a strong emphasis on customer-centricity. Google's adoption of a user-focused approach to product development allows them to prioritize features and improvements based on customer feedback and data, therefore enabling rapid and efficient delivery of value to users. This customer-driven mindset is deeply ingrained in Google's culture and is a guiding principle in the organization's decision-making process.

Now, with these additional insights into Google's Agile culture, let us examine the key aspects and strategies that have contributed to its success:

Table 16: Google's Agile Culture – Key Aspects and Strategies

Aspect	Strategy
Goal Alignment	Google employs Objectives and Key Results (OKRs) to align goals and track progress. This system ensures that teams and individuals have clear objectives, enabling them to prioritize tasks and maintain focus on the most important goals
Employee Empowerment	Google empowers its employees by giving them the autonomy to make decisions and take risks, fostering an environment where innovation and experimentation can flourish
Innovation and Creativity	Google's "20% time" policy encourages employees to spend 20% of their working time on side projects that interest them. This nurtures innovation and allows employees to explore new ideas, contributing to Google's Agile culture
Continuous Learning and Development	Google emphasizes the importance of continuous learning and development, offering various training and development programmes and promoting a culture of knowledge-sharing and learning from failures
Talent Management	Google's hiring and talent management approach focuses on recruiting individuals with diverse backgrounds and skills, contributing to their Agile culture and ensuring the organization has the right mix of expertise and perspectives to drive innovation and adaptability

In addition to Google, numerous other companies across diverse industries have successfully adopted Agile principles to drive innovation and adaptability. For example, ING Bank has restructured its operations around Agile ways of working in the financial sector, resulting in improved customer satisfaction and accelerated time-to-market. Similarly, the retail giant Amazon has built its success upon Agile practices, allowing it to adapt to rapidly changing market trends and customer needs.

Key Takeaways from the Case Study

1. **Creating alignment with clear objectives** – The application of OKRs at Google has streamlined focus, propelled progress and maintained strategic alignment across the organization.
2. **Empowering employees and encouraging autonomy** – The autonomy encouraged by Google's Agile culture has propelled innovation and expedited adaptation to market shifts.
3. **Fostering a culture that encourages innovation** – The creative and adaptable mindset promoted by Google's culture has enabled continuous delivery of value to customers, securing their industry leadership.
4. **Promoting learning and professional development** – Google's emphasis on continuous growth and learning has fostered a culture of knowledge-sharing and leveraging failures as learning opportunities.
5. **Implementing effective talent management strategies** – The diverse skills and backgrounds prioritized in Google's hiring and talent management strategy have nurtured its Agile culture, driving innovation and enhancing adaptability.

Exercise: Assessing and Shaping Your Organization's Agile Culture

Following a structured approach that aligns with your goals and objectives is essential to effectively evaluate and improve your organization's Agile culture. Systematically assessing and shaping your culture can result in an environment that supports Agile principles and practices.

Consider the following steps:

1. **Conduct a cultural assessment** – Use surveys, interviews and focus groups to gather insights into your organization's culture, values and

behaviours. This will help you understand the current state of your culture and how it aligns or diverges from Agile principles.

2. **Identify gaps and opportunities** – Analyse the assessment results to identify areas where your organization's culture aligns with Agile principles and areas that require improvement. Recognizing these gaps and opportunities will allow you to create targeted interventions to build a more Agile culture.

3. **Define your desired Agile culture** – Develop a clear vision of the Agile culture you wish to create, including the values, behaviours and practices that will support your organization's Agile transformation. This vision will serve as a guiding light for your cultural change efforts.

4. **Create a culture change road map** – Develop a detailed plan for implementing the desired Agile culture, including strategies for addressing cultural gaps, fostering new behaviours and reinforcing Agile values. A well-defined road map will help ensure a smooth and successful transition to a more Agile culture.

5. **Monitor progress and adjust as needed** – Regularly evaluate your organization's progress toward building an Agile culture, adjusting your strategies and tactics to ensure continued growth and improvement. Embrace a continuous improvement mindset, making adjustments based on learnings and feedback from your teams.

6. **Engage leadership and employees** – Involve leaders and employees in shaping and fostering an Agile culture. Encourage open communication, collaboration and shared ownership of the transformation process, ensuring that all levels of the organization are invested in building a more Agile culture.

Remember these steps as you assess and shape your organization's Agile culture. Utilize the insights and best practices gained throughout this book to create a supportive environment that encourages continuous learning, improvement and the removal of barriers to Agile adoption.

Chapter Summary

This chapter underscored the significance of cultivating an Agile culture for business agility. It investigated the critical components of an Agile culture, such as trust, transparency and a spirit of experimentation. The chapter further examined how organizational values and beliefs shape the culture and suggested aligning these with Agile principles. It provided best practices for establishing an Agile culture and drew examples from diverse industries. An Agile culture facilitates quick responses to changes and value delivery, making it attractive to top talent who seek engagement and empowerment.

Further Readings and Resources

1. Book: *The Culture Code: The Secrets of Highly Successful Groups,* by Daniel Coyle, 2019, Random House Business.

2. Book: *Creating Great Teams: How Self-Selection Lets People Excel,* by Sandy Mamoli and David Mole, 2015, O'Reilly.

3. Website: Management 3.0 – www.management30.com

Part 3

Building and Managing Agile Teams

6

Building and Managing Agile Teams

Picture this: you've just attended a conference where Agile ways of working were hailed as the future of business. Inspired, you return to your organization, eager to implement what you've learned. You start with a single team, hoping they'll be the beacon for the rest. But a few weeks in, something's off. The team struggles, unsure of their roles and lacking cohesion. They're a far cry from the Agile teams you heard about. What went wrong?

Perhaps it wasn't the idea but the execution. The cornerstone of an Agile organization is its teams. They're the engine rooms, driving projects forward. But, without the right components, these engines splutter and stall.

Building Agile teams results in increased adaptability, shorter time-to-market and enhanced collaboration, ultimately leading to greater customer satisfaction. Agile teams can be a business leader's secret weapon for success in a constantly evolving market. Comprised of cross-functional and self-organizing members, Agile teams concentrate on providing customer value by employing Agile approaches and practices.

Emphasizing customer value via iterative development and constant feedback allows Agile teams to adjust their tactics, stay on target and achieve their objectives. Empowered to decide and act, Agile teams may foster increased innovation and creativity as members are urged to experiment and explore new ideas.

Agile teams can be adopted across various departments, not just confined to software development. Importantly, while team members are empowered, the manager's role is crucial as a facilitator and servant leader. Managers guide, support and remove roadblocks, creating an environment where Agile teams can flourish. Their role shifts from traditional command-and-control to nurturing, mentoring and fostering collaboration and open communication, making them indispensable in the Agile transformation journey.

Top-down pressure can impair Agile teams and stifle innovation. The so-called "Agile Harry Potter Syndrome", where teams are expected to work magic overnight, is a common misstep. Also known as faith-driven development, this expectation harbours the illusion of waiting for something magical to rectify the situation. Understanding what Agile can realistically deliver is key to fostering an environment that encourages creativity rather than suppressing it.

Regrettably, some organizations fail to view Agile in a long-term vision, resulting in isolated Agile experiments without a strategic plan for organization-wide adoption. This is a common challenge. This short-sighted approach can curtail the benefits of Agile transformation, keeping it a mere drop in the ocean instead of a sweeping tide of change.

Transforming a group of individuals into a high-performing Agile team requires more than just good intentions. It demands the right mindset, understanding and an environment that promotes collaboration, experimentation and learning.

Realizing the full potential of Agile isn't merely a matter of attending a seminar or reading a book. It's about actualizing that knowledge within the complex dynamics of your organization's existing teams. Are you prepared to turn good intentions into actionable strategies for high-performing Agile teams?

This chapter guides you on how to build and manage Agile teams capable of achieving swift and effective outcomes. Explore how team composition, structure, performance and roles impact Agile team success, emphasizing collaboration, communication and continuous learning and improvement culture. With this knowledge, you will be equipped to build high-performing Agile teams that consistently deliver value to your organization and customers.

Key Factors for Building and Managing Agile Teams

As business leaders delve into the key factors for building and managing Agile teams, they will gain valuable insights into fostering a collaborative, adaptable and high-performing work environment. Leaders who understand the importance of team values, principles, composition, structure, performance, metrics and feedback can establish empowered teams that deliver consistent value to customers.

Also, leaders will learn to support Agile team members through training, coaching and maintaining an environment that promotes open communication, innovation and continuous improvement. Adopting Agile approaches beyond software development teams and across various departments enables the entire organization to respond quickly to changing market conditions, ensuring a competitive edge in their respective industries.

As with the broader Agile culture, teams must own their Agile processes rather than merely adopting a pre-existing model or framework. By encouraging teams to define their unique approach, we empower them to innovate and evolve in line with the spirit of Agile.

Let us inspect some key factors for building and managing Agile teams:

Team Values and Principles

Incorporating the Agile Manifesto's values and principles into a team's culture and practices is vital for building and managing successful Agile teams. As discussed in Chapter 2, four key values are emphasized: individuals and interactions over processes and tools, working solutions over comprehensive documentation, customer collaboration over contract negotiation and responding to change over following a plan.

The Agile approach is guided by 12 principles that address customer satisfaction, embracing change, sustainable development and technical excellence, among other areas. Nurturing a team culture that reflects these values and principles allows business leaders to align their Agile teams with core Agile concepts, setting them up for success.

Promoting and maintaining Agile values and principles in daily practices can be done by establishing regular team meetings, fostering open communication and encouraging a growth mindset. Team members must be reminded of these values and principles during meetings, retrospectives and decisions. Incorporating Agile values and principles into the team culture helps members stay aligned with the Agile approach, leading to consistently delivering value to customers.

Team Composition

Agile principles stress the significance of diverse teams. Agile teams must comprise individuals with various skill sets and backgrounds, including members skilled in development, testing, design and product management. The benefits of this diversity are manifold, bringing together a broad range of perspectives, fostering more creative and innovative problem-solving and ensuring a wider range of experiences and knowledge to be drawn upon in tackling complex tasks. By incorporating different viewpoints and skill sets, an Agile team becomes a melting pot of ideas, sparking innovative solutions and propelling the team toward success. Such a diverse team can offer unique perspectives and ideas, leading to more innovative solutions, and possessing the skills required to achieve its goals. This may involve offering training and development opportunities to team members, enabling them to gain new skills and stay current with the latest technologies and Agile approaches.

Balancing technical and soft skills is essential for an Agile team. While technical skills are necessary for problem-solving and product development, soft skills such as communication, teamwork and adaptability contribute to better collaboration and decision-making. A diverse team with a mix of technical and soft skills can better navigate complex problems and foster a productive and innovative work environment.

Team Structure

Efficiency and effectiveness are paramount in Agile team structures. Teams are generally designed to be small to enable effective communication and collaboration, often comprising around three to nine members, although this is more of a guideline than a strict rule. Such a size enables team members to work closely, better manage their tasks and keep track of progress.

Teams must have decision-making autonomy and clearly understand their roles and responsibilities. This empowers team members with daily interdependence and motivation to experiment with new approaches and ideas, cultivating an environment of innovation and continuous improvement.

Different Agile team structures offer various advantages and challenges, such as Scrum, Kanban or a hybrid approach. Scrum provides a highly structured framework with set roles and ceremonies, promoting organization and predictability. In contrast, Kanban is more flexible and focuses on continuous flow and prioritizing work based on demand. When choosing an Agile team structure, consider project complexity, team size and organizational culture. Experimenting with different structures and adapting based on feedback can help you find the most suitable approach for your team.

In addition to the choice between Scrum, Kanban and hybrid models, the physical structure of an Agile team plays a crucial role in determining its dynamics and effectiveness. This structural arrangement can be vertical, horizontal, matrix or even a blend of these, known as a hybrid structure. Each layout has its key roles, communication methods and unique benefits.

A vertical structure provides a clear hierarchy and direct lines of communication, while a horizontal structure encourages peer-to-peer collaboration and skill-sharing. Information exchange across departments is emphasized in a matrix structure, balancing specialization with broad coverage. Hybrid structures, combining elements from all others, focus on flexibility and adaptability.

The appropriate choice of team structure is as much an important consideration as the Agile approach adopted. This decision should be guided by your project's specific needs, the unique characteristics of your team, and the prevailing culture within your organization. Understanding these different structures and their benefits helps establish teams that can optimally operate within the Agile framework. Table 17 outlines these structures, enabling leaders to assess the potential fit for their specific context.

Table 17: Structure of Cross-Functional Teams

Team Structure	Key Roles	Communication Channels	Benefits
Vertical	Project Manager, Developers, Testers, UX Designers	Regular stand-ups, collaborative tools (e.g. Jira, Slack)	Clear hierarchy, direct lines of communication
Horizontal	Product Owner, Scrum Master, Agile Team Members	Regular stand-ups, sprint retrospectives, collaborative tools (e.g. Confluence, Trello)	Encourages peer-to-peer collaboration, enhances skill-sharing
Matrix	Business Analyst, Team Lead, Developers, Testers, UX Designers	Regular cross-departmental meetings, collaborative tools (e.g. MS Teams, Asana)	Balances specialization with broad coverage, facilitates information exchange across departments
Hybrid	Product Owner, Project Manager, Scrum Master, Agile Team Members	Regular stand-ups, sprint reviews, collaborative tools (e.g. GitHub, Google Workspace)	Combines the best practices from other structures, encourages flexibility and adaptability

Team Performance

Agile teams must focus on delivering customer value encompassing workflow, product or feature quality and relevance. A team's performance hinges on its capacity to produce functional software, or other deliverables, that addresses customer requirements and offers tangible advantages.

Aligning the delivered products with client expectations and ensuring their satisfaction is key. Regular communication with clients and stakeholders, getting feedback and integrating it into subsequent iterations are essential. Prioritizing the most significant features or functionalities guarantees that customers derive maximum benefit.

Ensuring teams possess the required resources, tools and leadership support is vital. Agile teams can achieve optimal performance and customer satisfaction by nurturing an environment that prioritizes workflow efficiency and the value of deliverables.

Team Feedback

Agile teams can track progress and assess performance using a variety of metrics, including cycle time, sprint burndown, cumulative flow diagrams and lead time. For example, a sprint burndown represents the amount of work remaining in a sprint, plotted against time. It's a powerful tool that allows teams to visualize their progress and pace, enabling them to adjust as needed for optimal efficiency. These metrics reveal efficiency, effectiveness and areas for improvement. Regular retrospectives are crucial for continuous enhancement alongside metric monitoring.

Retrospectives provide a platform for reflecting on finished iterations, pinpointing successes and growth opportunities and strategizing for future improvement. Metrics and retrospectives allow Agile groups to refine their processes constantly and achieve better results.

Qualitative metrics include customer satisfaction, team morale and collaboration quality. Quantitative metrics may include defect rates, code coverage and task completion rate. To interpret the results, compare your team's metrics against industry benchmarks or historical data from past projects. Analyse trends and correlations to identify areas for improvement or recognize team successes. Agile teams can better understand their performance and make data-driven improvements using qualitative and quantitative metrics.

Team Empowerment

Empowering team members is crucial to an Agile team's success. They must be able to make decisions and assume responsibility for their work. Autonomy and encouragement to experiment are essential, as empowered groups are more likely to take ownership and deliver quality outcomes.

Providing the resources and support for accomplishing objectives is crucial. This encompasses access to learning opportunities, growth, tools and technologies that streamline work.

Training and Coaching

Supporting Agile groups in reaching their potential requires proper training and coaching, especially for Agile newcomers. Agile coaches are instrumental in guiding and assisting groups in understanding and adopting Agile principles, practices and mindset.

Continuous training and professional development access are vital for team members, enabling them to gain new skills, remain current with emerging technologies and Agile approaches, and consistently develop in their roles. Investing in Agile team members' growth allows business leaders to foster a culture of continuous learning and improvement, driving team success.

Team Collaboration

A well-designed team structure fosters collaboration, which is essential for the success of Agile teams. Collaborative Agile practices include pair programming, code reviews and daily stand-ups. Encouraging open sharing of ideas and concerns promotes trust and transparency.

Constructing and managing Agile teams demands a focus on constant progress and adaptability to changing situations. Providing necessary support and resources and fostering innovation and collaboration are key to ensuring team success.

Collaboration tools and technology are crucial in supporting communication and collaboration among team members. These tools, such as project management software, communication platforms and document-sharing systems, facilitate sharing ideas, progress updates and feedback. Adopting suitable collaboration tools that cater to the team's needs and preferences enables business leaders to promote efficient teamwork and keep everyone informed and engaged.

Promoting Open Communication

Business leaders can cultivate a culture of open communication by establishing regular team check-ins, retrospectives and maintaining continuous feedback channels. At the heart of this culture lies the principle of psychological safety, a state in which team members feel comfortable sharing ideas, expressing their thoughts and taking calculated risks without fear of judgement or criticism. This sense of security is critical, as it is closely knit with the team's environment, fostering a holistic framework that encourages open and transparent dialogue.

To facilitate seamless interaction within the team, leaders should implement instant messaging platforms, virtual meeting software and collaborative project management systems. These tools are indispensable for maintaining regular communication not only among team members but also with stakeholders and customers, ensuring everyone is aligned and informed.

An "open door" policy can be metaphorically extended to virtual spaces as well, where leaders actively seek and welcome feedback during team meetings. Such practices underscore the value placed on transparent communication, which is fundamental in Agile teams that rely on swift and honest exchanges to adapt and align with shared objectives continuously.

Team Environment

Agile teams might experience conflicts because of differing opinions, priorities or personalities. To preserve a positive team atmosphere, business leaders must create conflict resolution guidelines and, as just discussed, promote transparent communication among team members.

Encouraging a culture where disagreements are tackled constructively and team members feel comfortable expressing their thoughts and concerns respectfully can prove beneficial. Emphasizing healthy communication and conflict resolution supports Agile teams in maintaining a strong sense of collaboration and trust, as facilitated by business leaders.

Cultivating psychological safety is paramount for Agile teams, as it fosters an intricate tapestry of trust, risk-taking and creative exploration. Psychological safety is the undercurrent that nurtures an environment where team members can share their ideas, challenge assumptions and learn from failures without trepidation. This vibrant atmosphere pulsates energy and promotes an innovative mindset, driving the team's collective intelligence to unprecedented heights. To foster psychological safety, leaders must celebrate the diversity of thought, encourage respectful debate and acknowledge individual contributions. Intertwining these elements allows Agile teams to create a rich, dynamic work environment that fosters limitless growth and resilience.

Agile Roles

Agile teams may include various roles. In this example, the roles for Scrum teams: Product Owner, Scrum Master and Developers are shared. Each role has specific responsibilities as defined by Agile approaches.

Table 18: Example of Agile Roles (Within Scrum Teams)

Role	Primary Responsibilities	Collaborative and Cross-Functional Aspects
Product Owner	Defining and prioritizing product requirements, creating and maintaining the product backlog and collaborating with stakeholders.	Works closely with all stakeholders, ensuring alignment between business and team goals. Utilizes diverse skills to maintain product vision.
Scrum Master	Facilitating Agile ceremonies, coaching the team in Agile practices and removing obstacles to the team's progress.	Collaborates with the Product Owner and Development Team to streamline processes, using facilitation skills to ensure efficient collaboration.
Developers	Designing, building, testing and delivering high-quality, customer-focused products incrementally.	A truly cross-functional unit, drawing on diverse technical skills to deliver value. Promotes an open, collaborative culture.

Cross-functional collaboration and understanding the interdependence of these roles are crucial in achieving project goals and ensuring the team's success. The Product Owner sets the product vision and priorities, the Scrum Master facilitates the Agile process and eliminates obstacles, and the Development Team creates the product and achieves sprint goals.

Addressing Team Building Challenges: Obstacles and Solutions

Addressing challenges often encountered is crucial in our exploration into building Agile teams. Recognizing these hurdles allows us to prepare effective countermeasures, ensuring successful team development.

Let us delve into two key challenges and their potential solutions:

1. **Resistance to change** – The shift to Agile often implies a significant cultural change, which might trigger resistance among team members. To navigate this, it's imperative to communicate clearly and openly about the reasons for the change and the benefits it will bring. Create a safe space for employees to express concerns and provide adequate training to facilitate the transition.
2. **Balancing autonomy and alignment** – Agile teams require autonomy to maintain speed and adaptability. However, too much autonomy can lead to a lack of alignment with the company's broader goals. Creating structures like those of Spotify's "tribes" and "chapters" (without copying them like for like) can facilitate achieving this balance, allowing teams to operate independently while staying aligned with the organization's mission.

Additionally, beware of "Agile camouflage", a pitfall or challenge where teams wear the Agile tag without truly understanding or living its core values. It's like dressing up as a superhero but having no powers. It might look good on the surface, but the lack of substance will soon show.

Each Agile team will encounter distinctive challenges on their journey. Leaders must stay attentive and responsive to these issues, nurturing their teams toward a more Agile, productive and harmonious operation.

Agile Beyond Development Teams

Agile teams are not limited to a company's software development sector. Adopting Agile strategies across various divisions like people teams, marketing and senior management is not merely an option; it's an imperative for achieving overall business agility. This comprehensive alignment allows the entire organization to act in concert, swiftly pivoting to meet market demands, delivering unprecedented value to customers and capitalizing on emergent opportunities. Embracing Agile across the board sets the stage for an adaptive organizational culture where cross-functional collaboration becomes the norm rather than the exception.

Agile Marketing Teams

For example, businesses can significantly enhance the value of their releases by seamlessly incorporating Agile practices within their marketing teams. These Agile marketing teams are well-positioned to pivot as swiftly as their development counterparts. This ensures that customers are always in the loop about the latest features and enhancements, maximizing the value of each release. Agile marketing teams can readily adapt to shifting customer needs, evolving market trends and dynamic business objectives, maintaining a competitive advantage in a constantly changing environment. They can adopt iterative campaign planning and data-driven decision-making to improve adaptability and efficiency.

Agile People Teams

Likewise, Agile practices offer transformative potential when applied to people teams or human resources. It's not just about recruiting new talent and expertise but also eliminating bureaucratic business barriers that often plague the new employee onboarding process. Agile people teams can streamline recruitment and onboarding workflows. This efficiency guarantees that the organization is always people-ready, possessing the talent and human capital needed to meet its goals and rapidly respond to fresh, untapped opportunities. With the help of Agile tools like Kanban boards, people teams can visualize, manage and improve the recruitment process with unprecedented efficacy.

Agile in Sales and Customer Support Teams

Agile practices can also be applied in sales and customer support teams to facilitate quick responses to client needs and market shifts. Adopting Agile approaches in sales teams can help them prioritize leads and opportunities, manage their sales pipelines more efficiently, and enhance customer relationships. Similarly, customer support teams can leverage Agile methods to prioritize customer issues, streamline ticket resolution and continuously improve their support processes. Sales and customer support teams that adopt Agile practices can enhance their adaptability, customer-centricity and efficiency. These teams can use Agile tools like Scrum to prioritize tasks, improve collaboration and track progress.

Agile Financial and Operations Teams

Similarly, Agile principles are not just for product development or customer-facing teams; they offer substantial benefits to financial and operations sectors as well. Implementing Agile budgeting methodologies empowers organizations to pivot from rigid, predefined financial plans swiftly, allowing for more dynamic resource allocation in line with real-time needs and opportunities. This fluid approach to financial planning is deeply in line with Beyond Budgeting principles, which advocate for decentralized decision-making and adaptive planning. By employing Agile budgeting techniques, organizations can improve their responsiveness to market changes, thereby maximizing resource utilization and financial performance. Financial and operations teams can use Agile tools such as rolling forecasts and real-time dashboards to monitor financial health, adapt to variances and make informed decisions rapidly. Such Agile practices bring financial agility, enabling organizations to seize emerging opportunities and to adapt to market downturns with minimal disruption.

Besides the above factors, there are a few more crucial aspects for building and managing Agile teams:

Purpose and Direction

A clear purpose and direction are vital for Agile teams. Business leaders must collaborate with their teams to shape the product vision and set priorities, ensuring the team understands the organization's overall strategy and objectives. This approach keeps the team focused and aligned with broader business goals.

Instilling Accountability and Ownership

To cultivate a sense of accountability and ownership in Agile teams, business leaders must set clear expectations regarding project outcomes, timelines and individual responsibilities. Providing timely feedback and celebrating small wins can reinforce the team's commitment to achieving their goals. Leaders must encourage team members to take responsibility for their work and support their efforts to learn from mistakes, fostering a culture of continuous improvement and growth. Practical tools like tracking individual and team progress using visual management tools like task boards can help promote accountability and keep everyone on track.

Agile teams carry responsibility for their successes and failures, holding accountability for addressing customer requirements. Business leaders must offer the support and resources for success while maintaining high performance and quality standards.

Measuring Team Performance and Progress

Tracking team performance using relevant metrics and key performance indicators (KPIs) is essential to manage Agile teams effectively. Business leaders must monitor customer satisfaction, team engagement and product quality to ensure their teams deliver value. Continuously evaluating performance enables leaders to work with teams to identify areas for improvement and make data-driven decisions, optimizing productivity.

Ongoing Support

Ongoing support and guidance from leadership are essential for Agile teams. This involves offering regular feedback, monitoring team performance and providing direction when needed. Business leaders must also be open to adjusting team structure or processes to ensure the delivery of value and goal achievement.

Team Health

The well-being of an Agile team, which includes physical, mental and emotional health, is critical for success. Business leaders must ensure a balanced work–life environment, preventing overwork or burnout. Providing resources like counselling or mental health support can be beneficial. Promoting work–life balance through flexible working hours, remote work options and regular breaks helps maintain team morale and prevent burnout.

Encouraging Experimentation and Risk-Taking

By celebrating learning from failures, implementing a "blameless culture", and providing resources for team members to pursue innovative ideas, business leaders can foster a culture of experimentation and risk-taking. For instance, leaders can allocate a percentage of work hours to pursue side projects or encourage team members to experiment with new techniques or tools. Google encourages experimentation by allocating 20% of employees' time to work on innovative side projects, resulting in ground-breaking products like Gmail and Google Maps. Leaders who share stories of failures and subsequent learnings can showcase the value of experimentation and risk-taking within the organization.

CLEAR Lens for "Building and Managing Agile Teams"

We can apply two CLEAR Model® principles to Building and Managing Agile Teams:

Culture: The formation of a truly Agile team goes hand in hand with cultivating a culture that embodies the values of the CLEAR Model®. This entails creating an environment that supports flexibility, collaboration and continuous learning. It's an environment where individuals feel safe to venture beyond their comfort zones, experiment with new ideas and embrace the learning that comes from the occasional misstep.

Leadership: The role of Leadership in building and managing Agile teams is paramount. Agile leaders serve as navigators on the journey of Agile transformation. They provide a clear vision, promote Agile values, inspire their teams and offer unwavering support in facing challenges. The CLEAR principle of Leadership underscores the importance of strong leadership in guiding the team toward a successful Agile transformation.

Reflection Prompts

1. Reflect on your team's current structure and dynamics. What adjustments could be made to enhance agility?

2. How can you encourage cross-functional collaboration within your team or organization to foster innovation and problem-solving?

Case Study: Agile Teams at Spotify and Atlassian

Spotify and Atlassian are two industry-leading companies that have effectively constructed and managed Agile teams, leading to increased adaptability and efficiency in their respective domains. Examining their approach enables business leaders to gain valuable insights into forming and managing Agile teams for outstanding results.

We delve deeper into these two companies' Agile team management strategies, identifying their key success factors, challenges faced, and lessons learned. Business leaders who examine these unique approaches can draw inspiration, adapt these practices to their organizations and ultimately drive improved performance and outcomes.

Table 19: Spotify and Atlassian Agile Team Management Comparison

Aspect	Spotify	Atlassian
Team Structure	"Squads" – Small, cross-functional, autonomous teams	Agile teams with decision-making autonomy and risk-taking opportunities

Key Success Factors	Autonomy, cross-functional collaboration, continuous improvement, supportive culture	Empowerment, experimentation, continuous learning, open communication
Challenges and Lessons Learned	Balancing autonomy and alignment with the overall strategy	Adapting Agile practices as the company grows, scaling Agile practices effectively

As discussed in Chapter 1, Spotify, the Swedish music streaming and media services provider, is renowned for its unique Agile team structure, known as "squads". These small, cross-functional teams have the autonomy to work independently and make decisions about their work while still collaborating with other squads when necessary. This structure enabled Spotify to respond quickly to changes in the market and continuously deliver value to its customers.

Spotify's Agile team management relies on a system of tribes, chapters, guilds and their squads. This organizational structure encourages collaboration and knowledge-sharing across the entire company. Tribes are collections of squads working on related areas, while chapters represent functional groups within tribes that share knowledge and best practices. Guilds are informal, cross-tribe networks of people with similar interests who collaborate and share expertise. This framework has allowed Spotify to balance autonomy and alignment, driving innovation and cohesion throughout the organization.

Atlassian, a leading software development and collaboration tools company, has also successfully adopted Agile approaches and is committed to continuous learning and improvement. Atlassian can adapt quickly to a changing business environment by fostering a culture of experimentation and granting employees decision-making autonomy and risk-taking opportunities.

They have also developed an internal system called "Health Monitor" for their Agile teams to evaluate their performance and identify areas of improvement. This evaluation process involves team members coming together to discuss and rate their performance on key attributes, such as shared understanding, decision-making and balance of skills. Regular Health Monitor sessions enable Atlassian teams to identify and address any obstacles hindering their effectiveness, therefore ensuring continuous growth and improvement. Atlassian's open company culture emphasizes transparency and collaboration, fostering an environment that supports knowledge-sharing and learning.

Key Takeaways from the Case Study

1. **Autonomy and decision-making** – Spotify and Atlassian empower their Agile teams by giving them the autonomy to make decisions and take risks. This approach encourages innovation and allows teams to adapt to industry changes quickly.
2. **Cross-functional collaboration** – The Agile teams at both companies comprise members with diverse skill sets, allowing them to collaborate effectively and develop innovative solutions to complex problems.
3. **Emphasis on continuous improvement** – Both companies are committed to continuous learning and improvement, which helps them stay ahead of their competition and deliver value to their customers.
4. **Supportive culture** – Spotify and Atlassian have cultivated environments that encourage experimentation, learning from failure and open communication. This type of culture enables Agile teams to thrive and adapt to changes in the market.

Challenges and Lessons Learned

Spotify faced challenges balancing team autonomy and alignment with the company's overall strategy. They overcame this by implementing the concept of "bounded autonomy", which ensures that squads can innovate within a defined framework.

Atlassian learned the importance of continuously adapting its Agile practices as the company grew. Scaling Agile practices involved investing in coaching, creating internal Agile champions and developing frameworks to support effective communication and collaboration across teams.

In comparing the approaches of Spotify and Atlassian, fostering autonomy, encouraging cross-functional collaboration and promoting a culture of continuous improvement are key drivers of their success. Other organizations can learn from these examples and tailor their Agile implementation to fit their unique needs and circumstances.

Exercise: Building High-Performing Agile Teams

Creating high-performing Agile teams within your organization is essential to drive innovation, collaboration and success. To achieve this, it's important to establish a solid foundation for teamwork and adaptability.

Consider implementing the following guidelines:

1. **Assemble cross-functional teams** – Bring together members with diverse skills and expertise to encourage collaboration, innovation and shared ownership of work. Diverse perspectives can lead to more creative solutions and a better understanding of customer needs.

2. **Foster a culture of trust and psychological safety** – Promote open communication, mutual respect and a supportive environment where team members feel comfortable sharing ideas and concerns. Psychological safety empowers individuals to take risks and learn from failure, which is key to Agile success.

3. **Establish clear goals and expectations** – Align team objectives with organizational goals and ensure team members understand their roles and responsibilities. Providing clear direction and purpose helps maintain focus and motivation within the team.

4. **Encourage self-organization and autonomy** – Empower teams to make decisions and manage their work, fostering a sense of ownership and accountability. Autonomous teams are more agile and can adapt to changing circumstances more quickly.

5. **Regularly review and iterate** – Conduct frequent retrospectives to evaluate team performance, identify areas for improvement and implement changes as needed. Continuous improvement is a cornerstone of Agile, and retrospectives provide an opportunity to learn from successes and failures.

6. **Promote collaboration and knowledge-sharing** – Encourage team members to share their expertise and collaborate on problem-solving. This fosters a learning culture and helps to break down silos within the organization.

7. **Invest in training and development** – Provide team members with the resources and opportunities to develop their skills and knowledge. Ongoing learning and development contribute to a more capable and adaptable workforce.

Utilize these guidelines to build high-performing Agile teams within your organization. Continuously monitor team dynamics and performance, making adjustments as necessary to ensure teams remain effective and adaptable. As you progress in your Agile journey, refine your approach to team building to maximize efficiency, collaboration and delivery of value.

Chapter Summary

This chapter focused on building and managing Agile teams to achieve business agility. It explored the key characteristics of Agile teams, including cross-functional collaboration, self-organization and continuous improvement. The chapter also discussed the importance of team dynamics and guided on creating and maintaining high-performing Agile teams. The chapter covered common challenges that teams may face when adopting Agile practices and provided strategies for overcoming these challenges.

Further Readings and Resources

1. Book: *The Five Dysfunctions of a Team: A Leadership Fable,* by Patrick Lencioni, 2002, John Wiley & Sons.

2. Book: *The Art of Agile Development,* by James Shore and Shane Warden, 2021, O'Reilly Media.

3. Website: Scrum Alliance – www.scrumalliance.org

Part 4

The Agile Process

7

Agile Planning

Think back to the golden age of railroads. The tracks were laid out, plans set in stone and trains ran on rigorous schedules. But imagine a world where those rails could spontaneously adjust to faster routes or evade unexpected obstacles. That's the essence of Agile planning in the business world.

Agile planning significantly impacts the creation of flexible and responsive organizations that can skilfully steer through changing market scenarios and cater to customer needs. For leaders aiming to prosper, mastering the basics of Agile planning and comprehending its role in driving achievement is paramount.

Picture this: you're at the helm of a vessel, sailing through uncharted waters. Suddenly, the weather shifts, casting dark clouds and strong winds. Traditional navigation methods, reliant on clear skies and mapped courses, would leave you adrift. But with Agile planning, you're equipped with dynamic tools and strategies that adjust in real time, ensuring you weather the storm and find optimal paths previously unseen.

Rather than being a one-off activity confined to a project's outset, Agile planning is an ongoing process occurring throughout the entire project or product life cycle. It's a common misnomer that there is less planning in Agile. Agile approaches often involve more frequent planning to ensure responsiveness to change. Various techniques and tools designed to keep projects on track and meet their objectives fall under the umbrella of Agile planning.

Agile planning isn't just about breaking down work into manageable chunks; it's also about incorporating Agile's core values of iteration and experimentation. The difficulty is that organizations, while adopting Agile approaches, sometimes fail to assimilate these values. This can cause a rigid, unyielding mindset that stifles Agile's adaptive and innovative spirit.

Have you ever played a game of chess? Every move you make is based on anticipating your opponent's next action. Agile planning can be likened to playing this strategic game. However, instead of a single opponent, you're navigating against a myriad of market changes, consumer demands and potential risks.

Now, before we embark on an Agile transformation journey and introduce any form of Agile planning, let's pause and ask, "Why?". Understanding the "Why" behind our Agile adoption sets the compass for our journey and the tone for Agile planning. It provides a purpose, a direction and a measure of success for our transformation efforts.

Steering your organization without Agile planning is like piloting a ship without a compass – you might keep afloat, but are you truly navigating or just drifting? Are you ready to seize the helm and guide your organization through uncharted territories with confidence?

This chapter dives into Agile planning, a crucial component of business agility. As a leader, assuming your team will naturally understand how to implement this strategy is a mistake. Without guidance and clear permission to change their approach, they won't fully utilize Agile Planning. As a leader, you hold the authority to encourage new ways of working.

In this chapter, you'll learn how Agile Planning keeps your team sharply focused on delivering value and meeting goals. We will also explore how this approach enhances continual improvement and boosts overall business outcomes. This journey is critical for any leader aiming to fully leverage Agile Planning and guide their team to higher levels of success.

A Brief History of Agile Planning

As we moved toward the end of the 1990s, Agile planning started to take shape. This new way of planning solved the problems with existing planning methods. It came about because the software development industry was changing quickly. Technology was getting more complex, and customers wanted more, faster. Traditional methods like "Waterfall", which were slow and followed a strict path, couldn't keep up. Agile planning was different. It was about making plans in small steps and getting feedback quickly. The aim was to gradually deliver value to the customer and learn from each step. It also introduced the idea of "failing fast". This meant it was better to find mistakes or problems early in a project in order to fix them sooner. Agile planning was setting new standards for managing projects in the software industry and beyond.

What Is Agile Planning?

Agile planning is a dynamic, iterative process focusing on flexibility, adaptability and continuous improvement. This approach allows Agile teams to develop high-quality products that respond to transforming market conditions and customer needs. Unlike traditional planning, which focuses on extensive, inflexible plans, Agile planning enables teams to regularly re-evaluate and adjust their plans to stay aligned with organizational objectives and stakeholder expectations. Teams break work items into smaller, manageable increments known as iterations or sprints. This technique fosters enhanced cooperation, openness and agility, paving the way for more successful and timely outcomes.

Table 20 better illustrates the key differences between Agile and traditional planning:

Table 20: Agile vs. Traditional Planning

Aspect	Agile Planning	Traditional Planning
Flexibility	High, adapts to change quickly	Low, resistant to change
Time-to-market	Shorter, with frequent releases	Longer, with infrequent releases
Collaboration	High, emphasizing team and stakeholder input	Lower, often siloed
Risk Management	Continuous, proactive	Periodic, reactive
Customer Involvement	High, with regular feedback loops	Low, typically limited to start and end

In traditional planning, a project is divided into distinct phases, such as initiation, planning, execution and closure, and the work is planned upfront with a detailed project plan. This approach assumes that requirements and conditions remain relatively stable throughout the project and that a thorough final examination can assure quality. Any changes that occur can prove costly and time-consuming, which is why such processes use stage gates and sign-offs to keep the project moving forward in pre-determined phases.

In contrast, Agile planning focuses on iterative development, delivering value to customers frequently and embracing change throughout the project life cycle. Agile planning acknowledges the uncertainties and complexities in project requirements and aims to adapt and respond to changes effectively. This approach enables teams to remain flexible, prioritize customer value and continuously refine their processes based on feedback and learning.

Agile Planning for Non-Agile Businesses

For non-Agile businesses or those new to implementing Agile practices, adjusting operations may appear daunting. However, comprehending the advantages and core principles of Agile approaches can ease this transition. Start by educating your team on Agile approaches (refer to Chapter 3) and explaining how these can enhance your business through heightened efficiency and customer satisfaction. Engage with expert Agile professionals through workshops or coaching sessions; these resources will offer valuable insights into effectively incorporating Agile planning into your organization.

Once you understand Agile planning, you can begin implementing it. To maximize the benefits of your efforts, ensure that all stakeholders comprehend their roles within the process. Collaboration between team members is essential for swiftly achieving successful outcomes. Concentrate on Agile processes that prioritize customer demands – this guarantees that valuable time is not wasted on tasks with little impact while ensuring customer needs are addressed.

Key Agile Planning Components

Grasping the fundamental concepts and techniques presented in this chapter will prepare leaders to understand and implement Agile planning effectively, fostering a culture of continuous improvement and collaboration within their teams.

As we delve into the components of Agile planning, business leaders will gain insights into prioritizing and managing work, streamlining communication and leveraging various tools and approaches to support their team's efforts. You will learn how to customize Agile planning to suit your organization's unique needs, ensuring your team remains focused on delivering exceptional value to customers.

Incorporating Agile planning components into your organization's processes will bolster efficiency, enhance customer satisfaction and equip your team to navigate the complexities of an ever-changing business environment with confidence and agility. This will drive an improvement in overall business performance.

Table 21: Example Agile Planning Components

Component	Purpose	Characteristics
Product Backlog	A prioritized list of features, enhancements and fixes for a product	Evolving, prioritized and refined based on customer feedback and business needs
Business Value Backlog	A list of tasks and user stories ranked by their business value	Continuously re-prioritized, focused on maximizing the value delivered
Release Plan	A high-level plan for delivering product increments	Provides a road map for product development, subject to change based on feedback and priorities

Value Streams	Visualization of the process steps and flow to deliver value	Highlights inefficiencies, creates awareness of value flow and assists in process improvements
Visual Management Techniques	Tools to visually represent progress and workflow	Enhance transparency, highlight bottlenecks and help teams monitor their progress

Let us inspect some of the key Agile planning components:

Product Backlog

At the heart of Agile planning is assessing the priority of work to be done. Once the most critical outcomes have been identified, the work must be broken down into small, independent units. These are placed in the product backlog, a prioritized list of requirements or user stories describing the features, functionality and enhancements the Agile team needs to address to achieve valuable customer outcomes. Typically maintained by a Product Owner, the product backlog constantly evolves based on customer and stakeholder feedback.

The backlog is integral to Agile planning, as it ensures the team tackles the most critical tasks and features first. The Product Owner collaborates with the team to refine and update the backlog, breaking larger features into smaller, more manageable parts that can be completed quickly, ideally within one or two days. This evolving artefact guides the team's work, focusing on delivering customer value and adapting to changing priorities and requirements.

Business Value Backlog

Just as the Product Backlog is critical to guiding an Agile team's operational work, the Business Value Backlog aligns the team's efforts with strategic objectives. This ranked list of goals, initiatives or features represents the organization's overarching priorities based on their estimated business value. The higher an item's position on the backlog, the greater its contribution to the business strategy and overall value generation. Typically, the business stakeholders, such as business analysts or product managers, are responsible for maintaining and evolving the Business Value Backlog.

The Business Value Backlog is a guidepost for the Product Owner in determining which features or requirements should populate the Product Backlog. By linking the Agile team's work to broader business objectives, the Business Value Backlog helps ensure that every effort supports strategic growth and drives the business forward.

The iterative refinement of the Business Value Backlog is essential, as business priorities can change due to market dynamics, customer needs or competitive pressures. By regularly revisiting and updating this list, the organization can respond to changing conditions effectively, ensuring that the team's efforts continually focus on initiatives that deliver the most substantial business value. In essence, the Business Value Backlog serves as a strategic compass, helping to navigate the path to sustainable success.

Visual Management Techniques

Agile planning also employs a range of visual management techniques to manage a product backlog, providing transparency across the team. Here are some examples of effective methods:

1. **Kanban boards** – These visually represent the workflow, with columns showing various stages such as "To Do", "In Progress", and "Done". Team members move tasks or user stories through the columns as they progress, making it easy to observe work and identify bottlenecks.
2. **Scrum boards** – Similar to Kanban boards but specifically used in Scrum, these boards showcase the work of the current sprint. Columns may include "Sprint Backlog", "In Progress", "Testing", and "Done", demonstrating the flow of work during the sprint and helping to track progress and completion.
3. **Burndown charts** – These are graphical representations of work left to do versus time left in a sprint or a release. The downward slope of the line indicates the team's progress toward completing the planned tasks, which helps identify whether the team is on track to meet the sprint goals.
4. **Cumulative flow diagrams** – These visualize the status of work items over time and provide an overview of the project's health. They show the number of tasks in different stages and the rate of progress, making it possible to spot bottlenecks and balance the workload effectively.

Each of these visual techniques offers a different perspective on the progress and health of the project, enabling better project management and decision-making.

Iteration Planning and Continuous Workflow

Agile methodologies and frameworks, such as Scrum, Large Scale Scrum (LeSS), Scaled Agile Framework (SAFe) and Kanban, have different approaches to planning and managing work. Scrum and its variants use iterations called sprints and planning ceremonies. Kanban focuses on continuous workflow and flow-based planning.

In an iteration-based approach, the entire Agile team gathers for planning sessions at the beginning of each sprint, typically lasting two to four weeks. During these sessions, they select items from the product backlog to work on during the upcoming iteration or sprint. The team breaks down the selected user stories into tasks and estimates the effort required to complete them. This process helps the team focus on what they can realistically accomplish during the sprint while maintaining high quality.

In a continuous workflow approach, akin to the practice in Kanban, tasks are pulled from the backlog by the team upon completion of other tasks. There is no fixed time-box for completing work items; the primary focus is maintaining a steady flow of work through the system. The team uses metrics such as lead time, cycle time and throughput to measure progress, identify areas for improvement and optimize the flow of work.

Release Planning

Release Planning schedules the incremental delivery of value to customers, typically via product increments or iterations. This process involves setting objectives, defining the scope of each increment, planning tasks and identifying key milestones and project goals.

Release Planning, which typically kicks off during a project or product development cycle, considers market trends, customer requirements and resource availability. It is essential for release plans to remain flexible and adaptable as project priorities and requirements change. The Product Owner works with stakeholders and engineers to regularly review and update the release plan, ensuring it accurately reflects project progress and priorities. Also, it is important to establish a feedback loop with customers to validate that the product increments are meeting their needs and expectations.

Value Streams

Continuing our exploration of Agile planning, it is essential to understand the concept of Value Streams. This term refers to the series of steps an organization undertakes to deliver a product or service to a customer. Mapping these Value Streams provides a clear view of the flow of value from the initial request to the customers experiencing the value of what has been delivered – "Idea to Value". It forms a critical part of business agility as it allows for the identification of bottlenecks, redundancies and wastes in the process. By eliminating these hindrances, we pave the way for streamlined operations and enhanced efficiencies, leading to an increased value proposition for customers. This optimization directly correlates to the core tenet of Agile – delivering maximum value.

Quarterly Planning

Let us consider the role of regular planning cycles in maintaining business agility. One such cycle, Quarterly Planning, is crucial for adjusting business direction based on new insights, changes in the market or customer feedback. Regular review and re-planning enable the organization to react more efficiently and effectively to changes, reinforcing the principle of responsiveness and facilitating continuous improvement. This brings us to another vital aspect of Agile planning, where we align Agile leaders' roles in aligning planning with Agile objectives and transforming strategic goals into actionable tasks.

Continuous Delivery as an Alternative Approach in Agile Planning

In software development, Continuous Delivery (CD) has surfaced as an alternative to Release Planning. CD focuses on automating software delivery to facilitate frequent and predictable delivery of value to customers. This approach reduces the time between developing new features or fixing bugs and deploying them to customers.

CD and Release Planning share common principles: adaptability, responsiveness and a customer-centric approach. The primary difference lies in the frequency and granularity of releases. While Release Planning schedules incremental value deliveries and often involves more comprehensive planning, CD aims for a seamless and continuous release process, enabling rapid deployment of new features and fixes with reduced planning overhead.

Agile Estimation

Agile Estimation is often a crucial part of Agile planning. It's not just about predicting delivery dates; it's about aligning the team's capacity to the amount of work they undertake, managing expectations and controlling work in progress. Agile estimation forms the basis for informed decision-making and resource allocation by evaluating the scope and complexity of tasks.

Various techniques, such as relative sizing, T-shirt sizing and time-based estimates, are often employed in Agile estimation. The purpose here is to help plan teams' workload that maximizes the likelihood of delivering value within the iteration or release time frame. When organizations implement appropriate Agile estimation techniques, they stand a better chance of improving their planning processes and delivering high-value products and services to customers.

Agile estimation, while often necessary, can sometimes prove unreliable. An alternative approach involves forecasting based on historical trends. This method recognizes the uncertainties inherent in project planning and sets more realistic expectations. Analysing past data and trends enables teams to forecast completion times more accurately. Also, offering a date range with a confidence index instead of rigid milestones helps manage risks better.

The "No Estimates" approach, a variation of traditional Agile estimation and forecasting, emphasizes the importance of breaking tasks into small, manageable parts. By focusing on deliverables that can be completed within a short time frame, such as one or two days, teams lessen the need for extensive numerical estimates. Instead, they concentrate on delivering value quickly and iteratively. Incorporating the "No Estimates" approach in Agile planning can streamline processes, reduce the risk of delays or scope creep and ultimately enhance the delivery of value and customer satisfaction.

Agile estimation encourages team collaboration. Prerequisites such as psychological safety are vital for this collaboration to be effective. When team members feel safe to express their thoughts and ideas without fear of judgement, they can contribute their expertise and perspectives more genuinely. As a result, collective estimates are worked out, making them more accurate. This fosters a sense of ownership and accountability among team members, reinforcing the core Agile principle of self-management.

Agile Metrics

In Agile planning, project progress and performance transparency are essential. Agile metrics (see Chapter 9) function as key performance indicators (KPIs), allowing teams to make data-driven decisions and adjust plans accordingly. Common examples of Agile metrics include:

1. **Progress tracking** – A measure of the team's work completion rate during an iteration, typically represented in story points or hours. This helps teams predict future performance and adjust their workload accordingly.
2. **Work remaining** – A visual representation of the remaining work in an iteration or release, displaying progress over time. This metric lets teams quickly determine whether they are on track to meet their iteration or release goals.
3. **Work item flow** – Diagrams that depict the flow of work items through various stages of the development process, providing insights into potential bottlenecks and areas for improvement.

Continuous Planning

Continuous planning is an ongoing process integrated into all aspects of an organization. It involves regularly reviewing and updating plans and adapting to change and priorities based on feedback from customers and stakeholders. Continuous planning ensures that the team remains value-focused and adaptable to change.

This approach also promotes cross-functional collaboration, as teams work closely with stakeholders to identify emerging needs and update plans accordingly. Continuous planning helps organizations align their development efforts with customer needs and market trends, ultimately enhancing their ability to stay competitive and deliver products that meet customer expectations.

Agile Planning Tools

A range of tools, such as Jira, Kanbanize and Asana, for example, support Agile planning and execution. These tools assist teams in managing product backlogs, planning sprints, looking at the flow of work and identifying bottlenecks. They also offer transparency into the team's work, enabling stakeholders to view task status and monitor progress towards goals. Other popular Agile tools include ClickUp, Monday.com and GitLab. Each tool has strengths and weaknesses, so evaluating which best aligns with your organization's needs, goals and preferences is crucial.

Agile planning tools empower teams to collaborate, prioritize and adapt to changes throughout the project life cycle, aiding workflow visualization and identifying potential bottlenecks.

Agile Planning Challenges

Agile planning offers many benefits, but it has challenges. Common pitfalls and difficulties in Agile planning include:

1. **Estimation challenges** – Estimating the size and complexity of work items can be difficult, particularly when dealing with new or unfamiliar tasks. To improve the estimation accuracy, consider using different techniques such as planning poker, affinity estimation, t-shirt sizing, dot voting or ideal days, which involves team collaboration and leveraging collective wisdom.
2. **Resistance to change** – Organizational resistance to Agile adoption can hinder planning efforts. To overcome this hurdle, concentrate on articulating the advantages of Agile planning, provision of training and resources and active involvement of stakeholders in the planning process. This will foster buy-in and commitment.
3. **Balancing flexibility and discipline** – Agile planning requires balancing adaptability and maintaining discipline in execution. Encourage teams to regularly revisit and adjust their plans while adhering to Agile principles and practices.
4. **Adapting to different Agile frameworks** – Agile planning can be more challenging when teams adapt to various Agile frameworks, such as Scrum or Kanban. Ensuring the team is familiar with and comfortable using different approaches can improve planning efforts and lead to more successful project execution.
5. **Distributed team challenges** – With the rise of remote work, teams often face challenges related to time zone differences, cultural barriers and communication. To overcome these challenges, organizations can:
   a. Implement virtual collaboration tools to facilitate communication and collaboration among team members.

b. Schedule regular video conferences and stand-up meetings to maintain alignment and shared understanding of project goals.

c. Establish clear communication protocols and expectations to ensure timely responses and updates from team members.

d. Consider time zone differences and plan meetings or collaboration sessions accordingly to ensure the active participation of all team members.

e. Foster a culture of trust and accountability, encouraging team members to be transparent about their progress and any potential roadblocks.

Organizations can successfully implement Agile planning methodologies and maintain effective collaboration across distances by addressing the unique challenges of remote and distributed teams.

Customizing Agile Planning for Your Organization

To tailor Agile planning to your organization's unique needs and goals, follow these steps:

1. Assess your organization's current processes and structures to identify areas where Agile planning can be most beneficial, such as workflows, communication channels and project management practices.

2. Choose an Agile framework that aligns with your organization's needs, goals and culture as discussed in Chapter 3.

3. Involve key stakeholders in the planning and implementation process to ensure they understand the benefits of Agile planning and are committed to making necessary adjustments.

4. Provide training and support for your team to develop the skills and knowledge necessary to adopt Agile planning practices effectively. Offer workshops, training sessions or coaching to enable your team members to become proficient in Agile planning techniques.

5. Review and adjust your Agile planning practices as your organization evolves and grows. Regularly refine and adapt your processes to ensure they remain effective and aligned with your business goals. The Shu-Ha-Ri model of learning, which progresses from following rules (Shu) to adapting rules (Ha) and ultimately transcending rules (Ri), aligns well with the Agile mindset of continuous learning and adaptation.

6. Engage with your customers to inform them of the changes they will experience. Listen to their concerns and work with them to make the agile change happen.

7. Monitor and measure the effectiveness of your Agile planning practices through regular reviews and retrospectives, ensuring continuous improvement and alignment with your organization's goals.

Benefits and Outcomes of Agile Planning

A significant benefit of Agile planning is enabling teams to supply working software to customers in small increments. This tactic can ease risk by detecting and tackling issues early in development. Segmenting the project allows the team to concentrate on delivering a high-quality product that fulfils customer expectations.

Customers who can provide feedback and observe progress more frequently will experience higher satisfaction and find better alignment with their requirements as smaller increments of working software are delivered regularly.

Integrating supplementary Agile ceremonies, like frequent progress updates, completed work assessments and opportunities for reflection and enhancement, can foster communication, cooperation and continuous improvement. These practices guarantee that teams stay on course, adjust to changes and refine their processes. Some examples of these Agile ceremonies include Sprint Planning, Daily Stand-up, Sprint Review and Sprint Retrospective.

Efficient Agile planning demands collaboration, communication and openness. Business leaders must promote this among team members and stakeholders, providing the tools and resources to support Agile planning processes. For example, in Scrum, the Product Owner, Scrum Master and Developers must collaborate closely to ensure the product backlog is appropriately prioritized and the team works toward well-defined goals and objectives. Organizations that embrace Agile planning practices can attain heightened flexibility, swiftness and responsiveness, delivering increased value to customers. It is also essential to involve stakeholders in planning, ensuring their input and feedback are considered and integrated into product development.

While Agile planning offers many advantages, it is important to be aware of common pitfalls, such as overcommitting and lack of stakeholder engagement. To avoid these issues, consider the following tips:

1. **Align objectives with the strategic vision** – Ensure that your Agile planning aligns with your organization's strategic vision and goals to promote coherence and focused execution.
2. **Involve all stakeholders** – Engage all relevant stakeholders in the planning process, including team members, product owners and customers, to create a shared understanding of goals and expectations.
3. **Prioritize customer needs** – Focus on delivering value to the customer by prioritizing their needs and continuously adapting to their feedback.

4. **Set realistic expectations** – Avoid overcommitting to timelines or deliverables; instead, establish realistic expectations based on your team's capacity and resources.

5. **Break down work into smaller tasks** – Divide large projects into smaller, manageable tasks that can be delivered incrementally, allowing continuous progress and improvement.

6. **Encourage flexibility and adaptability** – Embrace change and encourage team members to be open to adjusting their plans based on new information or feedback.

7. **Create a feedback loop** – Establish a continuous feedback loop between team members, stakeholders and customers to ensure that progress is regularly assessed and adjusted as needed.

8. **Measure progress with relevant metrics** – Track your team's progress using appropriate Agile metrics, such as cycle time, throughput and customer satisfaction, to ensure that improvements and goals are achieved.

9. **Encourage open communication** – Promote transparency and open communication within the team, allowing for constructive discussions and sharing ideas and challenges.

10. **Continuously learn and improve** – Reflect on your team's performance and processes regularly, identifying areas for improvement and implementing changes as needed to drive continuous improvement.

This checklist offers valuable insights and guidance on avoiding common Agile planning pitfalls organizations may encounter during their Agile transformation. When these potential challenges are addressed, businesses can ensure a smoother transition and greater success in their Agile journey.

Agile Planning for Smaller Organizations and Startups

Small companies and startups can greatly benefit from Agile planning. Take the example of Satago, a fintech firm based in the UK and Poland. They used a blend of Agile planning techniques from the Disciplined Agile toolkit in a context-sensitive manner for their organization. Just three months into adopting these new ways of working and Agile planning, Satago delivered over 300% more outcomes and customer deliverables than they had in the prior three months with traditional methods. This swift response allowed them to quickly adapt to changes in the market and effectively scale their product and technology operations. By prioritizing work based on customer feedback and rapidly iterating on its products, Satago accelerated growth and customer outcomes. It was named as one of the Top 10 Fast-Growing Fintech firms in the UK for 2023.

For smaller organizations and startups, it is essential to:

1. Ensure clear communication and alignment of goals among team members and stakeholders.
2. Focus on delivering the highest-value features to customers first.
3. Adopt lightweight Agile frameworks such as Scrum or Kanban, easily adapted to suit the organization's specific needs and requirements.
4. Foster a culture of continuous improvement and learning to stay agile in a competitive market.

Smaller organizations and startups can effectively leverage Agile planning to navigate uncertainties and rapid changes. These organizations can deliver high-quality products and services quickly and efficiently, positioning themselves for long-term success by focusing on customer value, maintaining flexibility and continuously refining their processes.

CLEAR Lens for "Agile Planning"

We can apply two CLEAR Model® principles to Agile Planning:

Leadership: In Agile planning, effective leadership is critical. Agile leaders champion adaptability for emergent work, such as new feature development and bug-fixing, using iterative inspection and adaptation rather than traditional predictive planning. For repeatable processes like onboarding new customers and staff, leaders focus on refining these processes. This balance helps teams navigate uncertainty, prioritize tasks and make informed decisions. It also fosters a responsive, Agile environment. In this way, Agile leaders ensure that the planning process aligns with the broader Agile goals of the organization, exemplifying the Leadership principle in the CLEAR Model®.

Execution: Agile planning extends beyond theoretical strategies to emphasize the CLEAR principle of Execution. It's about bridging the gap between strategic objectives and actionable tasks and delivering them efficiently. The dynamic, interactive and adaptable nature of Agile planning ensures that the team remains equipped to adjust to evolving requirements and shifts in the business environment, making the principle of Execution integral to the process.

Reflection Prompts

1. Assess your organization's current planning processes. How can they be adapted to better align with Agile principles?

2. How can you involve your team in planning to ensure shared understanding and ownership of the plan?

Case Study: Microsoft and IBM's Agile Planning Success

Agile planning has helped to achieve business agility for major corporations such as Microsoft and IBM. We can glean valuable insights into effectively planning and implementing Agile projects by examining their strategies.

Microsoft's Agile Planning Journey

Microsoft embraced Agile planning and experienced improvements in productivity and teamwork. The company used Agile approaches like Scrum to prioritize work based on customer value, foster collaboration and streamline processes. This enabled Microsoft to adapt to the fast-paced technology landscape and deliver innovative, high-quality products to their customers. Microsoft's Visual Studio Team Services (now Azure DevOps) also adopted Agile approaches, resulting in a faster release cycle and increased team collaboration. Every team within Azure DevOps manages their own product backlog and development cycle, with a production branch deployed every three weeks. The teams align their autonomy with organizational goals, ensuring a unified, high-quality product output.

Transition to Agile

Microsoft's transition to Agile planning was started by addressing long development cycles, low customer satisfaction and increasing competition. The company recognized that traditional planning methods no longer met the demands of a fast-changing technology sector.

Adopting Scrum

Microsoft began by implementing Scrum, an Agile framework, in some of their product teams. The teams worked in short, time-boxed iterations called sprints, focusing on delivering small increments of customer value. This allowed Microsoft to continuously gather feedback, iterate on their products and adapt to changing customer needs. The planning process at Microsoft includes various levels, like an 18-month plan with biannual calibrations, a 6-month seasonal plan, and more frequent sprint plans, aiding in scaling Agile practices.

Scaling Agile

As the benefits of Agile planning became evident, Microsoft extended Agile practices to more teams and projects, scaling their Agile practices across the organization. This enabled Microsoft to synchronize efforts across the organization and maintain alignment with strategic objectives. Feature chats were introduced to ensure team plans align with organizational goals, providing a platform for management and teams to stay informed and collaborate.

Challenges and Lessons Learned

During its Agile transformation, Microsoft faced challenges such as resistance to change, the need for organizational support and the importance of continuous learning. They overcame these challenges by investing in Agile training and coaching, fostering a culture of experimentation and promoting transparency and collaboration.

Table 22: Microsoft's Agile Planning Framework

Aspect	Strategy
Prioritization	Focus on customer value and data-driven decisions
Collaboration	Encourage cross-functional teams and open communication
Streamlining	Eliminate unnecessary steps and focus on efficiency
Continuous Improvement	Constantly evaluate and refine processes

IBM's Agile Planning Transformation

Similarly, IBM has harnessed Agile planning methodologies to accelerate and streamline the delivery of top-notch software products. Through Agile planning practices, IBM has adapted quickly to market changes, responded to customer feedback and fostered a culture of continuous improvement. This has allowed the company to maintain its competitive edge in the software industry. IBM's adoption of Agile practices for their cloud services development has also led to quicker response times to market demands and streamlined delivery processes.

Enterprise-Wide Adoption

IBM's Agile transformation began with pilot projects in software development teams. As the benefits of Agile planning became clear, the company adopted Agile practices across the entire organization, involving over 350,000 employees.

Agile Centers for Enablement (ACEs)

IBM established "Agile Centers for Enablement" (ACEs) to support this massive transformation. The ACEs, established in strategic locations globally, served as hubs of Agile expertise and knowledge dissemination. They provided extensive coaching, training and resources to support Agile adoption, which is crucial in helping teams develop a deep understanding of Agile principles and values. These centres also served as platforms for knowledge exchange, allowing different teams across IBM to learn from each other's experiences and refine their Agile practices.

Innovation and Adaptation

IBM's Agile planning transformation prioritized process improvement and nurturing a culture of innovation. The company consolidated its z/OS development tools into a single delivery pipeline to deliver better client value and function faster. They achieved monthly releases for fixes and small functionalities, integrating 17 separate products into this pipeline.

Challenges and Lessons Learned

IBM faced several challenges during its Agile transformation, such as scaling Agile practices across a large, complex organization and overcoming resistance to change. To address these challenges, IBM provided extensive training, established executive buy-in and promoted a culture of continuous learning and improvement. IBM's experience highlighted the importance of giving teams time for adaptation and education, with a focus on long-term productivity gains.

Table 23: IBM's Agile Planning Framework

Aspect	Strategy
Prioritization	Align with market changes and customer feedback
Collaboration	Promote stakeholder involvement and shared understanding
Streamlining	Simplify processes and reduce time-to-market
Continuous Improvement	Encourage innovation and learning from mistakes

Key Takeaways from the Case Study

1. **Prioritizing customer value** – Microsoft and IBM focused on delivering customer value by prioritizing work and making data-driven decisions. This approach helped them stay aligned with customer needs and adapt to market changes.
2. **Fostering collaboration** – Microsoft and IBM emphasized collaboration between teams and stakeholders to ensure alignment and shared understanding of project goals. This collaborative approach enhanced decision-making and facilitated efficient project execution.
3. **Streamlining processes** – Agile planning enabled both companies to streamline processes, eliminating unnecessary steps and improving overall efficiency. This allowed for quicker adaptation to market changes and faster delivery of high-quality products.
4. **Culture of continuous improvement** – Embracing Agile planning practices encouraged a culture of continuous improvement at both Microsoft and IBM. The companies could optimize their operations and maintain a competitive edge in their respective industries by constantly evaluating and refining their processes.
5. **Embracing change and learning from mistakes** – Agile planning encourages adaptability and learning from errors, allowing Microsoft and IBM to respond to changing market conditions and continuously refine their processes.

Exercise: Agile Planning Techniques for Success

Adopting planning techniques that align with your organization's goals and objectives is crucial to planning Agile projects and initiatives effectively. Incorporating these techniques enables you to establish a clear direction, prioritize tasks and ensure efficient resource allocation throughout the project life cycle.

Consider incorporating the following Agile planning techniques:

1. **Product vision** – Establish a clear and compelling vision for your product or project, outlining the desired outcomes and guiding principles. This vision serves as a foundation for decision-making and goal-setting throughout the project.

2. **Product road map** – Develop a high-level strategic plan that aligns your product vision with organizational goals, outlining the key features, milestones and priorities. This road map helps communicate the project's direction to stakeholders and ensures a shared understanding of objectives.

3. **Release planning** – Identify the features and functionality delivered in each release, considering factors such as customer needs, resource constraints and dependencies. This planning enables you to manage expectations and allocate resources effectively.

4. **Iteration planning** – Plan the work to be completed during each sprint or iteration, breaking down larger tasks into smaller, manageable pieces. This approach promotes transparency and ensures that team members understand their responsibilities.

5. **Daily stand-ups** – Facilitate brief daily meetings where team members share progress updates and discuss obstacles, promoting transparency and collaboration. These meetings encourage accountability and enable teams to identify and address challenges promptly.

6. **Backlog refinement** – Continuously review and update the product backlog to accurately reflect current priorities and requirements. This practice ensures that the team focuses on the most valuable tasks and maintains alignment with the project's goals and vision.

Utilize these Agile planning techniques to create a solid foundation for your projects and initiatives, adapting them to suit your organization's unique context and requirements. As you gain experience with Agile planning, continuously refine your approach to maximize efficiency, delivery of value and overall project success.

Chapter Summary

This chapter delved into the importance of Agile planning in helping achieve business agility. We explored the differences between traditional and Agile planning and examined how Agile planning could help organizations respond more to change and deliver value to customers quickly. We also discussed the key principles of Agile planning, such as iterative development and prioritization, and provided practical guidance on implementing Agile planning methodologies in your organization. We looked at real-world examples of companies like Microsoft and IBM that successfully leveraged Agile planning methodologies to deliver better value to their customers. Remember that the key to success in Agile planning is continuously refining and adapting these practices to your organization's unique needs and context, ensuring that you stay ahead and maintain a competitive edge.

Further Readings and Resources

1. Book: *User Stories Applied: For Agile Software Development,* by Mike Cohn, 2004, Addison-Wesley Signature Series.

2. Book: *Agile Project Management: Creating Innovative Products,* by Jim Highsmith, 2009, Addison-Wesley Professional.

3. Website: Project Management Institute – www.pmi.org

8

Agile Execution

Imagine piloting a high-tech aircraft soaring through the unpredictable skies of the business world. Just when you think you've reached cruising altitude, turbulence appears out of nowhere, jostling your plans and altering your trajectory. Now envision Agile execution as your skilled co-pilot and the aircraft's cutting-edge guidance system, perpetually primed and prepared to adapt to these sudden shifts, guaranteeing a secure and successful flight.

A team's ability to apply Agile approaches, provide customer value and attain objectives is significantly impacted by their execution of Agile principles. As a business leader, it is vital to grasp the critical aspects of Agile execution, such as iterative planning, daily coordination, feedback mechanisms and ongoing enhancement.

Acknowledging the significance of effective leadership and support is akin to realizing that, in the midst of a storm, your crew looks to you for direction and assurance, trusting in your skills and vision. Similarly, your Agile teams need your guidance to manoeuvre through challenges and seize opportunities.

Agile execution, a continuous process throughout a project or product's lifespan, entails using diverse techniques and strategies to maintain agility and deliver customer value effectively. Grasping its nuances and challenges allows business leaders to cultivate a more adaptable and responsive organization that is well equipped to navigate fluctuating market conditions.

Business leaders must accept that Agile practice may vary among organizations, depending on unique goals, priorities and market circumstances. Adopting a tailored approach while considering industry-specific factors can considerably enhance an organization's success and growth in the fiercely competitive market.

In Agile execution, the focus is not merely on the tools or systems but crucially on delivering business value, fostering customer collaboration and achieving the desired outcomes. However, a persistent challenge is keeping antiquated methodologies from resurfacing. When intermingled with Agile, these traditional methods can act as obstructions, slowing progress and making it more difficult to optimize the benefits of Agile.

While rolling out software as a service (SAAS) solutions like Oracle, SAP or Salesforce across individual business units may initially seem to provide the needed outcomes, overlooking the bigger picture often leads to the realization of inefficiencies. There are numerous instances where departments, after independently implementing these solutions, have been forced to retrofit workarounds to genuinely achieve the outcomes they need, exemplifying the importance of a holistic Agile approach.

Let's debunk a common misconception: Agile isn't just about coding. If you think so, you're merely scratching the surface. True Agile execution is holistic, encompassing every project facet, weaving them together into a seamless tapestry of efficiency and innovation.

Flawless execution is the linchpin that transforms an Agile blueprint into a resounding success. Are you confident that your organization can navigate the labyrinth of Agile execution without losing its way?

This chapter explores the important aspect of Agile execution and how it helps organizations deliver maximum customer value. The chapter offers insightful discussions on the key elements that drive Agile success and provides strategies to perfect Agile execution. When these strategies are implemented, organizations can consistently provide high-quality products and services, surpassing customer expectations.

What Is Agile Execution?

Agile Execution is a vital component of Agile methodologies or frameworks that focus on effectively implementing Agile approaches to deliver maximum value to customers while navigating the complexities of transforming markets.

It's crucial to maintain an uncompromising focus on this commitment and not allow the shadow of old methodologies to cloud our vision. Any traces of these outdated methods infiltrating the Agile workspace can hinder progress, creating obstacles in harnessing Agile's full potential.

Effective Agile execution is critical to an organization's Agile transformation and overall agility. A well-executed Agile approach equips organizations to adapt to rapidly changing market conditions and aligns closely with the key stages of the Product Development Cycle. This alignment ensures a harmonious integration of Agile principles within the organizational structure, thereby enhancing long-term success and competitiveness.

Table 24: Example Agile Product Development Cycle

Stage	Description
Ideation	Ideas are brainstormed, often with the involvement of customers or end-users. This is the initial stage where the vision for the product or feature is created
Planning and Prioritization	Teams organize ideas based on their viability and impact and decide on the product backlog. This includes prioritizing the tasks based on the potential value delivered to the customer
Prototyping	A minimum viable product (MVP) is created. This is a basic version of the product, enough to gather user feedback and validate the idea
Testing	The MVP is tested internally and externally. Feedback is collected from users and bugs are identified
Iteration	Based on user feedback and testing results, the product is improved and refined. This step is repeated until the product meets customer needs
Review and Retrospective	The team reviews the completed work and reflects on the process, identifying areas for improvement in the next sprint. This ensures that lessons learned are applied to future iterations
Release	The product is released to the end-users. Even after this stage, the Agile cycle continues with the collection of user feedback and continuous improvements

Key Elements of Agile Execution

Executing Agile well means teams can employ Agile approaches effectively (see Chapter 3), deliver customer value and achieve their goals. Business leaders must understand the following key principles and elements of Agile execution to help build and grow an Agile culture that promotes transparency, communication and continuous learning and improvement.

Agile execution is not just a tick-in-a-box exercise. It is a crafted approach that caters to your organization's unique needs. Understanding these key elements will allow you to gain a deep appreciation for the importance of each aspect and how they interconnect with one another. The insights and pragmatic guidance offered empower you to create an Agile environment that can adapt to the market's demands and consistently deliver exceptional customer value.

Table 25: Agile Execution Principles Overview

Principle	Description	Real-life Example
Continuous Delivery	Delivering small, incremental improvements frequently to customers	Amazon's rapid release of new features and updates
Collaboration	Working together to solve problems and create innovative solutions	Spotify's cross-functional squads collaborating on projects
Empowerment	Enabling team members to make decisions and take ownership of tasks	Google allowing engineers to allocate 20% of their time to personal projects
Adaptability	Responding to changing circumstances and incorporating feedback	Netflix pivoting from DVD rentals to streaming services
Transparency and Visibility	Openly sharing information and progress within teams and the organization	Atlassian's use of public dashboards to share project updates

Let us look at some key elements of Agile execution:

Iterative Planning

Iterative planning is a fundamental component of Agile execution, ensuring teams are focused on the goals for the upcoming iteration. As discussed in Chapter 7, in planning sessions, the teams examine the backlog items and select those to work on during the iteration. Time-boxed and focused planning sessions ensure teams maintain momentum and avoid getting bogged down in the planning process. Subsequently, team members break the items into smaller tasks and estimate the effort for completion. Iterative planning guarantees that they work on the most valuable tasks and understand the required actions. It also encourages cross-functional collaboration as team members discuss dependencies, risks and potential solutions.

Daily Stand-Ups

Daily stand-ups are short meetings where team members get together to share their progress and ask for ideas or help if they need it. These meetings must ideally be around 15 minutes to keep them efficient and focused, reflecting Agile's principles of simplicity and respect for others' time, keeping the team aligned and focused on the iteration goals. Regular check-ins help teams swiftly identify and tackle challenges or roadblocks, maintaining consistent progress throughout the iteration.

Feedback Loops

Feedback loops are a continuous process of gathering, analysing and incorporating stakeholder input to improve a product or project throughout its development cycle iteratively. They are also crucial for verifying the team's delivery of customer value and alignment with the project or product goals. Internal feedback (from team members) and external feedback (from customers) must be considered, balancing both perspectives to achieve optimal results. Agile teams can continually deliver solutions that satisfy customer needs and expectations by engaging with end-users and incorporating their insights into the product or project.

Continuous Improvement

A key aspect of Agile execution is continuous improvement. Throughout iterations, teams reflect on their performance and pinpoint areas to improve. When cultivated, a culture of continuous improvement and learning allows teams to discover more effective ways to work and achieve their objectives efficiently. Continuous improvement is not just about identifying areas for improvement but also about celebrating successes and acknowledging progress to maintain team motivation. Retrospectives are vital for nurturing progress and enabling teams to assess iterations, identify successes, pinpoint improvements and formulate action plans. Continually reviewing and adjusting processes boosts overall performance.

Agile Development Practices

Applying Agile development practices like continuous integration, continuous delivery and test-driven development is key to successful Agile execution. Integrating these practices into the team's workflow can increase efficiency and quality, ensuring high-quality work aligned with project or product objectives. Continuous integration promotes collaboration and reduces the risk of integration issues by merging code changes frequently. Continuous delivery ensures that software is always in a releasable state, enabling faster deployment and reduced time-to-market. Test-driven development enhances code quality by writing tests before implementing the actual functionality. Adopting these practices helps teams to swiftly respond to shifting requirements, minimize defect risks and deliver a sturdy, dependable product.

Cross-Functional Collaboration

Agile execution hinges on cross-functional teamwork, with developers, testers, designers and business analysts pooling their expertise. This synergy overcomes silos, fosters knowledge exchange and cultivates a shared understanding of project goals. To maximize this synergy, it is essential to create a psychologically safe environment where team members feel comfortable sharing their ideas and concerns without fear of judgement or reprisal. United, cross-functional teams can exceed customer expectations with top-notch products and services.

Regular Communication with Stakeholders

Regular communication with stakeholders is vital to ensure alignment and promptly address any changes in priorities or requirements. Open communication channels foster transparency, enabling stakeholders to voice their concerns, provide updates and contribute to decision-making. Establishing a clear communication cadence, such as weekly or bi-weekly meetings, can facilitate more effective information exchange and keep stakeholders informed and involved in the project. Agile teams can use tools like Slack, Microsoft Teams or Google Chat to facilitate real-time communication and collaboration. Agile teams can focus on delivering value and ensuring that the end product meets customers' needs and expectations when stakeholders are engaged throughout the project.

Prioritizing Customer Value

Constantly re-evaluating what is most valuable to customers is essential for Agile execution success. Regularly reassessing the product backlog based on customer feedback and market demands helps teams focus on high-value features. Leaders must empower team members to make decisions that align with customer needs and promote a shared understanding of customer value throughout the organization. This customer-centric approach yields superior products and services and bolsters customer satisfaction and loyalty. Business leaders must champion customer-centricity and prompt teams to make data-driven decisions catering to customer needs.

Embracing a Growth Mindset

In Agile execution, a growth mindset is indispensable for perpetual improvement and adaptation. Agile teams must learn from experiences, accept change and welcome feedback. Encourage team members to share their learning experiences and seek individual and collective growth opportunities to foster innovation and resilience. A growth mindset enables team members to view challenges as opportunities for advancement, fostering innovation and resilience throughout the project's life.

Balancing Flexibility and Discipline

Agile execution encourages adaptability, but discipline and focus must counterbalance this flexibility. Agile teams must adhere to structured planning and task execution, ensuring accountability for their commitments and delivering quality work within set time frames. Implement time-boxed activities, enforce team agreements and establish well-defined goals to balance flexibility and discipline in Agile execution. Harmonizing flexibility and discipline allows teams to navigate an ever-changing business environment while controlling project outcomes.

Risk Management

Agile execution success hinges on effective risk management, an often unsung hero of Agile, yet its influence is profound. It's about vigilantly mitigating risk in every Agile move. Agile teams ought to pinpoint potential risks and craft proactive mitigation plans, ultimately safeguarding the project and its success. Leaders must ensure that risk management is an ongoing activity embedded in the team's processes, with regular reviews and updates to the risk register. This tool is vital for identifying and assessing potential risks as new information emerges or situations change, highlighting its role in proactively empowering teams to manage risk. Risk-centred backlog prioritization, set-duration iterations and regular inspection and adaptation are Agile practices that facilitate proactive risk identification and management.

These practices not only guide the course of the project but also act as the guardrails that protect it from unnecessary disruptions. Continuous assessment and plan adjustments empower Agile teams to reduce risk impacts on project results, delivering value to customers. It's this persistent attention to risk that fortifies Agile execution, helping to ensure that the delivery of value to customers isn't just a goal but a predictable outcome.

Agile Tools and Technologies

Employing appropriate tools and technologies can improve Agile execution. Select tools well suited to your organization's needs and size, and provide training and support to ensure team members can effectively leverage these tools in their daily work. Project management and collaboration software like Jira, Kanbanize and Asana enable communication, task monitoring and reporting, bolstering Agile teams' efforts to provide customer value. Also, modern development practices, such as continuous integration and deployment, can streamline development, reduce errors and ensure prompt, high-quality software delivery.

Distributed Teams and Remote Work

Examining the effect of distributed teams and remote work on Agile execution is vital in our current globalized work setting. Business leaders must utilize collaboration tools and virtual meeting platforms that facilitate real-time communication and updates. This will ensure smooth collaboration across time zones and locations. Clear communication protocols and expectations are crucial to avoid misunderstandings or project delays. Establishing regular "virtual water-cooler" sessions or dedicated channels for informal interactions can help remote team members build stronger relationships and improve collaboration. Regular team-building activities help maintain team cohesion and morale, fostering effective collaboration even with physical distance. Nurturing a supportive remote work culture and utilizing technology to bridge distances enables Agile teams to execute projects successfully, irrespective of location.

Cultivating Agile Excellence through Leadership and Culture

Successful Agile execution is deeply influenced by both leadership and organizational culture. Leaders must demonstrate Agile values, providing a clear vision and creating an environment where trust and psychological safety are prevalent. They should engage with teams, particularly in sprint reviews, to offer support. Simultaneously, fostering an organizational culture that prizes transparency, collaboration, and a learning mindset is essential. This dual focus ensures that team members feel empowered to share ideas and learn from each experience, driving the organization towards Agile excellence.

Agile Coaching and Training

Agile coaching and training positively impact teams adopting Agile practices and processes. Agile coaches guide teams through the process, sharing insights and expertise and addressing any challenges or roadblocks. Ensure that Agile coaches and trainers are well-versed in your organization's unique challenges so that they can tailor their approach to provide targeted, actionable guidance for your teams. Providing ongoing training and development opportunities helps team members maintain their skills and stay up to date with evolving Agile practices, reflecting the organization's dedication to Agile principles.

Challenges and Pitfalls in Agile Execution

Organizations may face challenges and pitfalls during Agile execution, such as resistance to change or a lack of management support. To overcome resistance to change, fostering a supportive culture that encourages open communication, collaboration and learning from mistakes is crucial.

Consider the following steps to facilitate this process:

1. **Communicate the vision** – Clearly articulate the benefits of Agile approaches and the reasons behind the transition. Ensure that all team members understand the goals and expected outcomes of Agile execution.
2. **Engage stakeholders** – Involve employees in the Agile transformation process, encouraging their input and addressing concerns. This inclusive approach can help to build buy-in and minimize resistance.

3. **Offer training and support** – Provide comprehensive training on Agile practices and offer ongoing support to help team members adapt to new processes and ways of working.
4. **Encourage a growth mindset** – Foster a culture that embraces change and supports continuous learning, allowing team members to feel comfortable experimenting and adapting to new approaches.
5. **Be patient and persistent** – Change takes time, and setbacks may occur. Remain patient and persistent in your efforts to drive Agile adoption, continually emphasizing the benefits and supporting your team through the transition.

Another common misconception about Agile is that it lacks structure or discipline. Agile requires a different discipline, one centred on adaptability and iterative progress. Overcoming this misconception is crucial in achieving successful Agile execution. Leadership plays a vital role here, setting the tone for the team, facilitating communication and ensuring alignment with Agile principles.

In Agile execution, much like driving a high-performance car, it's also crucial to clear any blockers or "traffic" that may impede the team's progress. Creating a frictionless environment for our "Ferrari-like" Agile teams will enable them to deliver their best without unnecessary organizational obstacles slowing them down.

Identify and address potential challenges, such as insufficient resources, constant late changing requirements from the customer, unrealistic expectations or communication breakdowns. Gaining management support is crucial for Agile success; you need to make sure the leaders understand the benefits of being Agile and how it will deliver more customer value.

Remember, our goal is not just to do Agile but to be "genuinely Agile". True Agile execution is like a well-orchestrated dance where each movement flows into the next, where adaptability and flexibility are at the heart of every step.

CLEAR Lens for "Agile Execution"

We can apply two CLEAR Model® principles to Agile Execution:

 Execution: Agile Execution embodies the soul of the CLEAR principle of Execution. It hinges upon delivering work efficiently, prioritizing tasks that maximize value creation and maintaining a sustainable work pace. Agile practices that promote transparency, enhance communication and foster a culture of continuous improvement are woven into the fabric of execution, acting as guiding threads in the complex tapestry of Agile Execution.

Responsiveness: Being nimble and adaptive to change is an inherent characteristic of Agile Execution, and this characteristic firmly underscores the Responsiveness principle in the CLEAR Model®. Agile Execution exemplifies a dynamic approach, illustrating how Agile teams calibrate their strategies based on insightful feedback, progressive learning and shifts in the market, thus bringing the principle of Responsiveness to the fore.

Reflection Prompts

1. Reflect on your team's recent project execution. What bottlenecks or inefficiencies did you find? How can these be addressed using Agile principles?

2. How can you improve communication and collaboration within your team to ensure smooth project execution?

Case Study: Salesforce and Siemens – Success Stories in Agile Execution

Adopting Agile approaches is essential for enhancing business agility and driving innovation in the modern commercial setting. Salesforce and Siemens, two global powerhouses, have demonstrated outstanding success in Agile execution by adapting unique strategies and fostering an enabling organizational culture. A closer look at their journeys provides business leaders with valuable insights into overcoming challenges and executing Agile projects effectively.

Salesforce: Agile Transformation for Improved Customer Value Delivery

Before embracing Agile, Salesforce, a leading customer relationship management (CRM) software provider, faced challenges in long development cycles, inefficient collaboration, and adapting to changing customer demands. In 2006, Salesforce began its Agile journey, transforming its entire R&D department from the traditional "Waterfall" SDLC to Scrum.

This iterative approach and a learning-oriented mindset have helped to achieve Agile excellence.

Salesforce tackled the challenge of scaling Agile practices by adopting a customized structured approach that suited their unique needs. This strategy improved communication, enhanced team collaboration and increased project visibility. Salesforce also implemented a robust measurement and reporting system to track progress, identify areas for improvement and drive Agile success. Salesforce has optimized its Agile execution and strengthened its competitive edge by customizing the Scaled Agile Framework (SAFe) framework to suit the organization's unique needs and continuously refining its practices.

As the advantages of Agile became apparent, Salesforce expanded Agile practices across the organization, resulting in increased productivity and heightened customer satisfaction. Salesforce ensured a consistent focus on delivering customer value by cultivating a culture of collaboration, continuous improvement and open communication. This success underscores the importance of aligning Agile execution practices with the organization's goals and priorities.

Siemens: Navigating Change Management in Agile Adoption

Siemens, a global technology leader, sought Agile transformation to accelerate innovation and adapt to fluctuating market conditions. During the initial phase, Siemens faced resistance from teams accustomed to traditional project management approaches. To overcome this hurdle, Siemens emphasized the need for continuous improvement in the Agile process and the integration of different software and hardware components seamlessly, including teams, tools and information.

To ensure ongoing improvement in Agile execution, Siemens regularly conducts Agile maturity assessments and emphasizes the importance of Agile coaching and mentoring. Siemens' shift of over 40 teams across three continents to Kanban resulted in a 33% increase in throughput and a 70% reduction in administrative maintenance time. This transition highlights the significance of patience, support and ongoing education during Agile transformation.

Siemens continues to execute Agile projects effectively by fostering a culture of transparency, accountability and collaboration. Embracing a growth mindset and striving for continuous improvement has enabled Siemens to navigate the complexities of Agile execution and achieve impressive results. This success demonstrates the importance of creating a supportive organizational culture and equipping employees with the training and resources to excel in Agile execution.

Table 26: Salesforce and Siemens
Agile Execution Comparison

Aspect	Salesforce	Siemens
Challenges	Long development cycles, inefficient collaboration, meeting changing customer demands	Resistance to change, balancing Agile with traditional project management
Unique Strategies	In-house Agile training programme tailored to team needs	Adapting Agile practices to organizational circumstances, combining Agile with traditional project management methods where appropriate
Organizational Culture	Collaboration, continuous improvement, open communication	Transparency, accountability, collaboration, continuous learning
Key Success Factors	Aligning Agile execution with overall goals, strong customer focus	Patience, support, ongoing education, adapting Agile to suit organizational circumstances

Key Takeaways from the Case Study

1. **Foster a culture of collaboration and continuous improvement** – Salesforce and Siemens achieved Agile success by nurturing a culture of collaboration, open communication and continuous improvement, enabling them to consistently deliver value to customers and stakeholders.

2. **Align Agile execution practices with overall goals** – Salesforce's increased productivity and customer satisfaction resulted from aligning Agile execution practices with the organization's overall goals and priorities.

3. **Establish a supportive organizational culture and provide resources** – Siemens' Agile success is attributed to a culture of

transparency, accountability and collaboration, along with equipping employees with training and resources.

4. **Learn from industry pioneers** – Studying the approaches of companies like Salesforce and Siemens offers valuable insights for organizations looking to effectively implement Agile approaches, ultimately enhancing business agility and competitive advantage.

5. **Customize strategies and tactics to suit your organization** – Salesforce and Siemens employed tailored strategies and tactics to ensure Agile success. These examples showcase that Agile execution can be adapted to an organization's unique circumstances, enabling optimal results.

Exercise: Implementing Agile Execution Best Practices

To enhance the execution of Agile projects within your organization, adopting best practices that align with Agile principles and foster a culture of continuous improvement is essential. Effective decision-making can be facilitated, and your teams can stay adaptable in changing circumstances by implementing these practices.

Consider adopting the following best practices:

1. **Iterative and incremental delivery** – Develop and deliver small, valuable increments of functionality, allowing for rapid feedback and continuous improvement. This approach enables your organization to respond quickly to customer needs and changing market conditions.

2. **Collaboration and communication** – Foster open communication and collaboration within and across teams to ensure alignment and facilitate effective decision-making. Encourage transparency, knowledge-sharing and a willingness to learn from successes and failures.

3. **Time-boxing** – Set strict time limits for each sprint or iteration, promoting focus, discipline and prioritization. Time-boxing helps teams manage their workload effectively and ensures that work is delivered on time.

4. **Continuous integration and deployment** – Streamline the development, testing and deployment processes to enable faster, more reliable software releases. Implement automation tools and practices to reduce errors, accelerate delivery and improve product quality.

5. **Monitoring and adaptation** – Regularly review project progress, adapting plans and strategies to address changing circumstances, challenges or opportunities. Embrace a continuous learning and adaptation culture, using feedback and data to inform decision-making and guide future actions.

6. **Risk management** – Proactively identify, assess and mitigate risks associated with your Agile projects. Implement strategies for risk management, such as contingency planning and prioritization, to minimize the impact of potential issues on project outcomes.

Utilize these best practices as a foundation for your Agile execution efforts and continuously refine them to meet your organization's unique context and requirements. As you gain experience with Agile execution, be open to learning and adapting your approach to maximize efficiency and delivery of value.

Chapter Summary

In this chapter, we focused on the importance of the effective execution of Agile approaches for achieving business agility. We delved into the key principles, such as collaboration and the continuous delivery of Agile execution. We also provided practical guidance on implementing these ways of working in your organization and offered real-world examples from companies like Salesforce and Siemens, who have used these Agile approaches to deliver superior value to their customers.

Further Readings and Resources

1. Book: *Agile Retrospectives: Making Good Teams Great,* by Esther Derby and Diana Larsen, 2006, O'Reilly.

2. Book: *Continuous Delivery: Reliable Software Releases through Build, Test, and Deployment Automation,* by Jez Humble and David Farley, 2010, Addison-Wesley Signature Series.

3. Website: DevOps.com – www.devops.com

9

Measuring Business Agility

In our modern business world, even giants can stumble if they don't consistently gauge their agility. Remember Nokia? A titan in mobile communication, but when smartphones took the world by storm, its delayed reaction showcased the costs of not being Agile enough.

Assessing agility isn't just about acknowledging it but measuring it meticulously. Put yourself in the shoes of a leader at a flourishing e-commerce platform where responsiveness is of paramount importance. Sales are soaring, customers are pleased, and the road map looks promising. Then, seemingly overnight, a competitor innovates a feature your customers now view as essential. Could you measure how swiftly and efficiently your team could match or exceed that?

As we have discussed, business agility refers to an organization's ability to adjust quickly to market changes, meet customer needs, and consistently improve its products or services. As a business leader, understanding the responsiveness of your organization is critical to identifying areas for improvement. Making these improvements will boost your organization's adaptability and performance. This increases the probability of success in this challenging business environment.

Measuring business agility is key to assessing your organization's adaptability to change and its capacity to deliver value to customers promptly and consistently. There is no "one size fits all" regarding what to measure. Different organizations have unique priorities and goals. Choosing appropriate metrics for your organization is vital, considering the unique aspects of your industry and market.

However, evaluating Agile implementation success isn't straightforward. Companies often face difficulty quantifying whether Agile delivers as expected, not least because context and culture can have a greater impact than the choice of Agile methods. This measurement challenge underscores the importance of business agility, highlighting the need for flexibility in setting metrics that align with Agile's dynamic nature.

From the output of several global surveys carried out in the last five years, fewer than 10% of organizations consider themselves to be performing with a high level of agility. This statistic paints a stark reality and presents a challenge for us. How can we measure and improve our agility to find ourselves within that coveted 10%?

Envision the transformative journey, moving from uncertainty to a confident stride, as you equip yourself with the tools and metrics to survive and excel. The goal isn't just to be Agile but to clearly quantify that agility, ensuring it becomes a sustainable, tangible advantage.

As a leader, you navigate a maze of metrics, each vying for your attention, yet the pulse of agility could elevate your organization into an industry frontrunner. Are you ready to embrace the metrics that will definitively quantify your agility and set you on a path to long-term, sustainable advantage?

This chapter dives into the importance of measuring business agility and how it can be achieved. You can assess your organization's agility and make informed decisions by exploring various metrics such as cycle time, lead time, customer satisfaction, employee satisfaction and return on investment (ROI). For leaders seeking to improve their organization's agility to keep up with changing markets, it is crucial to understand these metrics' significance. With this knowledge, you will be better equipped to drive success and growth within your organization.

If we were to limit business agility to the confines of the Agile Manifesto, which says, "working software is the primary measure of progress", we risk developing tunnel vision. The measures of business agility need to extend beyond just software development. These measures must encompass how well the organization responds to change and delivers value.

The crucial aspect of measuring business agility effectively is considering the entire organizational ecosystem, including aligning and integrating individual teams, departments and processes. This holistic perspective can help identify potential gaps or misalignments hindering the organization's adaptability and responsiveness. When examining these interconnected elements, leaders can enhance their understanding of their organization's ability to respond to change and adapt to market demands. Another aspect is the relationship and interactions with customers and third parties.

Key Elements of Measuring Business Agility

Business leaders will comprehend various metrics and factors contributing to effectively measuring and enhancing their organization's agility once they examine the following key elements. This knowledge will enable leaders to select and employ the most relevant metrics for their specific context, ensuring an accurate and meaningful assessment of their organization's adaptability and performance.

Business leaders will also learn the importance of considering industry-specific factors, market trends and internal barriers when measuring business agility, as well as the critical role of leadership in fostering an Agile culture. They will discover strategies to establish effective feedback loops, create a culture of measurement and learning and leverage technology and automation to support their organization's agility goals.

Table 27: Key Performance Indicators for Business Agility

KPI	Description
Cycle Time	The duration from the moment work begins on a task or item until it is fully completed, commonly used to measure the speed and efficiency of a process in delivering outcomes
Lead Time	The time elapsed from the moment a customer request or order is received to when the product or service is delivering value to the customer
Customer Satisfaction	The degree to which customers are satisfied with a company's products, services and overall experience
Quality Indicators	Key metrics that measure various aspects of product and service quality, such as defect rates, customer complaints, and rework volumes
Employee Satisfaction	A measure of how content and engaged employees are with their work and workplace, often assessed through surveys or feedback tools
Return on Investment (ROI)	The financial gain or loss generated by an investment relative to its cost, used to evaluate the efficiency and profitability of the investment
Time-to-market	The duration from the initiation of a product or project to the point when it is available for sale to customers, indicating the organization's responsiveness to market demands
Adaptability Quotient (AQ)	A measure of an individual's or organization's ability to adapt effectively to changes in the market, technology, and customer preferences
Innovation Rate	A measure of an organization's output of new or significantly improved products or services, often reflected in metrics like the percentage of revenue from these innovations or the number of successful new offerings within a certain time period
Process Efficiency	A measure of how effectively a process uses its resources to produce outputs, often evaluated by comparing the quantity and quality of outputs relative to the inputs used

Let us inspect some key elements of measuring business agility:

Cycle Time

Cycle time measures how long it has taken for a team to complete a specific task or process. It is a vital metric for helping detect bottlenecks and inefficiencies in the development process. This helps organizations streamline their procedures and become more efficient. Organizations can identify areas needing extra focus or process enhancement by gauging cycle time.

Lead Time

Lead time measures how long it has taken to finish a project or product from inception to the customer experiencing value from the project. This helps organizations recognize opportunities to refine the development process and deliver customer value. Through lead time evaluation, organizations can identify where the teams struggle to deliver customer value or areas needing attention.

Customer Satisfaction

Customer satisfaction gauges how well the organization addresses its customers' requirements and delivers value. Assessing customer satisfaction helps pinpoint areas for improvement and ensures the organization provides value to its customers. High customer satisfaction can also bolster brand reputation and enhance customer loyalty.

Quality Indicators

Tracking quality indicators such as defect rates and code coverage (the percentage of code executed by a test suite) helps ensure that an organization delivers products and services that customers are confident will work effectively for them without error. Tracking quality can address potential product and service issues before customers experience them.

Employee Satisfaction

Evaluating employee contentment reveals the organization's ability to nurture a culture centred around cooperation, communication and continuous growth. Assessing employee satisfaction helps uncover areas needing enhancement and guarantees that top talent is attracted and kept. Also, elevated satisfaction levels contribute to heightened productivity, superior work quality and improved business results.

Return on Investment (ROI)

Calculating the return on investment for Agile endeavours offers a transparent view of the financial impact of Agile transformation efforts. ROI monitoring enables informed decision-making regarding resource distribution and project prioritization based on the value delivered to the organization. The investment in Agile coaching should also be evaluated like any other business investment. Calculate the ROI by contrasting the quantifiable benefits, such as increased delivery speed and product quality, against the costs of hiring and maintaining an Agile coaching position. This will give a clear picture of the financial viability of the coaching initiative.

Time-to-Market

Time-to-market refers to the time taken to introduce a new product or service to customers, from initial concept to final availability. This metric reflects an organization's ability to respond swiftly to changing market conditions and capitalize on emerging opportunities. Monitoring time-to-market allows organizations to identify areas for improvement, streamline development processes and enhance overall efficiency. Reduced time-to-market can lead to competitive advantage and faster revenue realization.

Adaptability Quotient (AQ)

Adaptability quotient measures an individual's or organization's capacity to adjust to changes in the market, technology and customer preferences. AQ highlights the resilience and flexibility in responding to disruptive forces and evolving customer needs. Individuals and organizations can uncover improvement areas and align their strategies and processes with shifting market conditions by assessing AQ. A high AQ helps businesses stay relevant and maintain a competitive edge in a rapidly changing environment.

Innovation Rate

The innovation rate quantifies the percentage of revenue generated from new products or services, showcasing an organization's ability to foster creativity and drive innovation. Evaluation of the innovation rate enables organizations to assess their innovation strategies' effectiveness, pinpoint potential improvement areas and maintain a market competitive edge. A healthy innovation rate demonstrates a company's commitment to continuous improvement, growth and long-term success.

Process Efficiency

Process efficiency, more than a simple ratio of outputs to inputs, can serve as a dynamic metric for detecting time delays and waste within the organization, in line with the principles of value flow mapping. This efficiency evaluation goes beyond resource utilization to uncover hidden inefficiencies, bottlenecks and potential for optimization in the product development process. It allows organizations to increase productivity and reduce costs, contributing to better resource allocation. Process efficiency can bolster the organization's aim of delivering consistent value to customers and stakeholders by minimizing waste and delays. It helps maintain a competitive edge by facilitating continuous improvement while aligning with Agile approaches.

Comparative Analysis

Measuring business agility also involves comparing your organization's performance to industry norms or rival companies. This comparison offers valuable insights into your organization's relative standing within the industry, unveiling areas that warrant the change. These contrasts allow for establishing practical objectives, better resource allocation and process enhancements.

Selecting the Right Metrics

For effective measurement, choosing suitable metrics that align with the organization's goals and objectives is vital. Consistent metric measurement over time is also necessary to detect trends and patterns that can facilitate continuous improvement. Effective measurement demands ongoing communication and collaboration among team members, stakeholders and customers to guarantee the tracking and measuring of relevant metrics.

Challenges and Pitfalls in Selecting and Implementing Metrics

While selecting the right metrics is crucial for measuring effectively, organizations must be mindful of potential challenges and pitfalls. These can include relying too heavily on vanity metrics that do not provide meaningful insights, choosing difficult metrics to measure or interpret, or focusing on too many metrics simultaneously. Psychological safety is also key. If, for example, people are blamed and given warnings that cycle times are longer than expected, they may game the system to hide the problem rather than working with others to reduce it. To avoid these issues, organizations must prioritize metrics that align with their strategic goals and provide actionable information for improvement. Measuring the results from chosen metrics also implies that you have a strategy and an operational framework for quality, which for a lot of organizations can often be rather thin.

A deeper understanding of these potential obstacles and strategies to overcome them is essential for organizations to maximize the outcomes of their metrics:

1. **Inaccurate or unreliable data** – Data accuracy and reliability are crucial for making informed decisions. Organizations must invest in data validation and cleaning processes to maintain the quality of the information used in their metrics.
2. **Overemphasis on certain metrics** – Maintaining a balanced approach when selecting metrics is important, as focusing too much on one area can lead to unintended consequences. Ensuring a mix of both leading and lagging indicators, as well as quantitative and qualitative metrics, helps maintain this balance.
3. **Resistance to change** – Employees may resist changes to existing processes or introducing new metrics. To overcome this challenge, organizations must involve employees in the development and implementation of metrics, provide clear communication on the purpose and benefits of the changes and offer training and support as needed. However, be prepared to change or abandon the metric if it produces undesirable consequences.
4. **Lack of alignment with strategic goals** – Metrics must closely align with an organization's strategic objectives. Regularly reviewing and updating metrics to ensure alignment with evolving goals helps maintain their relevance and effectiveness.

Steering Clear of Useless Agile Metrics

As just mentioned, navigating the world of metrics can be fraught with pitfalls. One of the most pernicious is the danger of "useless Agile metrics". While these metrics may seem beneficial, they provide little value and can lead to counterproductive behaviours. The allure of "velocity", for instance, can be tempting. Yet, an over-emphasis on velocity – the measure of how much work a team can complete in a sprint, used by the team to plan their capacity for the following sprint – can lead to an unhealthy focus on quantity over quality. Yes, being swift matters, but not at the expense of the effectiveness of our work. Velocity obsession can cause estimation inflation and a surge in technical debt as teams rush to complete tasks without due attention to quality or sustainability.

"Lines of code" is another classic useless metric. A high number of lines of code can be a smokescreen, masking poor quality or inefficient coding practices. Remember, more lines do not equate to better code; sometimes, the opposite is true. Similarly, utilization or "busyness" can be a misleading measure. A team member could be busy all day yet contribute little towards our strategic objectives. Instead, we must focus on "value delivered collectively" rather than individual activity.

Lastly, the "number of bugs fixed" can be deceptive. A large number of bugs fixed might just show that we're creating too many bugs. Let us not reward firefighting over prevention. Recognizing and steering clear of these useless Agile metrics is crucial to keep our focus on what truly matters – delivering value, maintaining quality and driving continuous improvement. The subsequent sections on balancing different metrics and aligning them with our strategic goals will provide further guidance on this.

Balancing Quantitative and Qualitative Metrics

When assessing business agility, it is important to consider quantitative and qualitative metrics. Quantitative metrics provide concrete, measurable data that can be easily analysed. In contrast, qualitative metrics offer insights into less tangible aspects of agility, such as employee satisfaction, changing culture, developing trust, job security or customer feedback. You can enhance your understanding of your organization's overall agility by incorporating both metrics into your assessment.

Holistic Metrics

Select a diverse array of financial, operational and customer-centric metrics to get a well-rounded view of your organization's agility. Overemphasis on one metric type may cause a distorted understanding of organizational performance, compromising the ability to make informed decisions. A balanced approach ensures that all crucial areas are monitored and enhanced.

Leading and Lagging Indicators

Both leading and lagging indicators are crucial when choosing metrics for business agility. Leading indicators like employee engagement, investment in innovation or the percentage of projects following Agile approaches can affect future performance. Conversely, lagging indicators, including customer satisfaction, market share or revenue growth, illustrate past organizational performance.

Table 28 showcases Agile metrics' leading and lagging indicators.

Table 28: Leading and Lagging Indicators

Type	Indicator	Description
Leading	Backlog Size	Provides insight into workload by showing the number of tasks waiting to be handled
Leading	Sprint Burndown	Tracks work completion during a sprint, facilitating early prediction of sprint outcomes

Leading	Defect Density	Gives insights into overall quality and future workloads via the number of known defects divided by the size of the software
Lagging	Net Promoter Score (NPS)	Gauges customer satisfaction and loyalty
Lagging	Revenue Growth	Reflects the success of past actions by comparing a company's sales with a previous period
Lagging	Return on Investment (ROI)	Evaluates the efficiency of an investment, revealing the financial benefits from specific changes or actions

These indicators allow organizations to assess the relationships between their actions and outcomes, facilitating informed decision-making. A balance between leading and lagging indicators aids in comprehending the progress in introducing business agility. They provide early insights for improvement and evaluate the effectiveness of implemented changes.

Tailoring Metrics to Business Size and Industry

When selecting metrics, considering your organization's size and industry is critical, as these elements can determine the appropriateness of certain metrics. For instance, small companies might focus on cash flow and client retention, while large enterprises could emphasize market share and cost efficiency. Similarly, a software firm may value code quality and deployment frequency, whereas a retail business could prioritize customer satisfaction and inventory turnover rates. Customization of metrics to suit your specific situation ensures the measurements are more accurate and relevant to your organization's objectives.

Benchmarking Performance

Organizations can identify their areas of excellence or lag, gaining valuable insights into their competitive positioning by comparing their agility metrics to similar businesses. This information can help inform strategies for improvement and drive ongoing growth.

Importance of Context

When examining metrics tied to business agility, consider the context in which they are measured. Market tendencies, industry shifts, internal governance and policies, culture and management behaviour and internal obstacles can significantly affect your organization's performance metrics. Factoring in these elements while interpreting metrics will give you a more accurate comprehension of your organization's agility, facilitating well-informed decisions.

Regular Metrics Assessment for Ongoing Refinement

Consistently evaluating metrics over time is vital. Organizations can discern trends and patterns that facilitate continuous improvement by regularly appraising metrics. Metrics must be reviewed frequently and adjusted to stay relevant and aligned with the organization's aims and objectives.

Establishing Effective Feedback Loops

Also, it is crucial to establish a transparent feedback loop within the organization. This loop enables teams to learn from the measured metrics, refine their processes and change their goals accordingly. This continuous feedback mechanism is vital for aligning with the organization's strategic objectives and ensuring efforts are concentrated on delivering value.

Table 29: Feedback Loop Stages

Stage	Description
Measure	Collecting data on performance and outcomes
Analyse	Evaluating data to derive meaningful insights
Learn	Extracting lessons from the analysis to improve understanding
Refine	Modifying goals and strategies based on learning
Modify	Implementing the changes in the actual process
Repeat	Starting the cycle again with the updated process

Aligning Metrics with Organizational Goals

It's paramount to ensure that the evaluated metrics align with the organization's goals and objectives. Measuring metrics not coinciding with the organization's aims can cause misdirected endeavours and squandered resources. As a leader, it is vital to convey the significance of the chosen metrics and how they connect to the organization's overarching strategy.

Customizing Metrics for Different Organizations

It is crucial to remember that the most effective metrics for measuring business agility may vary based on an organization's size, industry and unique characteristics.

Tailor your chosen metrics to suit your organization's needs and priorities, ensuring they provide actionable insights and drive continuous improvement.

Creating a Culture of Measurement and Learning

To fully capitalize on the advantages of measuring business agility, organizations must cultivate a culture that values measurement and learning. Urge teams to routinely evaluate performance metrics, engage in candid conversations and collaborate on tactics to enhance results. This learning and continuous improvement culture can considerably boost the organization's ability to adapt and thrive in an accelerated setting.

Alignment with Organizational Culture

To ensure that the chosen metrics are effectively integrated into the organization, aligning them with the organizational culture and employees' daily activities is essential. Encourage employees to understand the relevance of these metrics and how their contributions impact the organization's overall agility.

Role of Technology and Automation

In the present digital age, technology and automation notably influence the measurement and enhancement of business agility. Utilizing tools and platforms, such as Jira for project management, Tableau for data visualization and Splunk for log analysis, can simplify collecting, analysing and monitoring metrics. This enables your organization to respond more swiftly to market fluctuations or customer demands. When they tap into the technology's potential, business leaders can utilize real-time data and insights for quicker, more informed decisions that enhance their organization's agility and expansion.

Challenges Measuring Business Agility

While business agility is increasingly becoming a strategic imperative for organizations, measuring it can present its own challenges.

1. **Varying definitions of business agility** – Agility means different things to different businesses. For some, it's about speed and adaptability; for others, it's about workforce scalability or innovative capabilities. This variation complicates the measurement process as different organizations may require distinct metrics.
2. **Quantifying qualitative factors** – Some aspects of business agility, like the flexibility of decision-making processes or the adaptability of organizational culture, are qualitative and therefore challenging to measure. It's essential

to use a mixed-method approach to capture these agility dimensions, incorporating both quantitative and qualitative measures.

3. **Continuous change** – Business agility implies adapting to change. But as businesses evolve and adapt, so too do the measures of agility. It's vital to keep metrics updated and relevant to ensure they reflect the current state of agility in the organization.

Overcoming these challenges requires a tailored approach. Establish clear definitions of agility relevant to your organization, utilize mixed methods for capturing qualitative aspects and regularly review and update metrics to reflect changing organizational contexts.

Using DORA Metrics in Measuring Business Agility

Another approach to evaluate business agility is through DORA (DevOps Research and Assessment) metrics, concentrating on software development and delivery performance. DORA metrics provide a framework to evaluate the efficiency and effectiveness of your organization's software development and deployment processes and can be an important indicator of overall business agility.

DORA metrics are based on four key performance indicators (KPIs): "deployment frequency", "lead time for changes", "change failure rate", and "mean time to recover". Incorporating these metrics into your business agility measurement can provide insights into your organization's effectiveness in delivering value through software development and delivery processes.

DORA Metrics

1. **Deployment frequency** – The rate at which your organization deploys new software updates or releases is known as deployment frequency. Higher deployment frequency suggests your organization can promptly and consistently deliver customers new features, enhancements and fixes. This metric is crucial for measuring your organization's capacity to meet market demands and promptly address customer requirements.

2. **Lead time for changes** – When a change that has been committed to the code repository to when it is successfully deployed in production, it is called lead time for changes. A shorter lead time implies your organization can swiftly deploy and release new features and improvements, potentially increasing customer satisfaction and giving you a competitive edge.

3. **Change failure rate** – Change failure rate refers to the percentage of changes failing, such as service outages or performance degradation. A low change failure rate suggests your organization delivers high-quality updates and releases. This minimizes customer dissatisfaction and adverse business impacts.

4. **Mean time to recover** – Mean time to recover (MTTR) measures your organization's time to restore service after a failure. A shorter MTTR demonstrates your organization's ability to address and resolve issues quickly, reducing customer impact and ensuring service reliability and availability.

DevOps and Business Agility

The strong relationship between DevOps and business agility is truly illustrative of the transformative potential of business agility in practice. DevOps can be viewed as a vivid example of business agility. Efficient software development and delivery processes, at the heart of DevOps, directly contribute to an organization's ability to adapt and respond to change. Through DevOps performance improvement, organizations can boost their agility, echoing the essence of redesigning business operations in an agile manner. This transformative alignment and collaboration between development and operations teams ensure swift delivery of value to customers in a continuously changing market. This reshaping of business operations, empowered by DevOps, exemplifies the core of business agility in real-world operations.

Incorporating DORA Metrics into Business Agility Assessments

To successfully integrate DORA metrics into your business agility measurements:

1. Set clear software development and delivery performance objectives, aligning them with your organization's overarching strategy and priorities.
2. Utilize processes and tools that facilitate DORA metrics collection and analysis, such as continuous integration and continuous delivery (CI/CD) pipelines, automated testing and monitoring solutions.
3. Routinely review and discuss DORA metrics with your teams, pinpointing areas for improvement and implementing performance-enhancing strategies.
4. Foster a continuous learning and improvement culture, encouraging collaboration and shared accountability for software development and delivery success.
5. Merge DORA metrics with other KPIs measuring business agility, such as cycle time, customer satisfaction, employee satisfaction and return on investment (ROI).

Integrating DORA metrics into your business agility measurements can offer valuable insights into your organization's software development and delivery performance. This information helps identify areas for improvement and drives continuous enhancement of your products and services.

CLEAR Lens for "Measuring Business Agility"

We can apply two CLEAR Model® principles to Measuring Business Agility:

Execution: To measure business agility effectively, the CLEAR principle of Execution must be keenly observed. This involves tracking progress, assessing outcomes and meeting the organization's goals. It requires defining meaningful metrics, capturing accurate data and analysing this information to draw actionable insights. In doing so, the principle of Execution is reinforced and brought into sharper focus.

Responsiveness: Measurements act as the organization's compass, steering it towards making rapid, informed adjustments that keep the journey to increased agility on track. They provide invaluable insights into areas requiring enhancement and spotlight opportunities for innovation, thus resonating with the principle of Responsiveness within the CLEAR Model®.

Reflection Prompts

1. What KPIs do you currently use to measure success in your organization? How well do they align with the principles of business agility?

2. How can you integrate Agile metrics into your organization's performance measurement system?

Case Study: Amazon and Google's Approach to Measuring Business Agility

Amazon and Google, two of the most successful and innovative companies globally, offer valuable insights into effectively measuring and enhancing business agility. By scrutinizing various approaches, business leaders can enhance their understanding of selecting and applying the most appropriate metrics.

Amazon's Approach to Measuring Business Agility

Amazon's approach to measuring business agility involves assessing key factors such as cycle time, lead time, and incident recovery time. Amazon can assess the effectiveness of its Agile practices and identify improvement areas by consistently tracking these metrics. This focus on continuous evaluation and change enables Amazon to maintain its competitive edge in a fast-changing market.

One specific initiative implemented to improve business agility at Amazon is the "two-pizza team" concept, where teams are kept small and autonomous, enabling faster decision-making and increased innovation. This concept is straightforward: no team should be big enough that it would take more than two pizzas to feed them, typically comprising fewer than ten people. These smaller teams minimize lines of communication and decrease the overhead of bureaucracy and decision-making, which allows two-pizza teams to spend more time focusing on their customers and constantly experimenting and innovating on their behalf. Amazon also leverages its advanced technology infrastructure to streamline operations, automate processes, and reduce time-to-market for new products and services.

Another critical aspect of Amazon's business agility is its customer-centric approach. Amazon's "North Star" is being "Earth's most customer-centric company," and this customer-focused mindset allows the company to prioritize improvements that significantly impact the overall customer experience. Amazon maintains its agility and responsiveness to customer needs by continually gathering customer feedback and measuring satisfaction.

Amazon cultivates a culture of experimentation and learning, encouraging employees to take calculated risks and learn from successes and failures. Smaller teams also increase employee satisfaction, as shown in workforce studies, where organizations with fewer than ten employees scored engagement levels of 42% or higher compared to lower engagement levels in larger organizations. This environment fosters innovation and adaptability, improving the organization's overall business agility.

Google's Approach to Measuring Business Agility

Google's approach to sustaining business agility is deeply rooted in its strategic commitment to continuous improvement and meticulous performance measurement. This commitment is exemplified in its adoption and evolution of the DevOps and Site Reliability Engineering (SRE) models, which form the core of its operational philosophy. Rather than merely implementing Objectives and Key Results (OKRs), Google has been instrumental in advancing the DevOps Research and Assessment (DORA) principles. In its DevOps framework, Google underscores the synergy between development and operations, prioritizing collaboration, communication and automation to streamline software development and delivery processes.

The SRE model at Google integrates software engineering with operations disciplines to guarantee system reliability, performance and capacity. This combined focus on SRE and DevOps, characterized by regular reviews and refinement of procedures, empowers Google to concentrate effectively on high-impact objectives. This strategy has been pivotal in enhancing the company's ability to remain agile and consistently outpace its competition in the tech industry.

Moreover, Google adopts a rigorously data-driven approach to decision-making. Utilizing methodologies like A/B testing and advanced data analytics, Google shapes its strategies and initiatives with precise, data-backed insights. This data-centric mindset ensures that decisions are not only well-informed but also closely aligned with the company's overarching goals, thereby reinforcing its agility.

In addition to these technical strategies, Google places substantial emphasis on research and development. This investment enables the company to remain at the cutting edge of technology, fostering continuous innovation. Google also recognizes the critical role of employee engagement and satisfaction in cultivating an agile and responsive workforce. By focusing on maintaining a motivated and adaptable team environment, Google further solidifies its position as a leader in business agility.

Table 30: Amazon and Google's Approaches to Measuring Business Agility

Aspect	Amazon	Google
Key Metrics	Cycle time, lead time, recovery time	DORA and SRE metrics
Technology Infrastructure	Use of advanced technology and automation to streamline operations and reduce time-to-market	Heavy investment in R&D fostering continuous technological innovation

Organizational Culture	Emphasis on continuous evaluation and adjustment, fostering a culture of innovation	Focus on continuous improvement and employee engagement in decision-making processes
Employee Focus	Small, autonomous teams enabling swift decision-making; emphasis on team autonomy and customer focus	Prioritizing employee motivation, engagement and satisfaction to drive innovation and responsiveness

Examples from Different Industries

Organizations can measure business agility in the retail industry by tracking inventory turnover, customer satisfaction ratings and new product introduction rates. These metrics help retail companies understand how quickly they can adapt to changes in customer preferences and market conditions.

In manufacturing, metrics like production lead time, first-pass yield and equipment downtime can assess business agility. These metrics enable manufacturers to identify bottlenecks, streamline processes and improve efficiency.

For service-based industries, customer churn rate, response time to service requests and employee utilization rates are useful in measuring business agility. Service-based organizations can better understand how well they adapt to customer needs and maintain a competitive edge through metric tracking.

Key Takeaways from the Case Study

1. **Selecting appropriate metrics** – Amazon and Google demonstrate the importance of choosing relevant and meaningful metrics for measuring business agility. These metrics must align with an organization's overall objectives and provide actionable insights for improvement.
2. **Consistency in measurement and analysis** – Both companies emphasize the value of regular measurement and analysis to identify trends, uncover areas for improvement and drive continuous enhancement of their Agile practices.
3. **Learning from industry leaders** – Business leaders can enhance their understanding of measuring and improving their organization's agility

effectively by studying the approaches of successful companies like Amazon and Google.

In conclusion, measuring business agility is essential for any organization that wants to deliver value to its customers in a rapidly changing environment. Organizations can make informed choices and drive continuous improvement by understanding the importance of data-driven decision-making, selecting the right metrics and learning from industry leaders.

Data-driven decision-making is an essential component of a successful business agility measurement strategy. Organizations can make informed decisions that support their strategic objectives and promote continuous improvement through leveraging accurate and timely data. Data-driven insights can help organizations identify areas of strength and weakness, uncover trends and determine the effectiveness of their Agile practices. Embracing a data-driven culture also encourages transparency and accountability throughout the organization, fostering a mindset of continuous learning and improvement.

Action Plan for Implementing Business Agility Metrics

To begin implementing these concepts and metrics, organizations must:

1. **Assess their current level of business agility** – This involves analysing your organization's processes, culture and performance. Use surveys, interviews and data analysis to comprehensively understand your current agility level.
2. **Select and prioritize the most relevant metrics for their industry, size and strategic goals** – This might mean focusing on adaptability and employee engagement metrics for a tech startup. Production lead time and equipment downtime might be more relevant for a large manufacturing company.
3. **Establish a process for regularly measuring and analysing these metrics** – This could involve setting up a dedicated analytics team, using software tools or hiring an external consultant. Ensure that this process includes regular reporting and review sessions to discuss the results and decide on the actions.
4. **Learn from industry leaders and best practices** – Consider joining industry forums, attending seminars or hiring an Agile coach to learn from others' experiences and apply best practices to your organization.

Emulating the successful strategies of industry leaders like Amazon and Google can provide valuable guidance for organizations seeking to measure and enhance their agility. However, it's important to remember that each organization is unique, and what works for one may not work for another. Therefore, adapting these strategies to fit your specific context is crucial.

Exercise: Metrics and KPIs – Assessing and Monitoring Business Agility

To measure business agility effectively, tracking metrics and KPIs that align with your organization's goals and objectives is essential. Regular monitoring of these indicators allows you to gauge your progress, identify areas for improvement and ensure your organization stays on track in its Agile journey.

Consider tracking the following metrics and KPIs:

1. **Cycle time** – Measure the time to complete one process iteration from start to finish. Monitoring cycle time can help you identify bottlenecks and inefficiencies in your processes and drive continuous improvement.
2. **Lead time** – Track the time to complete a project, from the initial request to the customer experiencing value from the final product. Reducing lead time can help you respond quickly to customer needs and market changes.
3. **Customer satisfaction** – Assess the degree to which customers are satisfied with the products or services provided by your organization. Regularly gather feedback to inform continuous improvements in your offerings and processes.
4. **Product quality** – Measure the quality of your products and services by tracking key quality indicators, such as defect rates, user satisfaction and system reliability. High-quality products are crucial for maintaining customer satisfaction and driving business success.
5. **Employee engagement** – Assess employee engagement and morale within your organization. Engaged and motivated employees are more likely to contribute to a successful Agile transformation and drive innovation.
6. **Time-to-market** – Track the time to market new products or features. Reducing time-to-market is key to business agility, enabling

organizations to respond more rapidly to customer needs and competitive pressures.

7. **Adaptability** – Monitor your organization's ability to adapt to changes in the business environment, such as shifting market conditions, customer preferences or technological advancements. Adaptability is a core aspect of business agility and critical for long-term success.

Utilize templates, tools and dashboards to monitor these metrics and KPIs, allowing you to visualize progress easily and identify areas for improvement. As you continue your Agile journey, periodically reassess your chosen metrics and KPIs to ensure they remain relevant and aligned with your evolving goals and objectives.

Chapter Summary

Measuring the effectiveness of business agility is essential for driving continuous improvement. This chapter delved into the diverse metrics and methods organizations could employ to assess their business agility. We investigated the significance of making decisions based on data, contemplated the various types of metrics applicable and offered practical advice on adopting metrics-oriented strategies within your organization. We also looked at real-world examples of companies such as Amazon and Google that have established successful metrics for evaluating business agility.

Further Readings and Resources

1. Book: *Measuring and Managing Performance in Organizations,* by Robert D. Austin, 1996, Dorset House Publishing.

2. Book: *Evidence-Based Management: How to Use Evidence to Make Better Organizational Decisions,* by Denise M. Rousseau, 2018, Kogan Page.

3. Website: Business Agility Institute – www.businessagility.institute

10

Scaling Business Agility

Imagine leading a multinational corporation operating for decades. Its operations span continents, and the organization's structure is deeply rooted. Now, picture this behemoth trying to race against a nimble startup in today's digital age. It's akin to watching a colossal ship attempting to turn at the speed of a speedboat. This is the challenge many established corporations face when trying to implement and scale business agility across their vast expanse.

Scaling business agility is a persistent and intricate process, causing the continuous deployment of techniques and strategies throughout an organization's life cycle. This journey of scaling is not just about implementing practices but reimagining how vast structures, built over years or decades, can be moulded to be as adaptable and responsive as the newer, smaller entities in the market.

Business leaders must acknowledge that scaling business agility might differ among organizations because of distinct goals, priorities and market subtleties. Once leaders grasp these intricacies and challenges, they can build a more adaptable and responsive organization. This enables the organization to navigate fluctuating market conditions and consistently provide customer value. Embracing a customized approach to scaling agility while considering industry-specific factors can propel success and help organizations thrive in the increasingly competitive market.

Several well-established companies have experienced significant benefits from scaling Agile practices. These benefits include improved customer satisfaction, shorter time-to-market and increased employee engagement. For example, Philips, a global technology company, adopted Agile practices and scaled them across their organization, resulting in a 75% reduction in time-to-market for their healthcare products. Similarly, Spotify has pioneered implementing Agile ways of working and scaling them to maintain its competitive edge in a rapidly changing industry.

Scaling Agile without a firm understanding and effective implementation of its fundamental principles is like trying to run before you can walk. Scaling is important, but it should not be the first step. A house built on sand won't stand, nor will Agile scale without a firm foundation.

Scaling Agile also demands a long-term strategic vision. A pitfall some companies fall into is piloting Agile on small teams without plans for wider implementation. This limited scope can act as a bottleneck, preventing the full benefits of Agile transformation from permeating the organization.

Scaling Agile is the ultimate test, transforming not just teams but entire organizational ecosystems into Agile powerhouses. It's like orchestrating a symphony, aligning various departments and functions to work in harmony, creating a unified whole that's greater than the sum of its parts. Are you ready to conduct this grand transformation?

This chapter guides business leaders on how to effectively scale business agility, ensuring that their organizations can deliver value to customers at scale. It delves into strategies for aligning teams and departments, establishing clear communication channels and applying Agile practices to enhance overall agility and responsiveness. Fostering a continuous learning and improvement culture is emphasized, empowering organizations to adapt and grow in a highly competitive market.

Key Components for Scaling Business Agility

Before diving into the key components for scaling it is essential to understand the benefits business leaders will gain from studying these concepts. They will learn to streamline decision-making processes, enhance communication and collaboration and ensure their teams respond swiftly to changing market conditions. Once they embrace these components, leaders can improve their organization's overall performance and competitiveness while consistently delivering value to customers at scale.

Let us inspect some key components contributing to successfully scaling business agility:

Organizational Structure

Agile organizations typically feature flatter structures that empower teams to make decisions and take ownership of their work. Ensuring that the organizational structure aligns with its goals and objectives and supports adopting Agile approaches is important. A flatter structure fosters increased collaboration, faster decision-making and better responsiveness to change happening at scale, empowering teams to take ownership of their work and make decisions autonomously.

Establishing transparent communication channels across teams and departments is vital. This ensures alignment with the organization's objectives as it scales and encourages greater teamwork. Providing training and support to teams adopting Agile practices across the wider organization, along with promoting a culture of collaboration and continuous learning, is essential.

Cultivating a culture of trust, openness and shared responsibility encourages team members to take ownership of their work, share ideas and contribute to the organization's overall success. A robust culture of collaboration and ongoing improvement can significantly improve the organization's adaptability and performance in a high-speed environment.

Adapting existing organizational structures to support Agile practices better can still be a complex process. To navigate these challenges, consider the following approaches in Table 31.

Table 31: Organizational Structures and Their Impact on Agile Practices

Organizational Structure	Advantages for Agile Practices	Challenges for Agile Practices	Key Considerations
Hierarchical	– Clear lines of authority – Established reporting lines	– Resistance to change – Slow decision-making – Potential for silos	– Encourage top-down support for Agile transformation – Foster a culture of collaboration and empowerment
Flat	– Flexible and adaptive – Encourages collaboration – Faster decision-making	– Potential for ambiguity – May require frequent restructuring	– Clearly define roles and responsibilities – Maintain open communication channels
Matrix	– Cross-functional teams – Resource optimization – Enhanced collaboration	– Dual reporting lines – Potential for conflicts	– Establish clear priorities and goals – Encourage collaboration and open communication
Networked	– Access to specialized skills – Greater innovation – Scalable resources	– Dependency on external partners – Potential loss of control	– Build strong relationships with partners – Develop clear agreements and expectations

Aligning Culture and Leadership

It is crucial to align the organization's culture and leadership with Agile principles. Business owners and leaders must cultivate a culture that promotes innovation, experimentation and adaptability. Empowering employees at all levels in the business to make decisions, propose ideas and accept responsibility for their tasks is crucial. Leaders can imbue a sense of shared ownership and accountability throughout the organization, paving the way for scaling business agility successfully through a dedication to Agile approaches and principles.

Role of Middle Management

Middle managers are critical in aligning culture and leadership for scaling business agility. They act as a bridge between senior leaders and frontline employees, helping to facilitate communication and implement Agile practices throughout the organization. Middle managers can support Agile transformation by encouraging open communication, sharing best practices between teams and facilitating problem-solving sessions. They can also help dismantle silos by promoting cross-departmental collaboration and ensuring everyone comprehends their roles and responsibilities within the Agile process. Ensuring that middle managers are well-versed in Agile principles and empowered to drive change is crucial.

Portfolio Management

Portfolio management is integral to aligning an organization's investments with its strategic goals and objectives, ensuring a focus on the most impactful projects and initiatives that deliver customer value. This process involves a deep understanding of the organization's mission and vision, which is crucial for effectively scaling business agility. By establishing a robust process for evaluating and prioritizing initiatives and regularly reviewing and adjusting the portfolio, organizations can maintain their commitment to delivering substantial value to customers, guaranteeing that their strategic objectives are not just met but are also in harmony with their overarching mission.

Risk Management in Portfolio Management

Besides aligning investments with strategic goals and objectives, it is crucial to consider risk management when making portfolio management decisions. This involves evaluating potential risks associated with various initiatives and ensuring that the organization has appropriate measures in place to mitigate these risks. Effective risk management not only identifies potential challenges and uncertainties but also provides a framework for proactively addressing them, safeguarding the organization's interests. By incorporating risk assessment and mitigation strategies into portfolio management, organizations can make more informed decisions, enhancing the resilience and success of their strategic initiatives.

Programme Management

Programme management coordinates related projects to deliver benefits that individual project management cannot achieve. It involves managing dependencies and interactions between projects and ensuring alignment with the organization's goals. Programme management helps organizations maintain customer satisfaction on a larger scale and maximize investment benefits. This approach also allows for efficient resource allocation and risk mitigation across multiple projects, ensuring cohesive progress towards strategic targets. Also, programme management provides a framework for capturing collective insights and learnings, which can be leveraged to refine strategies and practices for future initiatives, thereby reinforcing the organization's capacity for continual improvement and innovation.

Resource Allocation in Programme Management

Effective resource allocation involves ensuring that the right resources, including personnel, technology and finances, are allocated to projects to support the organization's Agile objectives and maximize the return on investment. This entails a strategic balance between the available resources and the demands of various projects, prioritizing tasks based on their alignment with business goals. It also includes continuously monitoring and adjusting allocations to respond to evolving project needs and challenges, thereby ensuring that each project is optimally equipped for success within the broader framework of the organization's strategic agenda.

Cross-functional Teams

It is beneficial to promote cross-functional teams within the organization. These teams comprise members from different departments working together on a project or initiative, fostering collaboration and breaking down silos. This approach bolsters overall business agility and paves the way for more efficient decision-making and problem resolution. By integrating diverse skills and viewpoints, cross-functional teams are uniquely positioned to innovate and drive change. They enable a more holistic understanding of challenges and opportunities, leading to more comprehensive solutions that align closely with the organization's strategic objectives and customer needs.

Agile Metrics and Measurement

In scaling business agility, it's crucial to implement suitable Agile metrics and measurement techniques, which serve as a "compass" for an organization's progress. These metrics not only highlight areas for enhancement but also support informed decision-making, thereby boosting agility on a business-wide scale. Continuous monitoring and analysis of these metrics are essential to ensure effective implementation of Agile practices and swift adaptation to new challenges or opportunities. They act as a critical feedback mechanism, aligning business operations with strategic goals, fostering continuous improvement, and ultimately enhancing customer and employee satisfaction.

Customer Feedback and Collaboration

Actively engaging with customers and soliciting their feedback helps organizations get valuable insights, ensuring that their products or services align with customer requirements and expectations. Collaborating with customers throughout the development process enables organizations to adapt to shifting demands swiftly, establishing a robust feedback loop that contributes to ongoing improvement and heightened business agility. This approach of close customer collaboration not only enhances product relevance but also builds lasting customer relationships, fostering trust and loyalty, which are essential for long-term business success and market adaptability.

Agile Governance

Agile governance entails planning clear guidelines and policies for adopting Agile methodologies or frameworks and verifying their adherence across the organization. Agile governance can aid in consistently meeting customer needs as the organization expands, maximizing the advantages of its investments.

It is essential to strike a balance between governance and the need for autonomy and flexibility in Agile teams. While having transparent guidelines and policies is crucial, allowing teams to adapt their practices to their distinctive contexts fosters innovation and responsiveness. Agile governance must empower teams while ensuring alignment with the organization's goals and objectives.

Continuous Learning and Improvement

Scaling business agility requires a culture of continuous learning and improvement. It is vital to offer help and resources to teams, enabling them to expand their knowledge and fine-tune their practices. Periodic retrospectives are beneficial in pinpointing opportunities for enhancement and cultivating a culture of unwavering learning and progression. Creating a psychologically safe environment where employees feel comfortable sharing their thoughts and ideas fosters open communication and encourages continuous improvement.

Change Management in Scaling Business Agility

Successfully scaling business agility requires effective change management strategies. As organizations transform their processes and practices to become more

Agile, they must consider the potential impact on employees and stakeholders. This involves managing resistance to change, ensuring clear communication of the organization's vision and goals, listening to employee feedback, and providing necessary support and resources for them to adapt to new ways of working. When these challenges are addressed proactively, organizations can create a smoother transition toward greater business agility. To address common obstacles and resistance to change, organizations should provide training and support, establish a clear vision for the Agile transformation, acknowledge early successes and include employees in decision-making.

For instance, IBM adopted Agile approaches and scaled them across the organization by implementing a robust change management strategy. This strategy included clear communication of the Agile transformation vision, training and support for employees, and involving them in the decision-making. As a result, IBM reduced product defects by 50% and shortened development cycles by 30%, demonstrating the effectiveness of change management in scaling business agility.

To successfully scale business agility, it is imperative to supply coaching and reinforcement to teams, guiding them to embrace Agile approaches and grow their expertise. This ensures efficient collaboration and the ongoing improvement of their techniques. Investing in perpetual professional development and knowledge exchange throughout the company empowers employees to generate new ideas and contribute significantly to the organization's overall success.

Navigating the Challenges of Scaling Business Agility

Scaling Agile unveils a unique set of uncomfortable truths organizations must face to succeed. Mere implementation of scaling frameworks, such as Scaled Agile Framework (SAFe), does not automatically solve existing issues and aspiring to become Agile requires a fundamental shift in mindset and culture. Agile transformations are never process-driven but rely on cultural and mindset shifts, simplifying organizational structures, fostering autonomous teams and shifting focus from prescriptive processes to people-centric interactions.

One uncomfortable truth is that while Taylorism, an approach focused on work efficiency through the breakdown of tasks and scientific management, and top-down management styles may have worked well for simple, repetitive tasks in the past, they fall short when dealing with the complex adaptive problems that are prevalent in today's business environment. Agile practices, which promote team autonomy, self-management, cross-functionality, iterative and incremental development, and customer collaboration, are both better suited and indispensable.

Another uncomfortable truth is the need to descale the organization. While much attention is given to scaling Agile practices, descaling the organization can often be a more effective strategy. Descaling involves simplifying structures and processes, eliminating bureaucratic obstacles and promoting lean principles. This strategy empowers teams, reduces waste, increases speed and fosters a culture of continuous learning and improvement, ultimately leading to higher customer value. However, descaling may face resistance from stakeholders with vested interests in the existing hierarchical structure.

Empowering teams to solve customer problems is yet another uncomfortable truth. Agile is centred around empowered, autonomous teams that own their work, make decisions and solve problems. Instead of being directed and micromanaged, teams are given the autonomy to self-organize, collaborate and innovate. This approach increases motivation and job satisfaction and enables faster, more innovative solutions. However, this shift may challenge traditional command-and-control management styles.

Restraining from prescribing processes and tools is another uncomfortable truth in scaling business agility. While processes and tools have their place, they should be secondary to individuals and interactions. The Agile Manifesto emphasizes the importance of individuals and interactions over processes and tools. Organizations must foster a culture that empowers individuals, promotes collaboration and embraces change, rather than rigidly prescribing a one-size-fits-all approach.

It is also important to recognize that specific Agile methodologies or frameworks, such as Scrum or Kanban, are irrelevant in the long run. These methodologies are valuable tools but are not an end in themselves. Organizations must adopt a flexible approach that incorporates the aspects of various methodologies and frameworks to find the way of working that best suits their unique context and delivers the highest value to customers.

From Scaling Agile to Becoming Agile – The Visionary Transformation

Every component detailed in this chapter is crucial to scale business agility successfully. Addressing them in isolation will not suffice. To scale Agile is to embrace a holistic shift towards agility across every aspect of the organization – from its leadership style, culture, structures and methodologies to its interaction with customers. Each manager drives their respective areas towards this comprehensive vision of agility.

However, an intriguing phenomenon occurs as you progress in this transformative journey. Your organization evolves so significantly that the term "scaling Agile" becomes somewhat of a misnomer. Indeed, the very concept of "scaling" Agile implies that agility is an external methodology to be layered onto the organization. Yet, through this journey, Agile ceases to be an appendage and becomes the organization's DNA. You will no longer be a company trying to "scale Agile". You will be Agile incarnate. Agile's methods, values and principles will pervade every business stratum and dictate its every pulse.

The key takeaway is that these outlined components should not merely be a checklist for scaling Agile. They should instead shape the vision of the Agile organization you aspire to become. As a leader, your task is to instil this vision across every part of the business, inspiring and guiding all managers and employees in the collective pursuit of this vision. Ultimately, as the Agile principles take root and flourish in your organization, you will be astounded by the transformative power of agility. And therein lies the real triumph of scaling business agility.

CLEAR Lens for "Scaling Business Agility"

We can apply two CLEAR Model® principles to Scaling Business Agility:

Leadership: Agile Leadership plays a pivotal role in scaling Agile across the organization. Agile leaders act as change catalysts, propelling the transformation process, overcoming challenges and exemplifying leadership. They inspire and motivate their teams to adopt Agile practices at scale, manifesting the CLEAR principle of Leadership in its most dynamic form.

Execution: The effective scaling of Agile practices requires a laser-focused execution strategy that aligns process, people and technology. It entails maintaining a consistent approach to Agile implementation across different teams and levels of the organization, ensuring that agility permeates every facet of the business. This consistent approach aligns perfectly with the Execution principle of the CLEAR Model®, emphasizing its role in scaling Agile practices.

Reflection Prompts

1. Reflect on any previous attempts to scale Agile practices in your organization. What were the successes and challenges faced?

2. Identify one area of your organization that could benefit from scaled Agile practices. How would you approach implementing these practices?

Case Study: Scaling Agile Practices at Netflix and Salesforce

This case study will examine how Netflix and Salesforce, two leading companies in their respective industries, have successfully achieved this goal. We can gain insights into how to effectively scale business agility efforts in various contexts by analysing their approaches.

Netflix and Salesforce are two successful companies that have made significant strides in scaling Agile practices. While their industries and business models differ, both organizations have demonstrated the power of adopting Agile approaches to drive innovation, improve responsiveness to customer needs and maintain their competitive edge.

In 2006, Salesforce transitioned their entire R&D department from a traditional "Waterfall" SDLC to the Scrum agile framework, focusing on aligning its organizational structure with its business goals and objectives. This alignment has facilitated smooth communication and collaboration across teams and departments, enabling Salesforce to deliver value to customers on a larger scale and maintain its position as a leader in the CRM market.

Table 32: Netflix and Salesforce Agile Scaling Comparison

Aspect	Netflix	Salesforce
Organizational Culture	Experimentation, empowerment, adaptability	Alignment with business goals, collaboration, communication
Key Scaling Strategies	Decentralized decision-making, rapid adaptation to local market changes	Aligning organizational structure, streamlined communication across teams and departments
Scaling Challenges	Maintaining consistent quality across diverse teams, balancing experimentation with stability	Ensuring seamless collaboration, avoiding silos and bureaucracy

Salesforce's approach to Agile also involves the use of Kanban frameworks and a mix of processes, depending on the nature of the work item. Some teams at Salesforce continue to use the waterfall framework, demonstrating the organization's flexibility in choosing methodologies that best suit their projects.

Netflix, known for its innovative practices in the tech world, echoes Agile development principles in its operations. Their DevOps culture has enabled them to innovate faster, leading to many business benefits, including near-perfect uptime, pushing new features quickly to users, and increasing subscribers and streaming hours. After facing a major database corruption in 2008, Netflix chose to rewrite its entire application in the cloud, partnering with AWS, which fundamentally changed the way the company operated.

Netflix's transformation included converting its monolithic, data-centre-based Java application into cloud-based Java microservices architecture. This enabled their teams to be loosely coupled, build and push changes at a comfortable speed, and make independent decisions using self-service tools, thereby enhancing their agility and adaptability in the highly competitive streaming industry.

Key lessons learned from Netflix include integrating testing into every step of the software development lifecycle, embracing detailed user stories for better understanding customer preferences, and releasing content frequently to keep customers engaged.

Key Takeaways from the Case Study

1. **Culture of experimentation and empowerment** – Both Netflix and Salesforce have cultivated a culture that encourages teams to experiment, take risks and make decisions autonomously. This has enabled them to adapt quickly to market changes and deliver value to their customers.

2. **Alignment of organizational structure with business goals** – Salesforce's success in scaling Agile practices can be attributed to its alignment of organizational structure with business objectives. This has facilitated seamless communication and collaboration throughout the organization.

3. **Tailored approaches to scaling business agility** – The experiences of Netflix and Salesforce demonstrate that scaling business agility is a multifaceted endeavour, requiring customized approaches to portfolio and programme management, organizational structure, culture and leadership.

Achieving comprehensive business agility throughout the organization is crucial for delivering value to customers on a larger scale. Organizations must harmonize their portfolio and programme management processes with their strategic aspirations and targets, establish transparent communication pathways and enable teams to make informed decisions and take responsibility for their tasks. Proficient Agile governance, continuous learning and refinement are essential for effectively scaling business agility. Organizations can bolster business agility and maintain a competitive edge by fostering trust, cooperation and continuous development.

Scaling business agility offers many opportunities for further research and exploration. Topics such as measuring the impact of scaled Agile implementations on business performance, investigating the role of leadership in successful Agile scaling and examining the interplay between organizational culture and Agile scaling success warrant deeper investigation. As new Agile methodologies and frameworks emerge, there will be a continuous need to evaluate their effectiveness in different organizational contexts and understand how they can be best integrated to achieve comprehensive business agility.

Exercise: Key Considerations for Scaling Agile Practices

Successfully scaling Agile practices across your organization requires careful planning and attention to various factors. Focusing on these key considerations can ensure a smooth and effective transition as you scale Agile across teams and departments.

Consider the following key aspects when scaling Agile practices:

1. **Assessing organizational readiness** – Evaluate your organization's culture, leadership support, existing processes and team capabilities to determine whether you are prepared for scaling Agile practices. Identify and address any gaps or barriers that impede a successful Agile expansion.
2. **Aligning teams and processes** – Ensure that all teams within your organization understand and follow a consistent set of Agile practices, promoting alignment and minimizing confusion or inefficiencies.
3. **Training and coaching** – Invest in training and coaching resources to help teams develop the skills and knowledge to adopt and scale Agile practices effectively. Foster a continuous learning and improvement culture to maintain momentum as your organization grows.

4. **Building cross-functional teams** – Encourage forming cross-functional teams with representatives from various departments or disciplines, fostering collaboration and breaking down silos.
5. **Establishing Agile governance** – Develop a clear, comprehensive Agile governance model that outlines the roles, responsibilities and decision-making processes required to support a scaled Agile environment.
6. **Measuring and adapting** – Regularly assess the performance of your scaled Agile practices using metrics and KPIs, such as lead time, cycle time and customer satisfaction. Utilize data-driven insights to identify opportunities for improvement and guide ongoing refinements to your Agile scaling strategy.

Utilize these key considerations to scale Agile practices across your organization. As you encounter new challenges and opportunities, remain flexible and adaptive, continuously refining your scaling strategies to ensure sustained success and alignment with your evolving goals and objectives.

Chapter Summary

Scaling business agility is critical to achieving overall business agility. In this chapter, we examined the challenges of scaling Agile, discussed different approaches that could be used and provided practical guidance on effectively scaling Agile practices in your organization. We also looked at real-world examples of companies like Netflix and Salesforce that have successfully scaled their business agility initiatives.

Further Readings and Resources

1. Book: *Scaling Lean & Agile Development: Thinking and Organizational Tools for Large-Scale Scrum*, by Craig Larman and Bas Vodde, 2008, Addison-Wesley Professional.

2. Book: *SAFe 5.0 Distilled: Achieving Business Agility with the Scaled Agile Framework*, by Richard Knaster and Dean Leffingwell, 2020, Addison-Wesley Professional.

3. Website: PMI Disciplined Agile – Agility at Scale – https://www.pmi.org/disciplined-agile/agility-at-scale

Part 5

Overcoming Challenges and Looking Forward

11

Overcoming Challenges in Agile Adoption

It's not always smooth sailing in our world of constant change. Imagine a well-oiled machine, a company functioning at its peak, but suddenly it hits a series of bumps on the road – the challenges of adopting Agile. Picture Sarah, a top executive of a global company. Enthusiastically, she introduced Agile to her team, expecting immediate results. However, to her dismay, it wasn't the Agile approaches that posed a challenge but resistance from her team, rooted deep in tradition.

The ability to rapidly adapt to fluctuating markets, cater to customer requirements and continuously refine products or services is crucial. Organizations often encounter similar challenges. As a business leader, understanding these challenges and identifying strategies to overcome them is essential for successfully transitioning to a more Agile way of operating.

The journey toward business agility is ongoing and constant in a company's lifespan. Diverse tactics and approaches are needed to foster an agile and adaptable organization to tackle changing market conditions. Business leaders must grasp the complexities and challenges of Agile practices, creating a more Agile organization that consistently delivers customer value. Acknowledging that Agile transformations may differ among organizations with distinct goals, priorities and contexts, leaders must adopt a tailored approach to business agility. This approach accounts for industry-specific factors, therefore bolstering an organization's success and resilience against a demanding business environment.

Transitioning to Agile isn't merely about adopting a new method; it's akin to changing the very DNA of an organization. Old habits are hard to break, and established norms challenge the new. But with every challenge lies an opportunity to reshape, refine and rejuvenate.

Also, Agile adoption isn't without its hurdles. Resistance to change, particularly from those accustomed to traditional methodologies, poses a major challenge.

Embedding Agile's core values of iteration and experimentation into the organization's ethos is vital. If these values are ignored, the result can be a rigid mindset of anything but Agile.

A command and control mindset can create significant roadblocks to Agile adoption. Picture a highway with many toll booths, each one causing a delay and frustration. Understanding and overcoming these barriers is essential in order to reap Agile's benefits.

Facing these challenges head-on, Agile leaders must apply the same nimbleness and adaptability to their problem-solving as they do to their organizational structures. Are you prepared to tackle the hurdles that could disrupt your Agile transformation journey?

This chapter provides business leaders with an exploration of overcoming challenges in Agile adoption. It facilitates a smoother and more effective transition towards business agility by providing practical, results-driven strategies to address common obstacles and issues that may arise during Agile implementation. Leaders who understand and proactively address these challenges will be better equipped to adopt Agile principles and practices, successfully transforming their organizations into more adaptable, customer-centric entities.

Consider the tale of a CIO, freshly promoted and stepping into an organizational division he knew nothing about, that was less than two years into its Agile journey. The existing momentum towards Agile transformation was underway, but the arrival of the new CIO dramatically altered the course. Despite giving him coaching and the presence of Agile initiatives already in motion, his reluctance and scant effort to fully understand the Agile framework became a defining characteristic for him and, regrettably, for the entire organizational division. Compounding this were certain senior managers who, mistakenly believing they were Agile experts, managed to sway the CIO's opinions. This misguidance intensified friction and stymied the organization's transition to genuine Agile ways of working, near enough stopping the Agile Transformation in its tracks. This scenario vividly highlights the all-too-common barriers, misconceptions and voids in comprehension that frequently hamper a holistic Agile adoption within organizations.

Before diving into the intricacies of overcoming specific challenges, leaders must comprehend the broader landscape of business agility adoption. This foundational knowledge provides decision-makers with the context to proactively understand, anticipate and address potential obstacles. In the following sections, we examine each challenge in-depth, explaining the underlying factors and presenting actionable solutions tailored to the unique needs of modern organizations.

To provide a comprehensive overview, we have compiled Table 33, which outlines common Agile challenges and their corresponding solutions, serving as a reference and road map for your business agility journey.

Table 33: Common Agile Challenges and Solutions

Challenge	Solution
Resistance to Change	Communicate the benefits of Agile, involve employees in decision-making and provide training
Lack of Alignment	Establish transparent communication channels, conduct regular check-ins, and align goals and objectives
Inadequate Resources	Strategically allocate resources, prioritize initiatives delivering value to customers and seek external support if needed
Ineffective Governance	Establish a governance framework aligned with organizational goals and adapt policies as needed
Ineffective Communication within Agile Teams	Establish open communication channels, encourage feedback and hold regular team meetings
Insufficient or Inadequate Training	Provide comprehensive Agile training, coaching and ongoing support for employees
Difficulty Scaling Agile	Adopt a scaling framework, ensure cross-functional collaboration and prioritize alignment
Incomplete or Unclear Requirements	Use iterative planning, prioritize user stories and collaborate with customers
Inability to Measure Agile Performance	Use Agile-specific metrics and key performance indicators (KPIs) and adapt measurement strategies as needed
Balancing Agile with Traditional Methodologies	Implement a hybrid approach and customize the adoption process to fit the organization's needs

Common Agile Challenges and Solutions to Business Agility

Understanding common challenges organizations face during business agility adoption prepares business leaders to foresee potential obstacles and proactively devise strategies to overcome them. With the insights provided, business leaders will be well equipped to tackle challenges head-on and steer their organizations towards a successful Agile transformation.

Let us delve deeper into the common Agile challenges and solutions discussed above:

Resistance to Change

As mentioned throughout previous chapters, one of the most significant challenges for adopting business agility is resistance. People may resist new processes and practices, and managers may hesitate to give up control. Addressing the underlying reasons for resistance, such as fear of job loss or perceived loss of status, addresses those concerns. Emphasizing empathy, showing vulnerability and understanding employees' fears and concerns are crucial.

Another significant challenge when adopting Agile can be the tendency to fixate on established Agile brands or to clone another organization's way of working, such as the "Spotify Model". To overcome these pitfalls, we must remember that the essence of Agile is adaptation and evolution, not replication or imitation.

Clear communication of business agility benefits, alongside employee training and support, is crucial to overcoming this challenge. This can encompass educational sessions, workshops and coaching. Leading by example is also vital, with leaders embracing changes and exemplifying the conduct they wish to see. Encouraging open dialogue and addressing concerns can mitigate resistance and cultivate a more agile mentality across the organization.

Addressing Resistance to Change

Resistance to change can be a significant obstacle when implementing Agile practices. Consider the following change management strategies to overcome objections and secure buy-in from team members and stakeholders.

Table 34: Change Management Strategies for Agile Transformation

Strategy	Key Considerations	Potential Benefits
Top-down Approach	– Leadership commitment – Effective communication – Alignment with organizational goals	– Clear direction and support from the top – Faster decision-making and implementation – Stronger commitment to strategic objectives
Bottom-up Approach	– Empowering employees – Encouraging collaboration – Providing ongoing training and support	– Greater buy-in and engagement from team members – Enhanced innovation and creativity – Better adaptability to change and continuous improvement

Hybrid Approach	– Balancing top-down and bottom-up efforts – Fostering a culture of shared ownership – Adapting strategies to suit unique contexts	– Leveraging the strengths of both approaches – Improved collaboration and communication across the organization – Greater flexibility and responsiveness to changing needs and goals

Lack of Alignment

Organizations must also grapple with misalignment between teams and departments, causing confusion and delays in delivering customer value.

Establishing transparent communication channels and aligning everyone with the organization's goals and objectives are essential to overcome this challenge. This may involve regular meetings, check-ins and shared metrics. Fostering alignment ensures that everyone will grasp their role in delivering customer value. Forming cross-functional teams and promoting collaboration can dissolve silos and encourage a more integrated approach to achieving business objectives.

Inadequate Resources

While adopting business agility can be seen to require substantial resources like time, money and staff, presenting a challenge for many organizations, it is perhaps more beneficial to view this from a different angle. There is no denying that resources are essential, but necessity should serve as the primary instigator for change, not an abundance of resources.

Organizations need to use what they already have more effectively, employing strategic resource allocation and prioritizing initiatives that deliver value to their customers. This may involve a hard look at how resources are currently used, possibly shedding wasteful processes or functions akin to shedding excess weight for greater agility. This transformation might require concentrating on high-priority areas, optimizing resource usage through better team and department collaboration and continuously overseeing resource allocation to ensure alignment with organizational goals and objectives.

Implementing Agile practices, such as value-based work prioritization and minimum viable product (MVP) delivery focus, can be instrumental in this shift, helping organizations maximize resources and guarantee efficient customer value delivery. The drive to become lean and agile does not always equate to needing more resources but rather using what's already available more effectively and efficiently. Organizations should seek external funding or partnerships to support the Agile transformation if internal resources prove insufficient. This approach speaks to the core of Agile approaches, making the most of what you have to deliver the greatest value.

Ineffective Governance

Effective governance is key to expanding business agility. Governance encompasses decision-making processes, resource distribution, risk management and tracking and reporting progress.

Establish a governance framework aligned with the organization's goals and objectives. Regularly revising and adapting these guidelines and policies is crucial. Explore different governance models suitable for Agile organizations, such as "Agile or Adaptive Governance", to find the best fit. Engaging stakeholders in creating the framework enhances its relevance, efficacy and acceptance.

Ineffective Communication within Agile Teams

Effective communication is the lifeblood of Agile teams and the foundation for shared understanding, transparency and successful collaboration. However, ineffective communication can often obstruct the Agile transformation journey.

To address this, it's crucial to establish open and transparent communication channels that promote regular exchanges, share insights and foster an environment of continuous learning. Encourage feedback and active participation from all team members, therefore ensuring that everyone's voice is heard and valued. Regular team meetings, facilitated by tools such as daily stand-ups and retrospectives, can provide a structured approach to sharing updates and addressing concerns. Overcoming this hurdle will significantly enhance team cohesion, improve decision-making and bolster the overall efficiency of Agile practices.

Insufficient or Inadequate Training

In the journey toward business agility, insufficient or inadequate training can pose a significant challenge. Agile principles and practices represent a shift from traditional ways of working and require a new set of skills and mindsets.

To overcome this, comprehensive training and ongoing support are crucial for all employees, not just those directly involved in project execution. This training should cover the fundamentals of Agile methodologies and frameworks, the benefits of Agile, specific practices relevant to their roles and how to apply Agile principles effectively to their work. Incorporating Agile coaching, workshops and practical exercises can further solidify learning. Agile is a continuous learning journey, so ongoing education, mentoring and support must be a cornerstone of any Agile transformation strategy.

Difficulty Scaling Agile

Scaling Agile practices beyond individual teams to an organization-wide level can be a daunting task. It involves synchronizing multiple Agile teams, aligning them with strategic objectives and ensuring seamless collaboration across different parts of the organization.

Adopting a suitable Agile scaling framework can help to overcome this challenge. These frameworks offer a structured approach to scaling Agile, ensuring cross-functional collaboration and alignment at all levels. Fostering a culture that promotes open communication, breaks down silos and encourages shared ownership of goals can help smooth the scaling process. Always remember that scaling Agile is not a one-size-fits-all approach; it must be tailored to the organization's unique context and needs.

Incomplete or Unclear Requirements

Another common challenge in Agile adoption is dealing with incomplete or unclear requirements. This can lead to confusion and misalignment, resulting in deliverables not meeting customers' needs and major delays for expected products.

To overcome this, Agile embraces iterative planning and continuous refinement of requirements. Prioritizing user stories and involving customers in defining and refining requirements is essential. Practices such as backlog grooming and sprint planning can help ensure clarity and a shared understanding of requirements. Always remember, in Agile, requirements are not set in stone but evolve as the team gains a better understanding and receives feedback.

Incomplete or unclear requirements can also lead to last-minute changes, adding significant pressure on teams. Such late shifts in requirements can strain resources and affect team morale, as they may have to work intensively to meet the original deadlines, impacting psychological safety. To mitigate these challenges, Agile promotes active stakeholder engagement and frequent communication. This approach ensures that changes are incorporated systematically, allowing teams to adjust their workload and timelines realistically. It's crucial to foster an environment where team members feel safe to express concerns about workload and deadlines, ensuring sustainable delivery without compromising team well-being.

Inability to Measure Agile Performance

Measuring Agile performance can be challenging given its iterative nature and focus on delivering customer value over adhering strictly to planned tasks and schedules. However, it becomes difficult to assess progress and improve without effective metrics.

Using Agile-specific metrics and KPIs can provide a clear view of how well the Agile practices are being implemented and their impact. These can include metrics like lead time, cycle time and customer satisfaction. Regularly reviewing and adapting measurement strategies is critical to ensure they remain relevant and supportive of your Agile journey. Remember, the goal of measurement in Agile is not merely to track but to inspire continuous improvement.

Balancing Agile with Traditional Methodologies

Implementing Agile does not mean completely dismissing traditional methodologies. The challenge lies in finding the right balance and tailoring the approach to suit the organization's unique needs.

This balance can be struck through a hybrid approach, where Agile methods are implemented alongside traditional ones, allowing the organization to enjoy both benefits. This involves understanding where Agile methods will be most beneficial and where traditional methods may still hold value. It's about customizing the adoption process, allowing Agile and traditional methodologies to complement each other in the organization's unique context. The focus should always be on delivering customer value, enhancing flexibility and encouraging continuous improvement, irrespective of the methodologies used.

Selecting Appropriate Agile Approaches and Tools

Organizations may need help selecting the ideal Agile approaches and tools that cater to their specific requirements and context. This difficulty can create confusion and obstruct the successful adoption of business agility.

Cracking the code of picking the ideal Agile approaches and tools can often feel like navigating through a labyrinth, posing a significant challenge on the journey towards successful business agility adoption. To outmanoeuvre this, it becomes paramount to research and comprehend the strengths, weaknesses and differences of various Agile frameworks and methodologies (see Chapter 3).

Agile Coaches

Engaging external Agile coaches or consultants is a strategic move in any organization's transition to Agile ways of working. These experts bring vital insights and guidance for selecting appropriate Agile approaches and tools. Their expertise ensures these methods remain relevant and effective, even as the organization grows and evolves.

Table 35: Comprehensive Overview of
Agile Coaches and Their Roles

Type of Agile Coach	Role and Responsibilities
Team Coach	Focuses on team dynamics, collaboration and Agile practices within individual teams
	Helps teams become self-organized and high-performing
	Facilitates Agile ceremonies and assists in resolving team conflicts
Technical Coach	Guides technical aspects of Agile development, such as continuous integration, test-driven development and automated testing
	Assists teams in adopting Agile engineering practices and improving code quality
	Mentors and trains team members in new technologies and tools
	Works at the organizational level to support Agile transformation across multiple teams
Enterprise Agile Coach	Collaborates with senior leadership to align Agile initiatives with business objectives
	Facilitates the scaling of Agile practices across the organization
	Helps to establish and maintain an Agile Centre of Excellence (CoE)
Transformation Coach	Focuses on organizational change management and helps organizations transition to Agile
	Collaborates with leadership and stakeholders to manage resistance and drive change
	Develops and executes Agile transformation strategies and road maps
Agile Portfolio Coach	Supports the alignment of Agile practices at the portfolio level
	Assists in prioritizing and managing projects, programs and products in an Agile manner
	Ensures the strategic alignment of Agile initiatives across the organization
	Facilitates cross-team coordination and collaboration

Agile Leadership Coach	Provides coaching and mentoring to leaders and executives on Agile leadership principles
	Helps develop an Agile mindset at the leadership level
	Supports the creation of an environment that fosters collaboration, learning and innovation
	Enhances leaders' ability to support Agile teams and drive organizational change effectively

Assessing the Quality of an Agile Coach

The effectiveness of Agile coaches can vary significantly. It's vital for organizations to rigorously assess the skills and experience of potential coaches. Through practical interviews and a review of past case studies, an organization can gauge a coach's impact. The right Agile coach can be a key differentiator, transforming an Agile adoption from a theoretical exercise into a practical, impactful transformation.

The Pitfalls of "One-Size-Fits-All" Agile Coaching

While recognizing the essential role of proficient Agile coaches, there is a growing concern about coaches who rigidly adhere to a "little black book" approach. This term symbolizes a coaching style that relies heavily on predefined frameworks and methodologies, without adequately considering the unique context of the organization. Such a "cookie-cutter" approach can potentially hinder, rather than help, an organization's Agile transformation.

Contextual Application of Agile Principles

The effectiveness of Agile coaching lies in its contextual application. Agile is less about rigid adherence to a set of rules and more about flexible approaches tailored to meet specific organizational challenges. A skilled Agile coach recognizes this and applies principles flexibly and thoughtfully. They tailor their coaching to align with the organization's specific goals, culture and operational style.

Hiring Agile Coaches

When hiring Agile coaches, it's crucial for organizations to look beyond certifications and theoretical knowledge. The focus should be on finding coaches who demonstrate a deep understanding of Agile principles and the ability to apply them contextually. This requires a combination of experience, adaptability, and a proven track record of successful, flexible Agile implementations in varied environments.

Questions to Consider When Hiring an Agile Coach

- How does the coach plan to adapt their approach to our organization's unique context?
- Can they provide examples of tailored coaching in varied organizational settings?
- What strategies do they use to ensure flexibility and responsiveness to our evolving needs?

Continual Learning for Agile Coaches

As Agile ways of working develop and change, so must the coaches. Mastery in Agile coaching is an ongoing journey marked by constant learning and skill enhancement. This commitment to continuous professional development is essential for Agile coaches to provide the most effective and current guidance to the organizations they assist.

The Exit Criteria for Agile Coaches

It's important to recognize that Agile coaches are not intended to be a permanent part of an organization. The ultimate aim is to foster a self-sustaining Agile culture. Setting clear 'exit criteria' for Agile coaches is crucial. These benchmarks indicate when an organization has fully embraced Agile ways of working and can continue its Agile journey independently. This strategic approach helps ensure that Agile coaching is a catalyst for lasting, self-reliant change.

Balancing Agility and Stability

Although adopting business agility is essential for organizations to adjust and thrive, maintaining stability in specific areas is equally important. Balancing agility and stability can be challenging, and organizations must be flexible and adaptable while offering a stable foundation for employees and customers.

To overcome this challenge, identify areas where stability is critical, such as core business processes, data security and regulatory compliance. Clearly defining and communicating these stable areas allows organizations to ensure that their pursuit of agility does not compromise the stability for long-term success. Adopting a flexible approach to Agile frameworks also helps maintain stability in vital areas while allowing adaptability. For example, Apple Inc. has maintained a balance between agility and stability, constantly innovating and adapting to market changes while preserving a stable core of products and services.

Fostering Trust and Psychological Safety

Cultivating a trust and psychological safety culture is essential for business agility success. This environment empowers employees to innovate, adapt and contribute to the organization's agility. Innovation and adaptability flourish when employees feel secure in taking risks, making errors and expressing their thoughts.

Leaders play a pivotal role in shaping a culture that supports business agility. To foster such a culture, they must lead by example, championing the values of transparency, collaboration and continuous improvement. Encourage employees to embrace change, learn from mistakes and celebrate collective achievements. A thriving Agile culture accelerates the organization's ability to navigate challenges and seize opportunities.

To tackle hurdles linked to trust and emotional safety, leaders must actively promote open dialogue, maintain transparency in decision-making and offer and accept constructive feedback. Recognizing and learning from mistakes and collectively applauding accomplishments can help create a trusting and emotionally safe space. This culture of trust and safety empowers employees to welcome change and enhance the organization's overall agility.

Encourage employees to give and receive feedback openly, fostering a learning culture. Setting up anonymous channels for expressing concerns can help create a safe environment for employees to share their thoughts without fear of repercussions.

Communities of Practice

Developing communities of practice within an organization supports incorporating business agility throughout. These communities encourage cooperation, innovation and ongoing learning. These provide a supportive setting where employees openly exchange ideas, recount experiences, and deliberate over challenges, failures and successes. As a valuable support system, practice-based communities enable individuals to learn from peers, experiment with innovative methods and collaborate to establish and refine best practices. These cooperative communities contribute to the organization's resilience and adaptability. This allows the organization to support Agile teams and effectively drive organizational change with individuals with different backgrounds and expertise. This enriches the exchange of ideas and fosters innovation.

These communities of practice can be supported by regular meetings, workshops and online platforms for collaboration, helping to drive innovation and continuous improvement.

Cultivating a constant learning and improvement culture is vital to overcoming the above challenges and embracing business agility. This includes offering support and resources for employees to grow their skills and knowledge and routinely examining and modifying processes and practices to guarantee customer value. It is also essential to foster a culture of experimentation and learning, urging employees to test and learn continually from new approaches and iterate and refine their processes and practices.

Economic Conditions and Agile Roles

One additional consideration to be mindful of is that Agile positions are often among the first to be cut during economic downturns or budget constraints. Organizations must be prepared to mitigate these risks by showcasing agility's intrinsic value, making it an indispensable part of the business strategy.

Personal Agile Adoption Experiences

In addition to those shared commonly faced obstacles of Agile adoption, I've encountered several repeating challenges over the years, resonating deeply with many professionals and colleagues navigating similar transformations. Recognizing and addressing these can be as crucial as overcoming the more widely acknowledged barriers.

1. **Confusion about complexity** – There's a prevailing belief that Agile is an insurmountable mountain of complexity. This misconception often wastes time and resources as teams scramble to decode what they perceive as a complicated set of rules and guidelines. In reality, Agile's essence is simplicity, flexibility and delivering value. The challenge then becomes educating team members and stakeholders effectively to alleviate these fears, ensuring the organization can move forward with a true understanding of Agile's benefits.

2. **Past bad experiences** – A general caution surrounds Agile, especially among those who've seen or been a part of failed Agile initiatives in the past. These past setbacks can significantly influence their willingness to embrace Agile again, often breeding scepticism or even outright resistance. It becomes imperative to showcase that when Agile is implemented correctly, it has the transformative power to elevate performance, increase customer satisfaction and drive business value.

3. **Thinking they know best** – Sometimes, the most formidable roadblock stems from non-Agile employees who are convinced their interpretation of Agile is superior. This self-assurance can lead these individuals to reject Agile methods recommended by experienced Agile coaches, which could benefit the organization's specific context more. This "I know best" mindset can cascade through entire departments, compromising the Agile transformation journey. Addressing this situation requires presenting compelling real-world success stories and evidence that illustrates Agile's

broader, proven benefits. This can help to challenge and, hopefully, reshape these misplaced convictions.

4. **Skill gaps** – The expertise in Agile across an organization is seldom uniformly distributed. This gap can create a tangible barrier to the effective roll-out of Agile practices. Failing to address this can result in a fractured approach, where some teams excel while others lag, therefore preventing the organization from realizing the full benefits of Agile. Hence, ensuring that comprehensive and consistent training is available for all is critical to bridging this skills and knowledge gap.

5. **Middle management's struggle for control** – A rather intricate issue often emerges from the echelons of middle management, particularly those in Project or Programme Management roles. These individuals can find it particularly challenging to relinquish old paradigms of command and control, bureaucratic measures or micromanagement. It's as if they instinctively attempt to manage the new Agile environment, possibly viewing it as challenging their established authority or expertise. In an Agile transformation, the focus should shift from managing to enabling, from dictating to supporting. Such a shift calls for coaches adept in Agile to guide the journey rather than having middle managers trying to corral it into their pre-defined structures.

6. **Agile fatigue** – A noteworthy challenge that has emerged recently is "Agile fatigue". This phenomenon typically arises in environments where Agile is adopted indiscriminately, without a firm grasp of its core principles. Such settings often lead to team burnout and financial strain, reflecting a misalignment between Agile practices and the organization's strategic objectives. Agile fatigue is further exacerbated when the focus shifts to rigidly adhering to processes, overshadowing the delivery of tangible value. To combat this, reevaluating key performance indicators to emphasize outcomes like customer satisfaction rather than just speed is crucial. This shift in focus can reignite the Agile spark within teams, steering them away from the pitfalls of burnout and disillusionment. It is also vital to understand that Agile is not a universal panacea but a strategic framework that requires alignment with the company's goals to be effective. Addressing Agile fatigue is not just about tweaking processes; it involves a holistic reexamination of how Agile principles are understood and implemented across the organization, ensuring they contribute meaningfully to the overall business objectives.

7. **The illusion of agility** – A troubling phenomenon making its rounds is what can be described as "Agile Theatre" – organizations profusely claiming to be Agile without substantiating such declarations through action or culture. They adopt Agile terminologies and even some processes to deflect scrutiny while operating under traditional bureaucratic methods.

This over-eagerness to self-identify as Agile has led to a dilution of what it truly means to be Agile, generating a facade of agility that exists in name only. Consequently, these organizations are merely "doing Agile" rather than "being Agile". To counteract this, it's imperative to employ rigorous assessment mechanisms that can sift the authentic from the superficial, thereby preserving the integrity of Agile philosophies.

A profound reflection I've carried through my experiences is this: the central challenge during any Agile transformation isn't solely in establishing a novel mode of operation. It's in discarding entrenched methodologies and conventions. We must not underestimate employees' profound connection with long-standing organizational structures and processes. Their very sense of identity can be intertwined with these frameworks. Consequently, this transformation becomes an operational shift and a deeply personal one. As we venture forth, acknowledging and addressing this connection is pivotal to nurturing a genuine, wholehearted embrace of Agile.

The Pretence and Reality of Agile Adoption

Now that we have looked at some common Agile challenges, the community is frustrated with organizations that merely feign an Agile transformation. As observed, many businesses desire change but are resistant when confronted with its reality. As discussed earlier, leadership often disengages from the required change processes, revealing a palpable absence of genuine intent.

It's not just organizational leadership under the scanner. Agile practitioners, armed with superficial knowledge from brief courses, frequently preach principles without the backing of practical experience. This has led to Agile being perceived as more of a "religion" largely based on faith rather than grounded practice. Sadly, this has culminated in Agile often failing to scale effectively, mainly because organizations are either ill equipped or unwilling to make the necessary adjustments.

What's even more concerning is the rise of roles within this Agile domain that appear effective on paper but, in reality, are far from it. There's a disconnect between the titles and the actual empowerment these roles bring, leading to diminished accomplishments and value. High-profile examples include the trend of firing Scrum Masters and coaches due to a perceived lack of value.

Agile, for many, seems like a brilliant idea turned industry buzzword, creating more noise than tangible results. And while there are shining exceptions, they are in the minority. This critical perspective underscores the importance of understanding and correctly implementing Agile rather than merely jumping on the bandwagon. It's essential to approach Agile with a clear understanding of its principles and a genuine intent for organizational change.

The Drift from Agile's Original Aspirations

It's intriguing to note how Agile, originally conceived to empower teams and enhance flexibility, has sometimes strayed from its founding principles. This drift is often a consequence of treating Agile as a set of rigid rules rather than a flexible approach to deliver value. It becomes a box-checking exercise, where the form takes precedence over function, missing the essence of what Agile aims to achieve: simplicity, collaboration and iterative progress. This distortion not only hampers the genuine adoption of Agile but also tarnishes its transformative potential. As we focus on continuous learning and adaptation, we must remember Agile's original aspirations and steer the course accordingly.

Continuous Learning and Adaptation

We have already discussed various challenges organizations may encounter during their Agile adoption journey. These challenges can be formidable: cultural resistance, lack of necessary skills or difficulty scaling. However, it's crucial to remember that the heart of Agile lies in learning and adapting continuously.

No organization will perfectly adopt Agile on the first attempt. There will be missteps, and there will be trials. And that is perfectly fine. Agile is not about perfection; it's about improvement. It's about building a mindset, attitude and culture that can adapt and improve continuously. When an Agile team encounters an obstacle, they take it as an opportunity to learn, adapt and improve.

In the words of Peter Senge, author of the book *The Fifth Discipline: The Art and Practice of the Learning Organization*: "Learning organizations are organizations where people continually expand their capacity to create the results they truly desire, where new and expansive patterns of thinking are nurtured, where collective aspiration is set free, and where people are continually learning how to learn together."

What's Still Missing from Agile?

While Agile approaches have revolutionized software development and organizational change, they are not without their blind spots. Certain key aspects often remain underdeveloped or entirely neglected, diminishing the efficacy and adaptability of Agile ways of working. From lapses in Systems Thinking to inadequate Value Stream Management, several facets still demand our attention. These aren't mere footnotes; they play a pivotal role in an Agile initiative's ultimate success or failure.

Systems Thinking

Agile approaches often fall short of incorporating Systems Thinking, a holistic approach that enables us to make sense of complex scenarios. It's a framework that moves us beyond the sum of the parts, inviting us to examine the intricate relationships that shape the whole project ecosystem. This concept is particularly relevant in our Agile journey, where we might excel at sprint planning, for example, but overlook the wider interconnections that influence project success.

Herein lies the essence of Systems Thinking: a panoramic perspective that appreciates the symbiotic relationships between various project facets. Far from being an optional appendage, Systems Thinking ought to be a cornerstone of Agile practices. Teams need to widen the lens, engaging in "big picture" retrospectives that transcend the limitations of a single sprint or project.

To address this, consider the introduction of bespoke Systems Thinking workshops. Tailored to the specificities of your project, these sessions are designed to unearth overlooked interdependencies and build a robust understanding of your project's broader ecosystem. Expert facilitators, well versed in Systems Thinking paradigms, can facilitate these transformative workshops.

Value Stream Management

Value Stream Management is a strategic approach to analyse, optimize and visualize the flow of materials and information required to deliver a product or service to customers. In the context of Agile, this often equates to understanding and improving the entire life cycle of a project.

Often lauded for its agility, Agile methodologies can inadvertently lead to tunnel vision, particularly when individual stages or processes within a project take centre stage. Herein lies the critical role of Value Stream Management: it transcends mere optimization of isolated elements, urging us to consider and enhance the entire process chain.

The urgency to embed Value Stream Management within Agile frameworks is palpable. We risk overlooking the collective Value Stream when engaged in the minutiae of individual process improvements. It's akin to meticulously tuning each instrument in an orchestra yet neglecting the harmonious output that only comes when all play in unison.

To address this, it's prudent to standardize Value Stream Mapping from sprint zero or during your project's initiation phase. But this is not a "one and done" activity. Continual updates to this map are essential. They serve as a visual reminder, ensuring every team member comprehends the bigger picture – how their tasks, however minute, contribute indispensably to overarching value delivery.

Double-Loop Learning

At the heart of truly overcoming the myriad of challenges in Agile adoption lies Double-Loop Learning. It's not merely about tweaking your actions based on observed outcomes; it's about fundamentally rethinking the very hypotheses that guided those actions in the first place.

In essence, the ability to question and reassess our underlying assumptions is a cornerstone for the enduring success of any Agile endeavour. It's what sets an Agile project on a path to sustainability rather than consigning it to a series of quick fixes that lack depth and durability.

To operationalize this principle, consider implementing "hypothesis-driven retrospectives" as a regular feature within your Agile cycles. These retrospectives do more than just review what transpired; they delve into the "why" behind the "what", dissecting the assumptions and beliefs that influenced your actions. Following this analysis, it's crucial to recalibrate both your actions and assumptions, aligning them more closely with the reality of your project or product.

By embedding Double-Loop Learning into your Agile practices, you're not just skating on the surface; you're diving into the deep end, where meaningful, long-term improvements are made.

Don't Shoot the Messenger: Misconceptions About Agile Failures

Too often, we also bear witness to the narrative that Agile is "broken", especially when its deployment is less than successful in bureaucratic settings. It's essential to understand that failure in Agile adoption often isn't a reflection on Agile itself but a mirror of the organization's underlying issues.

So, let's clear the air. If your Agile initiative is stumbling, cast a discerning eye on the broader organizational landscape – your culture, your management styles and governance structures. These are often the real culprits hampering Agile's success, not the Agile principles or frameworks you're striving to implement.

To remedy this, a diagnostic "organizational health check" could be invaluable. This isn't a box-ticking exercise but a deep, facilitated discussion designed to unearth structural and cultural roadblocks. Once identified, these issues can be systematically addressed, freeing your Agile initiative to thrive as it was meant to.

Challenges and the Future Path Towards True Agile Adoption

Achieving "genuine Agile" can seem like scaling a steep mountain. Avoiding the "Agile in name only" pitfall might feel like navigating a tricky precipice. But the rewards at the top are worth the climb. Overcoming these challenges clears our path toward true Agile adoption.

Here's a sobering thought – Agile in 2030 will be no different from now unless we resolve the challenges we've discussed. It's a powerful call to action for all leaders. The future of business agility is in our hands, and it's up to us to shape it.

CLEAR Lens for "Overcoming Challenges in Agile Adoption"

We can apply all five CLEAR Model® principles to Overcoming Challenges in Agile Adoption:

Culture: Creating a Culture that values and champions agility is critical in surmounting adoption challenges. It involves fostering open communication, nurturing an environment of trust and embracing change. Building this strong cultural foundation aids in overcoming resistance to change and paves the way for a smoother, more effective Agile transformation.

Leadership: In the voyage of Agile adoption, the principle of Leadership serves as the guiding star. Agile leaders inspire their teams, provide a clear vision and live the Agile values. By leading through action and displaying resilience in the face of setbacks, they play an instrumental role in overcoming Agile adoption challenges.

Execution: Agile Execution emerges as a critical ally in conquering adoption challenges. It enables swift and effective responses to setbacks, ensuring the Agile transformation process remains steadfastly aligned. By incorporating feedback and adapting accordingly, organizations can successfully transition from the theoretical principles of Agile to their practical application, proving crucial in overcoming Agile adoption hurdles.

Adaptability: In the dynamic path of Agile transformation, the principle of Adaptability serves as a crucial lifesaver, helping the organization float above unexpected obstacles. Nurturing adaptability empowers organizations to evolve their practices harmoniously with the Agile philosophy, seamlessly navigating through these challenges.

Responsiveness: The Responsiveness principle comes to the forefront as organizations strive to react swiftly and adjust to the challenges encountered during the Agile adoption process. It entails maintaining a readiness to reorient strategies and plans to address emerging needs and resolve challenges efficiently. By fostering a culture of responsiveness, organizations can ensure their journey to Agile is resilient and dynamic, capable of overcoming any hurdles that arise along the way.

Reflection Prompts

1. What obstacles or barriers have you encountered in adopting Agile practices in your organization? How have you addressed these challenges?

2. How can you leverage the lessons learned from previous challenges to improve the adoption of Agile practices in the future?

3. Can you spot any potential challenges that might crop up in the future, and how can you gear up to address these?

Case Study: Airbnb and Uber's Approach to Overcoming Business Agility Challenges

Companies like Airbnb and Uber have faced many challenges while adopting business agility, yet they have successfully overcome these obstacles to thrive in their industries. Examining their approach allows us to learn valuable lessons on addressing common challenges associated with business agility adoption within our organizations.

Airbnb and Uber, two revolutionary companies in the sharing economy, have harnessed the power of business agility to disrupt traditional industries and reshape how people travel and commute. Their journey towards embracing agility offers invaluable insights and learnings that can be applied across various sectors. In this case study, we delve into their challenges, strategies and key factors contributing to their successful adoption of business agility. When you understand their distinct approaches and draw parallels with your organization, you can craft a tailored road map to overcome potential obstacles and reap the benefits of a more agile, responsive and customer-centric business.

Airbnb addressed any issues with communication and collaboration by implementing core Agile practices. They encouraged cross-functional collaboration, promoted transparency and fostered a culture of continuous improvement. These efforts have allowed Airbnb to maintain a flexible, customer-focused approach, adapting to changes in the market and delivering value to its users. They introduced Scrum practices across product development teams and organized regular cross-functional meetings to ensure alignment with company goals.

Uber, conversely, surmounted resistance to change by implementing a comprehensive change management programme. This encompassed clear communication of the vision and benefits of Agile transformation

---

and providing training and support for employees during the transition. Uber established a culture of agility by involving all levels of the organization and addressing concerns, allowing them to adapt quickly to market shifts and customer needs. They rolled out an extensive training programme on Agile approaches and assigned Agile coaches to assist teams during the transition.

Table 36: Airbnb and Uber Business Agility Challenges Comparison

Aspect	Airbnb	Uber
Challenges	– Communication and collaboration issues – Market adaptation – Lack of customer focus	– Resistance to change – Lack of employee support during transition
Strategies	– Core Agile practices – Cross-functional collaboration – Transparency	– Change management programme – Agile training – Coaching
Organizational Culture	– Continuous improvement – Adaptability – Transparency	– Agility – Adaptability – Support during transition
Key Success Factors	– Alignment with company goals – Flexible approach – Customer focus	– Clear communication – Strong leadership – Comprehensive support

Besides the abovementioned strategies, Airbnb and Uber took specific actions to bolster their business agility further. Airbnb, for instance, established an "Airbnb Design Lab" to foster a culture of experimentation and innovation. This initiative encourages employees to test new ideas, iterate on existing ones and learn from failures. On the other hand, Uber focused on promoting knowledge-sharing and cross-functional collaboration among teams. They encouraged internal workshops and other learning opportunities to facilitate the exchange of expertise and help align the organization around common goals and values. Business leaders can glean valuable insights into creating a supportive environment that nurtures innovation, collaboration and continuous improvement by analysing these tailored initiatives, ultimately contributing to successful business agility adoption.

Key Takeaways from the Case Study

1. **Clear communication and collaboration** – Airbnb and Uber underscore the importance of clear communication and collaboration in overcoming challenges associated with business agility adoption.
2. **Addressing resistance to change** – Uber's comprehensive change management programme demonstrates the importance of addressing resistance to change and supporting employees during the transition.
3. **Fostering a culture of continuous improvement** – Airbnb's focus on continuous improvement and learning has enabled them to adapt and evolve in a dynamic business environment.
4. **Strong leadership and vision** – Business agility success hinges on decisive leadership and a compelling vision. Airbnb and Uber exemplify this by setting clear expectations, empowering teams, and consistently driving towards desired outcomes.
5. **Adaptability and resilience** – Airbnb and Uber's success demonstrates the value of adaptability and resilience in overcoming challenges and thriving in a constantly changing business environment.

Exercise: Navigating Common Agile Challenges

To tackle common Agile challenges and obstacles effectively, it's essential to employ various strategies that align with your organization's unique context and needs. Addressing these challenges proactively ensures a smoother Agile transformation and fosters a more resilient and adaptable organization.

Consider implementing the following strategies through practical, hands-on activities in your organization:

1. **Managing resistance to change** – Foster a culture of open communication, provide clear explanations of Agile benefits and involve stakeholders in the Agile transformation process. Empathize, address concerns constructively and demonstrate how Agile principles can improve the work environment.
2. **Aligning with non-Agile teams** – Establish cross-team collaboration mechanisms and ensure that Agile and non-Agile teams understand each other's processes and priorities. Develop shared goals and objectives and work together to resolve conflicts and ensure alignment with the organization's vision.

3. **Balancing flexibility and discipline** – Set clear boundaries and guidelines for Agile practices while focusing on continuous improvement and adaptation. Encourage teams to balance flexibility and discipline, empowering them to innovate while adhering to the organization's values and objectives.

4. **Scaling Agile** – Develop a tailored approach to scaling Agile practices across your organization, considering team size, project complexity and organizational structure. Invest in the right tools, processes and coaching to support the growth and evolution of Agile practices throughout the organization.

5. **Ensuring quality** – Incorporate quality assurance processes and practices throughout the Agile development life cycle, promoting a culture of shared responsibility for product quality. Implement regular feedback loops and continuously monitor key quality indicators to maintain high standards.

Utilize these strategies to proactively address your challenges and obstacles during your organization's Agile journey. As you progress, learn from setbacks and continuously refine your approach, ensuring that your organization remains resilient, adaptable and well-positioned to reap the benefits of Agile transformation.

Chapter Summary

In this chapter, we explored the common challenges organizations face when adopting business agility and provided strategies for overcoming them. We examined issues such as resistance to change, lack of alignment and cultural barriers. We provided practical guidance on overcoming these challenges and driving the successful adoption of business agility in your organization. We also looked at real-world examples of companies like Airbnb and Uber that faced and overcame many of these challenges.

Further Readings and Resources

1. Book: *Coaching Agile Teams: A Companion for ScrumMasters, Agile Coaches, and Project Managers in Transition,* by Lyssa Adkins, 2010, Addison-Wesley Professional.

2. Book: *Agile Transformation: Using the Integral Agile Transformation Framework to Think and Lead Differently,* by Michael Spayd and Michele Madore, 2021, Addison-Wesley.

3. Website: Agile Delta Consulting – www.agiledeltaconsulting.com

12

The Future of Business Agility

In a time of exponential technological growth, businesses that don't look ahead can quickly find themselves in the past. Let's revisit Blockbuster for a moment. Their downfall was not only due to a failure to acknowledge the present but also to visualize the future. Just as they missed the digital streaming boat, many businesses today risk overlooking the emerging trends in business agility.

Picture this: you've successfully integrated Agile practices within your organization. Your teams are harmonious, productivity is at an all-time high and customers are delighted. However, on the periphery, a new technological trend is emerging. Within months, competitors who've embraced this trend start to outpace you and market dynamics shift. This scenario underscores the relentless pace of change of the current Fourth Industrial Revolution and highlights why businesses must implement Agile ways of working and continuously evolve with its future.

Amidst this relentless pace of competition, businesses must stay on top of emerging trends and technologies within business agility. As a business leader, immersing yourself in the most recent developments that influence the future of Agile practices can strengthen your organization's resilience and performance, allowing it to prosper in the face of contemporary challenges.

Just as the business world constantly evolves, so must the Agile Manifesto. We must look at it not as an unchanging scripture but as a living document that adapts to modern business needs. This evolution is vital to stay relevant and responsive to new challenges and technological advancements. Embracing this adaptive approach allows the Manifesto to remain a foundational guide while also fostering innovation and forward-thinking strategies that align with an ever-changing global market.

As we gaze into the crystal ball to predict the future, it's also essential to acknowledge and address existing challenges. Over-emphasizing Agile artefacts and events at the expense of its core values can create a hollow Agile implementation.

Similarly, not investing in talent development can hinder the growth of an Agile environment. As we move forward, these issues demand our attention to foster a genuinely Agile future. Leaders must proactively identify and rectify these issues, ensuring their Agile implementation is robust and effective.

Having scaled the initial hurdles of Agile adoption, you might think your organization is set for long-term success. Yet, as the technological progress wheel continues, are you prepared to adapt and evolve your Agile practices to stay ahead of the curve?

This chapter invites business leaders to be part of the future of business agility, discussing emerging technologies and ways of working that will profoundly impact business agility and how organizations can stay ahead of the curve. This chapter offers a glimpse into the future of Agile practices and the technologies shaping the business environment, equipping leaders with the foresight and knowledge required to navigate the challenges and seize the opportunities that lie ahead.

We discuss various trends and technologies including Artificial Intelligence (AI), Blockchain, Internet of Things (IoT), data privacy regulations and advances in collaboration tools. We explore their potential applications and implications for organizations, providing a comprehensive understanding of the forces driving change in the business world.

Table 37: Potential Emerging Trends and Technologies Impacting Business Agility

Trend/ Technology	Description	Impact on Business Agility
Artificial Intelligence (AI)	Advanced algorithms and machine learning enable improved decision-making and automation	Enhances data-driven decision-making, automates tasks and improves efficiency
Internet of Things (IoT)	Network of interconnected devices collecting and sharing data in real time	Enables real-time data collection, enhances responsiveness and optimizes processes
Remote Work	Employees working outside the traditional office environment, leveraging technology	Encourages flexibility, adaptability and global collaboration
Sustainability and Social Responsibility	Focus on environmental, social and governance factors in business practices	Drives innovation, long-term resilience and stakeholder satisfaction

Key Trends and Emerging Technologies

Business leaders who understand these trends and technologies are better equipped to make informed decisions, identify growth opportunities and adopt innovative approaches to help their organizations stay ahead. This chapter provides actionable guidance for businesses seeking to capitalize on these innovations to bolster adaptability and agility in a swiftly evolving commercial setting.

Let us explore some key trends and emerging technologies:

Artificial Intelligence and Machine Learning

Artificial Intelligence (AI) and Machine Learning (ML) are revolutionizing how organizations function. These technologies optimize operations and enhance decision-making by automating mundane tasks and predicting outcomes based on data. They can detect patterns and trends in data, providing valuable insights for improving customer experiences. With these advanced tools comes the necessity for leaders to ensure workforce confidence and security. Employees must feel empowered to use these new technologies innovatively that further benefit the organization rather than perceive them as threats to their job security.

For example, American Express uses AI and ML to detect fraudulent transactions and analyse customer spending patterns. By employing these advanced technologies, the company enhanced its fraud detection capabilities and risk management processes. But beyond this, fostering an environment that encourages employees to leverage these tools in their roles further enhances business agility.

Internet of Things

IoT is a network of interconnected devices collecting and transmitting real-time data. It could transform industries such as healthcare, manufacturing and transportation. Harnessing IoT enables organizations to optimize operations, boost productivity and provide superior customer experiences. However, as with AI and ML, supporting the workforce in these transformations is essential, ensuring they can adapt and benefit from these technological advancements.

For example, John Deere, a leading agricultural machinery manufacturer, has harnessed the power of IoT to analyse data generated by its equipment. This has unveiled new growth opportunities. They collect valuable information on machine performance, soil conditions and crop health. The data analysis has led to the development of precision agriculture solutions, enabling farmers to improve crop yields, reduce waste and optimize resource utilization. In this context, it's essential to underline the role of the workers who leverage these technologies, transforming their daily tasks and contributing to the company's innovation.

Embracing these new technologies, underpinned by AI, ML and IoT, allows organizations to boost business agility and rapidly adapt to shifting market conditions and customer needs. However, this journey should be accompanied by proactive workforce empowerment, ensuring that the advent of technology is perceived as an enabler rather than a threat, fostering an environment where innovative use of these tools becomes second nature. In this way, we avoid creating a climate of "technological Ludditism", where workers resent new technology, and instead foster an environment of technological symbiosis where humans and technology harmoniously coexist and thrive.

Remote Work

One crucial aspect of the future of business agility is the burgeoning trend of remote work. In a digitized world, geographical boundaries no longer serve as restrictions in employment. Communication technologies and collaborative tools have opened up a world of possibilities, enabling individuals to work outside traditional office confines. Remote work has profound implications on business agility, fostering flexibility and adaptability and enabling global collaboration.

Remote work encourages flexibility by allowing organizations to tap into a global talent pool unbound by geographical constraints. This allows organizations to build diverse teams with varied perspectives, a critical ingredient for fostering innovation. It allows teams to operate across different time zones, enabling businesses to provide round-the-clock services or support if needed.

Regarding adaptability, remote work promotes a results-oriented work culture, prioritizing outcomes over processes. This resonates with Agile principles, which emphasize delivering value over adhering strictly to plans or procedures. Remote work compels organizations to focus on achieving results and creating value.

Global collaboration is yet another benefit of remote work. It exposes team members to different perspectives and ideas, fostering creativity and innovation. Collaboration tools and technologies enable seamless communication and collaboration among team members, irrespective of their location.

As more organizations embrace remote work, it's crucial to consider the potential challenges by employing these advanced technologies and devise strategies to mitigate them. These challenges may include communication barriers and difficulties in maintaining company culture and work–life balance for remote employees. With conscious effort and strategies, organizations can harness the benefits of remote work to boost their agility and adaptability.

Sustainability and Social Responsibility

As awareness of businesses' environmental and social impacts grows, organizations must consider sustainability and social responsibility in their pursuit of business agility. This involves adopting eco-friendly practices, ensuring ethical supply chains, and addressing the social implications of their operations.

Investors and other stakeholders increasingly consider environmental, social and governance (ESG) factors, making them a growing priority in business operations and decision-making. Company culture plays a crucial role in promoting sustainability and social responsibility. Aligning organizational values with these initiatives and fostering employee engagement contribute to the successful implementation and long-term commitment to sustainable practices. Integrating sustainability and social responsibility into business strategies enhances an organization's brand reputation, creates long-term value for stakeholders and allows for adaptation to the evolving expectations of customers, investors and regulators.

Implementing sustainability and social responsibility initiatives can present organizational challenges, such as balancing short-term financial goals with long-term sustainability objectives, managing supply-chain complexities and dealing with potential greenwashing accusations. It is essential for organizations to carefully plan and execute these initiatives to overcome these challenges and achieve lasting success.

Expanding the Horizon

Having explored the transformative impact of key technological trends and social shifts on business agility, we appreciate that our journey into the future of agility does not stop there. The broader digital landscape is teeming with more game-changing trends and powerful tools that leaders must be aware of.

An organization's agility is not just confined to adopting new ways of working or incorporating disruptive technologies. It is about creating an ecosystem where every function and every strategy is geared towards responsiveness, adaptability and innovation. It's about empowering the organization with the tools and capabilities to navigate the uncertain waters of the future effectively.

To that end, we now turn towards some other equally crucial elements shaping tomorrow's agile enterprises. Let us delve deeper into the importance of data analytics, cloud computing, cybersecurity and other factors contributing to building a resilient, agile and future-ready organization.

Data Analytics

Data analytics is vital to business agility, allowing organizations to make data-driven decisions and pinpoint growth opportunities. Utilizing data analytics tools like Tableau, Looker, QlikView, and Power BI, business intelligence and data visualization tools that enable users to transform complex data into meaningful insights can help optimize operations and improve decision-making capabilities. Data analytics helps organizations identify customer behaviour patterns and trends. This enables them to deliver personalized experiences and heighten customer satisfaction.

For example, the Coca-Cola Company uses data analytics to make informed decisions about its product offerings, marketing strategies and supply-chain management. The company can better understand consumer preferences and optimize its operations by leveraging data.

Adopting robust data analytics strategies is critical for organizations seeking to maintain business agility in a constantly changing world.

Cloud Computing

Cloud computing technology allows businesses to access computing resources on-demand without needing on-premises infrastructure. This technology significantly reduces costs and enhances agility, allowing organizations to scale their operations as needed. Also, it streamlines data storage and enables access from anywhere globally, therefore fostering collaboration and facilitating remote working.

In practice, a leader must know that with cloud computing comes the necessity for meticulous tooling and robust continuous deployment (CD) pipelines. Netflix, a leading streaming service provider, is a prime example. It migrated its entire infrastructure to the cloud to improve scalability, flexibility and reliability. For a leader, the lesson here is that it's not just about the technology but about the capabilities it enables. The agility in managing significant changes in demand, like those Netflix experiences, comes from a well-instrumented cloud environment and top-notch CD practices.

Cybersecurity

In today's digital era, cybersecurity is undeniably a critical priority for businesses relying heavily on technology. Cyber threats are ever-changing, requiring organizations to actively defend their information, systems and intellectual property. Leaders need to acknowledge that cybersecurity isn't just an IT concern; it's a business-wide responsibility that plays a vital role in business adaptability, securing assets while allowing for innovation and adjusting to the digital landscape.

Take IBM, for instance. It developed the IBM X-Force Incident Response and Intelligence Services (IRIS) to help organizations bolster their cybersecurity posture. This is more than just advanced threat intelligence and incident response capabilities. The practical takeaway is the importance of involving all employees in securing data access and spotting vulnerabilities as if protecting their most treasured possessions. Emphasizing best practices, like routine security assessments, employee education and advanced security tools, is crucial. Still, the people-centric security culture truly fortifies an organization's digital foundation.

So, while cloud computing and cybersecurity can augment an organization's agility and adaptability, the key is to view these technologies through leadership and employee engagement. That is how we ensure these tools serve us rather than merely acquiring technology for its own sake.

DevOps Culture

DevOps (a portmanteau of "development" and "operations") encompasses a cultural shift promoting collaboration, automation and continuous delivery, going beyond a simple set of practices. Organizations must invest in proper tools, processes and people to benefit from DevOps. This includes dissolving barriers between development, operations and other teams, adopting Agile approaches and automating key processes. Embracing DevOps allows organizations to enhance software delivery speed and efficiency, reduce costs and boost customer satisfaction. To fully utilize DevOps, leadership should promote a continuous learning environment where teams are encouraged to experiment, iterate and innovate. This leads to faster problem-solving and keeps the organization on the cutting edge of technology and market demands.

Human-Centred Design

Human-centred design (HCD) is a problem-solving strategy prioritizing users in the design process. HCD involves grasping user needs, preferences and feedback to create products and services that are intuitive, user-friendly and effective. Also, HCD nurtures empathy and understanding among employees and stakeholders, which is vital for successful collaboration and innovation. Organizations prioritizing user experience can more effectively cater to customer needs, increasing satisfaction and loyalty. HCD is a key driver of business adaptability, helping organizations efficiently develop and iterate on products and services that meet customers' evolving needs. Embedding HCD principles in design processes fosters innovation, experimentation and adaptation, which is essential for outpacing competitors in a changing business environment.

Customer-Centricity

Customer-centricity surpasses merely considering customer feedback in product development. It requires a deep understanding of customer needs, preferences and challenges, using this knowledge to guide business strategies and operations. Customer journey mapping is a valuable tool for visualizing and understanding customer experiences, enabling organizations to create more effective and customer-focused products or services. Building a customer-centric culture throughout the organization, from top executives to frontline employees, is essential. Prioritizing a customer-centric approach bolsters long-term customer loyalty, competitive edge and commercial expansion. Moreover, customer-centricity involves leveraging analytics and data insights to proactively solve customer issues even before they are aware they have them. In an age where customer preferences evolve at the speed of light, keeping a customer-centric ethos at the forefront of business decisions can be the difference between lagging behind and leading the pack.

The Future of Work and Remote Collaboration

The future of work is increasingly digital and dispersed, with remote collaboration becoming a vital aspect of business adaptability. As organizations adopt remote collaboration tools, they enjoy increased flexibility, reduced overhead costs and a wider talent pool. Instruments such as video conferencing, project management platforms and communication apps facilitate seamless interaction among team members, regardless of location. Organizations must foster a strong company culture to support remote work effectively and adapt their management and communication styles to accommodate remote employees. Leveraging these tools and nurturing a remote-friendly culture enables organizations to develop a more agile and adaptable workforce. This is crucial for staying ahead in a fast-changing business environment.

Business Collaboration and Partnerships

The business world is increasingly interconnected, highlighting the significance of collaboration and partnerships. Robust relationships with external partners encompassing suppliers, vendors and competitors can augment business agility by providing access to novel technology, resources and expertise. Open innovation and co-creation play a significant role in driving business agility.

For example, BMW, a leading automotive manufacturer, partnered with Local Motors, a smaller automotive company, to launch the Urban Driving Experience Challenge. This collaboration aimed to crowdsource ideas for future urban driving concepts. The challenge allowed BMW to tap into the creativity and expertise of a vast community of designers, engineers and enthusiasts, resulting in innovative vehicle designs and features that cater to urban mobility needs.

These approaches allow organizations to tap into external knowledge and resources, accelerating innovation and adaptability. Engaging with industry colleagues and utilizing knowledge-sharing platforms informs organizations about recent trends and best practices. Embracing collaboration and nurturing strategic partnerships allows businesses to access a broader resource and expertise pool, enabling them to adjust swiftly to market changes and customer demands.

Diversity and Inclusion

Promotion of diversity and inclusion in the global business environment is imperative for sustaining competitiveness. A diverse workforce provides various perspectives, experiences and ideas, leading to better problem-solving, innovation and decision-making. Monitoring and measuring the success of diversity and inclusion initiatives is crucial.

Organizations must track key performance indicators (KPIs) such as employee engagement, retention rates and diversity representation in leadership positions to measure the success of diversity and inclusion initiatives. Regularly monitoring these metrics enables continuous improvement and helps ensure the effectiveness of implemented strategies. Organizations that value diversity and inclusion can attract and keep top talent while enhancing business agility. This requires inclusive hiring practices, diversity and inclusion training and a supportive company culture that appreciates diverse perspectives and equal employment opportunities. Prioritizing diversity and inclusion strengthens agility and promotes a more fair and just society.

Organizational Culture

The future of business agility isn't limited to adopting new technologies and methodologies but also involves nurturing an organizational culture that welcomes change and encourages continuous improvement. A culture that embraces agility empowers employees to swiftly adapt to fresh challenges, take calculated risks and glean learning from setbacks. Organizations need to emphasize employee empowerment, open communication and collaboration. Transparency and trust are critical for fostering an Agile culture, as they promote open communication and collaboration. Fostering a growth mindset and stimulating experimentation allows organizations to create a resilient and adaptive workforce ready to face future uncertainties.

Continuous Learning

The concept of continuous learning extends beyond merely upskilling employees or providing training opportunities. It entails cultivating a learning culture that motivates employees to assume responsibility for their development and pursue learning and growth opportunities. This demands that leaders give regular feedback, acknowledge and reward learning and promote a growth mindset. Creating a safe environment where employees feel comfortable sharing their ideas, asking questions and making mistakes is essential for fostering a culture of learning and growth. Organizations must supply the tools, resources and support for continuous learning. Organizations can develop a more adaptable and innovative workforce prepared for future uncertainties by prioritizing continuous learning.

Digital Transformation

Digital transformation is an ongoing journey requiring constant investment, iteration and experimentation. Organizations must establish their digital objectives, including AI/ML, blockchain, IoT, data privacy and advances in collaboration tools, to excel in digital transformation. This is followed by developing a road map outlining the steps to achieve those goals. This entails embracing new technologies, building digital capabilities and investing in the right people and processes.

The growing importance of data privacy regulations, such as GDPR, significantly impacts digital transformation efforts. Organizations must adapt their strategies and processes to comply with these regulations, ensuring data protection and privacy for their customers and employees. Organizations adopting digital transformation can establish a more agile and resilient business, better positioned to compete in a fast-changing marketplace.

Resilience and Adaptability

Navigating through an increasingly unpredictable and uncertain business environment demands a heightened emphasis on the principles of resilience and adaptability. An organization's capacity to quickly recover from disruptions, adapt to new circumstances and maintain continuity of operations defines its resilience. Adaptability is the ability to alter course swiftly in response to changing market trends, customer needs or internal shifts.

For instance, Airbnb demonstrated notable resilience and adaptability during the COVID-19 pandemic when international travel restrictions profoundly impacted their business operations. They swiftly pivoted to offer virtual experiences and longer-term stays, therefore successfully navigating through the crisis. Hence, by cultivating resilience and adaptability, organizations can effectively mitigate risks, seize opportunities and maintain business agility.

Risks and Opportunities

Besides the key trends and emerging technologies mentioned above, it is essential to consider the potential risks and opportunities associated with the future of business agility. Table 38 outlines several potential scenarios and their implications for organizations.

Table 38: Future Scenarios for Business Agility

Potential Future Scenario	Risks	Opportunities	Implications for Organizations
Increasing Global Competition	Losing market share	Expansion into new markets	Need for agile strategies to stay competitive
Rapid Technological Advancements	Falling behind industry trends	Adopting cutting-edge technology	Continuous learning and upskilling of employees
Growing Focus on Sustainability	Reputational damage	Enhanced brand image	Integration of sustainability in Agile practices

Remote and Hybrid Work Environments	Communication breakdowns	Increased access to global talent	Adapting Agile practices for distributed teams
Regulatory Changes	Non-compliance penalties	Staying ahead of industry standards	Agility in adapting to new regulations

Business agility constantly evolves, and organizations seeking a competitive edge must stay informed about new developments and innovations. Incorporating these emerging trends and technologies into strategies and operations enables organizations to enhance their business agility and adapt rapidly to market changes and customer needs.

However, organizations must also know the challenges associated with digital transformation. As previously discussed, these may include resistance to change, integration of legacy systems, cybersecurity concerns and the need for additional skill sets within the workforce. Addressing these challenges proactively is crucial for successfully implementing digital transformation initiatives.

Addressing the Real Issues for a Sustainable Agile Future

As we gaze into the future of business agility, let's be candid – the path is not without its pitfalls. However, the common thread among organizations that master agility is their willingness to tackle the real issues head-on.

It's not enough to simply adopt Agile practices and hope for transformation. It's the culture, the structure, the very fabric of your organization that needs to be attuned to agility. Addressing these issues isn't just a necessity; it's the cornerstone of sustainable business agility.

Business Agility Maturity

The concept of this Agile philosophy that we have discussed throughout is not a fixed framework but a dynamic growth journey for teams and organizations. It is a road map, constantly evolving and responding to the organization's terrain. To distil it simply, it's the process of evolving our Agile practices to better align with the organization's strategic goals. It's akin to tuning a musical instrument, always aiming for that perfect harmony between Agile practices and the strategic symphony of the organization.

Much like tiers in a building, business agility maturity involves ascending levels of Agile sophistication. Each ascending level is like unlocking a new level of potential, harnessing more of the transformative power of Agile. At each stage, the organization reaps more substantial benefits from its Agile practices, continually refining them to increase value delivery. With each refinement, the organization extracts more value and squeezes more benefits out of its Agile practices – it's about getting better at getting better. It's a multi-dimensional approach, where teams choose one aspect to improve at a time, allowing for manageable, incremental progress rather than overwhelming transformation. This is not about overnight revolution but sustainable evolution, making consistent strides towards a more Agile future.

Business agility maturity must be intertwined into the organization's work rhythm, regularly reassessed and tweaked to foster ongoing improvement. It must be as routine as the daily stand-up, with a regular rhythm to the organizational heartbeat. This continuous refinement of Agile practices is the cornerstone of future business agility. As we move into the future, this ability to continually refine and improve is an added advantage and a fundamental requirement for business survival and success.

The Evolution of Agile

As we delve into the future of business agility, we must appreciate the current trends shaping this domain. These trends, dynamic and transformative in nature, aren't just passing waves; they herald the dawn of a new era of business operation. While Agile approaches were initially developed for software development, their relevance and applicability have been recognized across various sectors. Not merely restricted to the tech industry, Agile has crossed boundaries, being embraced by sectors as diverse as finance, healthcare and education. This cross-industry adoption of Agile principles is an encouraging trend that is expected to continue.

With technological advancements like AI and ML, as previously discussed, becoming pivotal in business operations, Agile practices will inevitably intertwine with these tech giants. The Agile of tomorrow might be enhanced with predictive analysis, automating backlog prioritization based on real-time market shifts or even customer sentiment analysis, ensuring even faster pivots.

The World Economic Forum, the global consortium of economic thought leaders, also recognizes agility as a critical driver for the future. In their eyes, agility is not a luxury but a necessity in the face of a rapidly evolving global economy. Their 2020 Future of Jobs report lists "agility" among the top skills needed for the future of work. This significance should not be understated – agility is considered a core competency for individuals and organizations. This implies a significant push towards agility not just at the organizational level but also at the individual level.

And it's not just about processes and methodologies; the next phase for Agile might centre on building an innate, almost intuitive Agile mindset for individuals. A future where agility is not a practice but an instinct deeply embedded into an organization's DNA and its employees. Training and development will shift from merely teaching Agile practices to nurturing an Agile psyche.

Agile will also likely play an integral role in digital transformation as we continue our journey into the digital age. The digital age is synonymous with change, a realm Agile knows only too well. With its iterative, flexible approach, Agile is the guiding star in the chaos of digital environment. Businesses must adapt and respond quickly to an ever-changing digital environment. Agile methodologies will remain instrumental in achieving this necessary adaptability.

Organizations will move further away from pre-packaged Agile frameworks and towards creating their own unique ways of working (WoW). This bespoke approach to Agile is a testament to its inherent flexibility – the capability of Agile to mould itself to fit the unique requirements and ethos of your organization. Embracing Agile means adopting a different approach to running your businesses, not just switching to a unique brand of management method.

As environmental and social governance (ESG) factors become increasingly pivotal in business operations and reporting, future Agile methodologies might deeply integrate these elements. Imagine Agile teams regularly prioritizing tasks based on business value, environmental impact, or societal value.

Experts predict a more holistic adoption of Agile principles in the future. Akin to a benevolent contagion, Agile principles will permeate every nook and corner of an organization. Rather than being confined to project management or software development, as discussed in Chapter 6, Agile principles will extend to all areas of an organization, from people teams to marketing and beyond, creating truly Agile organizations.

All these trends mentioned throughout the chapter point towards an exciting future where Agile principles will enable businesses to navigate an increasingly volatile, uncertain, complex and ambiguous (VUCA) world. While daunting to some, this future is an exciting challenge for those armed with Agile principles and practices. Agile is not just a toolkit for survival but a blueprint for thriving in a VUCA world.

As we consider the future, the term "Hyper Agility" emerges as a compelling descriptor for the next wave of Agile evolution. Far from merely intensifying current Agile principles, Hyper Agility suggests a metamorphosis, redefining agility to incorporate instantaneous adaptability supported by state-of-the-art technology. This form of agility aims for an unparalleled pace of change, serving as a beacon for organizations striving to excel in a world where the only constant is change.

CLEAR Lens for "The Future of Business Agility"

We can apply all five CLEAR Model® principles to The Future of Business Agility:

Culture: The pivotal role of Culture will continue to shape the future of business agility. Environments that value agility encourage continuous learning, and championing collaboration will help define business agility. Nurturing an Agile culture will drive innovation and maintain resilience as organizations evolve.

Leadership: Agile Leadership, imbued with the CLEAR principles, will continue to chart the course for the future of business agility. Leaders will set the strategic direction, guiding their organizations through the complexities and uncertainties of the future. Their foresight, dedication and capacity to motivate will remain at the heart of successful Agile approaches to transformation.

Execution: The principle of Execution will continue to be a critical element as Agile strategies are implemented. Successful execution ensures that the agility theory translates into a tangible reality, delivering results and enhancing business value. The ability to execute Agile approaches effectively will be a key factor in sustaining business agility in a continuously changing environment.

Adaptability: As the business environment transforms rapidly, the principle of Adaptability will gain even more significance. Agile organizations must expect and adjust their strategies to maintain their leading edge. This principle will continue to be a key driver of business agility, enabling organizations to thrive amidst uncertainty.

Responsiveness: As we traverse the path toward the future of business agility, the principle of Responsiveness cements itself as a fundamental pillar. Navigating the waves of evolving trends, advancing technologies and changing customer demands requires organizations to exhibit a rapid and assertive response mechanism. Hence, the ability to act swiftly and decisively is not just a requirement but a game-changer, helping businesses keep pace in the race.

Reflection Prompts

1. Reflect on the emerging trends and technologies that could impact your organization. How can your organization maintain its agility in the face of these changes?

2. How can you, as a leader, continue to develop your Agile skills and knowledge to support your organization's ongoing Agile journey?

Case Study: Google and Amazon – Leveraging Emerging Technologies for Agility and Innovation

In this case study, we examine how Google and Amazon harness the power of emerging technologies to drive business agility and foster innovation.

As global technology giants, Google and Amazon have demonstrated how embracing emerging technologies can enhance business agility and foster innovation. This case study will explore their approaches to integrating these innovations and discuss the role of organizational culture and leadership in driving their success.

Google, known for its search engine and diverse product offerings, has effectively leveraged AI and ML to automate many Agile processes. Doing so has allowed teams to focus on high-value tasks, increasing efficiency and enabling rapid response to market changes. This continuous improvement mindset has allowed Google to stay ahead of the competition.

Google's innovative approach, rooted deeply in its organizational culture, has made it a leader in applying emerging technologies. Google's famous "20% time" policy encourages employees to spend one-fifth of their working hours on passion projects, a significant driver of innovation and agility. The company has fostered a culture that values experimentation and risk-taking. In addition, AI and ML have been applied in various sectors, including environmental efforts like forecasting floods and wildlife conservation, demonstrating Google's commitment to using AI for social good. Google also provides fully managed AI services through Google Cloud, allowing businesses to leverage AI for innovation and customer experience enhancement.

Amazon, the world's largest online retailer, has pioneered cloud computing services with its Amazon Web Services (AWS) division. AWS offers various innovative services to businesses, including ML,

---

IoT and data analytics solutions. These services enable organizations to enhance their agility by leveraging the latest technologies and tools, ultimately improving their ability to adapt to market changes and maintain a competitive edge.

Amazon's innovative spirit is clear in the Amazon Web Services (AWS) division, which constantly develops and releases new services and features to cater to the evolving needs of businesses. AWS has become a driving force in the cloud computing landscape, pushing the boundaries of innovation and enabling clients to adopt innovative technologies, fostering agility and resilience in changing market conditions.

Amazon's culture promotes constant innovation and views failure as a necessary aspect of this process. The company's approach involves a willingness to fail and learn from these failures, constantly iterating based on customer feedback. Every employee, regardless of their role, is encouraged to innovate and focus on customer needs. This approach has enabled Amazon to quickly adapt and innovate across its various business functions.

Both organizational culture and visionary leadership are critical for successfully adopting and integrating emerging technologies, emphasizing a culture of experimentation, learning from failures and adaptability. Companies like Google and Amazon have demonstrated this by continuously pioneering new technologies to maintain a competitive edge.

Table 39: Google vs. Amazon Harnessing Emerging Technologies for Business Agility

Aspect	Google	Amazon
Technology	– AI and ML	– Blockchain
Application	– Automating Agile processes	– Supply-chain management
Benefits	– Increased efficiency – Rapid response to market changes	– Enhanced transparency – Security and efficiency – Swift adaptation to market shifts
Organizational Culture	– Experimentation – Learning from failures – Adaptability	– Experimentation – Learning from failures – Adaptability

This forward-thinking approach has permeated their organizations, creating a culture that values innovation, experimentation and adaptability, ultimately contributing to their ongoing success in leveraging emerging technologies for business agility and innovation.

Key Takeaways from the Case Study

1. **Embrace emerging technologies** – Google and Amazon demonstrate the importance of staying informed about new trends and technologies and proactively integrating them into their strategies and operations to drive business agility and innovation.
2. **Foster a culture of adaptability and continuous learning** – Encouraging adaptability, continuous learning and resilience within the organization enables companies to stay at the forefront and maintain a competitive edge in a fast-changing business environment.
3. **Leverage technology for process improvement** – Utilizing technologies such as AI, blockchain and IoT can enhance organizational processes and operations, allowing companies to swiftly adapt to market changes and deliver exceptional value to their customers.

The Google and Amazon case study highlights emerging technologies' vital role in shaping the future of business agility. Organizations can enhance adaptability, encourage continuous learning and foster resilience by staying informed about these developments and proactively integrating them into their strategies and operations.

Business leaders must remain vigilant in staying informed about these developments and integrate them into their organizations' strategies and operations. Organizations can maintain a competitive edge in an increasingly complex and fast-changing business environment by fostering a culture of adaptability, continuous learning and resilience.

In the final chapter, we delved into the future of business agility, examining upcoming trends and technologies poised to influence it significantly. The growing adoption of AI and ML, the surge of remote work and the ongoing expansion of cloud computing all highlight the swift transformation of the business arena. Organizations that proactively expect these shifts and adopt innovative tools and methodologies can maintain agility and responsiveness to customer demands in a perpetually changing environment. The aim has been to offer valuable insights, tactics and practical examples to help create an Agile enterprise capable of flourishing in the current high-speed business atmosphere.

> Throughout this book, we have covered the various aspects of business agility, from its definition and importance to the trends shaping its future. We have looked at the role of leadership and culture in fostering agility and examined how businesses can leverage emerging technologies to stay ahead in a fast-changing market. The case studies provided practical insights into how leading companies embrace agility, providing valuable lessons for other organizations. As we look to the future, business agility will continue to be a critical factor for success in the digital age.

Exercise: Preparing for the Future of Business Agility

As we contemplate the future of business agility, let us engage with some critical thinking exercises. Reflect on your organization's current state, and consider the following steps to expect and adapt to emerging trends, technologies and practices. Your organization can maintain its competitive edge and continue to deliver value in a rapidly changing market by proactively preparing for the future.

Consider the following steps to future-proof your organization:

1. **Embrace continuous learning** – Encourage your organization to stay informed about emerging trends, technologies and practices, fostering a mindset of ongoing growth and innovation. Provide opportunities for upskilling, training and knowledge-sharing to keep your teams at the forefront of industry developments.
2. **Invest in digital transformation** – Leverage the latest tools, platforms and technologies to enable more efficient, Agile ways of working. Evaluate your current systems and processes to identify opportunities for improvement and explore innovative solutions that drive digital transformation.
3. **Cultivate a culture of innovation** – Foster an environment where experimentation and calculated risk-taking are encouraged, and employees are empowered to develop new ideas and solutions. Recognize and reward creativity and provide resources and support for developing innovative projects.
4. **Build adaptive and resilient teams** – Equip your teams with the skills, knowledge and resources to navigate change and uncertainty effectively. Implement Agile team structures and provide ongoing coaching to ensure your teams can respond rapidly to shifting market conditions and customer needs.
5. **Stay focused on customer value** – Continually prioritize customer needs and expectations, ensuring your organization remains relevant and compet-

itive in a rapidly changing market. Regularly gather customer feedback to inform decision-making, product development and service delivery.

6. **Foster collaboration and partnerships** – Develop strategic partnerships and alliances to drive innovation and growth. Collaborate with other organizations, industry experts and thought leaders to learn from their experiences and gain fresh perspectives on your own business challenges.

7. **Monitor and adapt to regulatory changes** – Stay informed about changes in regulations, standards and best practices that may impact your industry. Adopt a proactive approach to compliance, ensuring your organization remains responsive and adaptable to evolving legal and regulatory requirements.

Integrating these steps into your organizational strategy allows you to remain Agile and prepared for the future of business agility. Continuously assess and refine your approach, ensuring your organization stays adaptable, innovative and well positioned to capitalize on new opportunities.

Chapter Summary

In this chapter, we looked at the trends and emerging technologies that will impact business agility in the future and explored how organizations can stay ahead of the curve. We examined various technologies, including AI, ML, IoT, data privacy regulations and advances in collaboration tools, and discussed how companies are already exploring leveraging these technologies to drive agility and innovation. We also provided practical guidance on preparing your organization for the future of business agility and looked at real-world examples of companies like Google and Amazon that are already leading the way in this area.

Further Readings and Resources

1. Book: *Project to Product: How to Survive and Thrive in the Age of Digital Disruption with the Flow Framework,* by Mik Kersten, 2018, IT Revolution Press.

2. Book: *The Age of Agile: How Smart Companies Are Transforming the Way Work Gets Done,* by Stephen Denning, 2018, Amaryllis.

3. Website: Business Agility Conference – www.businessagilityconference.com

Conclusion

In this book, we have explored the concepts, techniques and real-life examples of business agility, demonstrating how organizations can adopt agility to stay ahead, innovate and thrive in a changing, competitive environment. We have seen how business agility enables companies to deliver value to clients, enhance their processes and swiftly adapt to shifting market conditions with agility.

In our exploration, we have addressed the key aspects of business agility, including its necessity, underlying principles, approaches, impact on leadership, cultural implications, team dynamics, planning, execution, assessment, scaling, common challenges and future trends. Drawing upon real-world examples, we've illuminated the practical applications and benefits of Agile practices, providing actionable insights for organizations ready to embark on their Agile journey.

Throughout our discussion, real-world examples and case studies have been used to clarify the concepts and practices of business agility, highlighting how prominent companies have leveraged agility for competitive advantage. We have also explained essential terms, practical tips and actionable insights for organizations eager to adopt business agility.

In conclusion, business agility has evolved from being an optional approach to an indispensable necessity for organizations aiming to flourish in the highly competitive and constantly shifting commercial environment. Organizations adopting an Agile mindset, attitude, approaches and practices can become more adaptive, inventive and competitive, fostering a culture of ongoing learning and enhancement.

This book has provided valuable insights and motivation for organizations and individuals striving to lead the Agile transformation and establish an Agile organization.

We appreciate your time reading this book and wish you great success on your journey towards business agility.

Epilogue

The Phoenix Enterprise: A Tale of Transformation Through Business Agility

In a bustling city stood the towering headquarters of Phoenix Corp., a brand that had led its industry for decades. Its prowess was unmatched, its reputation renowned. Yet, in the underbelly of its operations, a storm was brewing, masked by its present glories.

The once-unchallenged Phoenix Corp. began to see the silhouettes of competitors on the horizon, not emerging from colossal corporations but nimble start-ups, tapping into the heartbeat of the modern consumer. The likes of Blockbuster flashed before their leadership's eyes. No longer was the past a guarantee of the future.

The first ripples of alarm were felt when a competitor, StellarTech, unveiled an innovative product. The market went berserk. Overnight, customer expectations transformed. Phoenix's age-old methodologies and operations seemed paralysed, unable to keep up with this new reality. The headlines whispered of the "fall of a giant". Desperation gripped Phoenix's corridors.

It was Sarah, an executive who had recently attended a conference on "Business Agility", who saw a glimmer of hope. Armed with insights from the book, *Clearly Agile: A Leadership Guide to Business Agility*, she presented a lifeline to the board.

To many, Agile was just a tech trend. The board was sceptical. But Sarah painted a vivid picture. Agile, she explained, wasn't just about tech. It was the compass to navigate treacherous business waters, a transformative mindset and attitude that could unshackle Phoenix from its self-imposed chains. The board took a leap of faith.

Phoenix's transformation began with reimagining leadership. They embraced lessons about vision realignment, being proactive, staying ahead of changes and steering the company with agility.

A cultural metamorphosis was crucial. Openness to change, experimentation and innovation became the lifeblood of Phoenix Corp. Feedback loops with customers were formed. When a new feature was demanded, Phoenix was swift to integrate it.

Scaling this agility was no small feat for a mammoth like Phoenix. They tapped into ways of working that ensured they remained as agile as smaller, more nimble competitors.

However, the path wasn't smooth. Resistance emerged, especially from veterans rooted in old business processes. But these challenges were stepping stones. By fostering a culture of collaboration and learning, the reluctant were slowly converted into Agile champions.

Agile planning and execution became Phoenix's North Star. They began to not only weather business storms but leverage them, uncovering opportunities in adversity. They measured their agility, ensuring it became a tangible advantage.

Months turned into years. Phoenix Corp., once on the brink of oblivion, emerged as a beacon of business agility. As competitors scrambled to react to market changes, Phoenix was already two steps ahead, capitalizing on them. And when new technological trends emerged, Phoenix was swift to adapt and integrate.

The final test came when another tech giant, InnovTech, challenged Phoenix's dominance. But Phoenix, now Agile to its core, was unfazed. They responded with agility, outpacing InnovTech at every turn, constantly innovating and listening intently to their customers. The market watched in awe as Phoenix not only defended its position but surged ahead, solidifying its legacy for the digital age.

From the ashes of its former self, Phoenix Corp. had truly risen, embodying the principles of business agility. Their tale was not just of survival but of rejuvenation, proving that with the right mindset, attitude and tools, even giants can dance to the ever-evolving beats of the business world.

Appendix A – Glossary

A/B Testing – A method of comparing two product or feature versions to determine which performs better based on user feedback or predefined metrics.

Adaptability Quotient (AQ) – A measure of how well an individual or organization can adapt to change. It complements IQ and EQ in assessing intelligence and skills.

Agile Attitude – The disposition or sentiment towards the principles of Agile, which may be nurtured and influenced but not strictly imposed. An attitude can be collective and can set the tone for the organization's approach to Agile.

Agile Coaching – A role that involves guiding and mentoring individuals and teams in adopting and implementing Agile principles and practices, helping them achieve higher levels of performance and adaptability.

Agile Culture – A culture that emphasizes flexibility, collaboration, continuous improvement and rapid feedback. An Agile culture is essential for successfully implementing Agile methodologies and frameworks.

Agile Governance – Establishing clear guidelines and policies for adopting Agile methodologies and frameworks and monitoring their implementation throughout the organization.

Agile Methodologies – A set of iterative and incremental approaches to software development and project management that emphasizes flexibility, collaboration and rapid feedback.

Agile Metrics – Quantitative measures used to track and assess the progress, performance and success of Agile projects and teams.

Agile Mindset – A set of attitudes and values that emphasize flexibility, collaboration, customer focus and continuous improvement. An Agile mindset is essential for successfully implementing Agile methodologies and frameworks.

Agile Teams – Teams that are cross-functional, self-organizing and empowered to make decisions and take ownership of their work. Agile teams are essential for successfully implementing Agile methodologies and frameworks.

Agile Transformation – The process of transitioning an organization from traditional project management methodologies to Agile approaches, involving changes in culture, processes and mindset.

Beyond Budgeting – A management strategy that seeks to replace traditional budgeting processes with more flexible, adaptive planning methods that are better suited for today's dynamic business environment.

Business Agility – The ability of an organization to adapt rapidly and cost-effectively in response to changes in the business environment. This includes innovating quickly, responding to customer needs and staying ahead of competitors.

Business Outcomes – The tangible or intangible results stemming from actions or decisions taken within a business context. In the realm of business agility, outcomes often refer to the achieved results from adopting specific approaches or tools.

Change Management – The process of planning, implementing and monitoring organizational changes to achieve successful outcomes and minimize the negative impacts of change on employees and stakeholders.

Cloud-based Infrastructure – Computing infrastructure hosted and managed remotely, usually by a third-party provider, and accessed over the internet.

Continuous Deployment – A software development practice that automates the release of software changes to production, ensuring faster, more reliable software delivery.

Continuous Integration – A software development practice that integrates code changes frequently, allowing for early detection and resolution of integration issues.

Continuous Integration and Continuous Deployment (CI/CD) – A set of practices designed to continually integrate code changes and deploy them to a production system automatically.

Continuous Learning and Improvement – A culture of ongoing learning and experimentation that emphasizes the identification and elimination of waste and the pursuit of continuous improvement in processes and practices.

Cross-functional Team – A team composed of members with diverse skills and expertise working together on a project or initiative to achieve a common goal.

Customer Relationship Management (CRM) – A technology for managing a company's interactions with current and potential customers. It involves using data analysis about customers' history to improve business relationships.

Customer Satisfaction – The degree to which customers are satisfied with the products or services provided by an organization.

Cycle Time – The time it takes to complete one process iteration, from start to finish.

Daily Stand-up – A brief meeting where team members provide updates on their progress and discuss any obstacles they face.

DevOps – A set of practices that combines software development (Dev) and information technology operations (Ops) to enable faster, more reliable software releases.

Digital Transformation – The integration of digital technologies into all aspects of an organization, leading to fundamental changes in how it operates and delivers value to its customers.

Distributed Teams – Teams that work together across different geographical locations, often relying on digital tools and remote collaboration practices.

DORA Metrics – A set of key performance indicators related to software development, including deployment frequency and lead time. They are used to measure the effectiveness of DevOps practices.

Feature Toggles – A technique for enabling or disabling specific features in a software application, allowing teams to test and release features incrementally and safely.

Holacracy – An organizational structure that replaces traditional hierarchies with a system of self-organizing teams. It aims to distribute authority and achieve agile governance.

Holistic Agile Approach – An approach that looks at Agile adoption not just in isolated departments or teams but across the entire organization, ensuring that Agile approaches and principles are consistently applied, and benefits are optimized.

Innovation – The development and implementation of new ideas, products or processes that create value for an organization and its customers.

Kanban – A system for visualizing and managing work that emphasizes limiting work in progress and focusing on continuous flow.

Lead Time – The time it takes to complete a project, from the initial request to the delivery of the final product.

Leadership in Business Agility – The ability of leaders to create a culture of agility within their organization and support adopting and implementing Agile approaches throughout the company.

Lean – A set of principles and practices for optimizing processes and reducing waste in production and other business operations.

Legacy Methodologies – Traditional or older methods and systems that may not align with Agile principles but persist within organizations due to their historical presence.

Mean Time To Recover (MTTR) – The average time it takes to restore a system or application after a failure. Lower MTTR is generally seen as an indicator of efficient incident response.

Minimum Viable Product (MVP) – A version of a product with just enough features to be released to early adopters, allowing for the collection of valuable user feedback to guide further development.

Net Promoter Score (NPS) – A customer loyalty metric that measures the willingness of customers to recommend a company's product or services. It's calculated based on responses to a single question.

Objectives and Key Results (OKRs) – A framework for setting and tracking goals and objectives that involves setting specific, measurable, achievable, relevant and time-bound (SMART) objectives and measuring progress towards those objectives through key results.

Organizational Structure – How an organization is designed and structured, including how departments and teams are organized, and decisions are made.

Outcomes Over Outputs – A principle that emphasizes achieving meaningful results (outcomes) rather than just completing tasks or producing deliverables (outputs). In Agile contexts, it highlights the importance of delivering genuine value.

Portfolio Management – The alignment of an organization's investments with its strategic goals and objectives.

Product Backlog – A prioritized list of features or items a development team works on during an Agile project.

Program Management – The process of managing a set of related projects in a coordinated way to deliver benefits that cannot be achieved by managing them individually.

Retrospective – A meeting at the end of each sprint in which the development team reflect on their performance and identifies areas for improvement.

Return on Investment (ROI) – A financial metric that is widely used to measure the likelihood of gaining a return from an investment. It calculates the ratio between net profit and the cost of investment.

SAAS (Software as a Service) Solutions – Cloud-based software applications that are provided to users over the internet. Their roll-out in organizations should be aligned with overall business objectives and be in harmony with other systems to avoid redundancies or workarounds.

Scaling Agile – Expanding Agile practices and principles across multiple teams, departments or the entire organization to improve collaboration, coordination and overall performance.

Scrum – A framework for implementing Agile approaches that emphasizes self-organizing teams and iterative development cycles called sprints.

Site Reliability Engineering (SRE) – A discipline that incorporates aspects of software engineering and applies them to infrastructure and operations problems. It aims for reliable, scalable and highly available services.

Sprint or Iteration – A time-boxed period of development during which a development team works to complete a set of items from the product backlog.

Sprint Review – A meeting at the end of each sprint where the development team demonstrate their work and gather stakeholder feedback.

System Integration – The process of ensuring different software systems, platforms and processes work together seamlessly. For businesses adopting multiple SAAS solutions, effective system integration is critical to avoid inefficiencies and achieve the desired outcomes.

Time-boxing – A technique for managing time by allocating a fixed amount of time to a specific activity, task or goal, ensuring that deadlines and priorities are met.

Unified Process – A software development framework that integrates various best practices in an iterative and incremental manner. It focuses on collaboration and rich architecture.

User Stories – A brief, informal description of a feature or functionality from an end-user's perspective, used to guide the development process and ensure that the product meets user needs and expectations.

Value Stream Mapping – A visualization tool used to analyse and optimize the flow of materials and information through a process, identifying areas of waste and opportunities for improvement.

Velocity – A measure of the amount of work a team can complete within a given time period, often used to predict the team's ability to deliver future work.

Waterfall Methodology – A traditional project management approach that involves completing each project phase sequentially before moving on to the next phase, in contrast to Agile approaches that emphasize iterative and incremental progress.

Work In Progress (WIP) – The number of tasks or features actively being worked on by a team at any given time, often limited to ensure focus and maintain a steady flow of work.

Workarounds – Temporary solutions to overcome limitations or issues in a system or process. Often a result of non-holistic approaches, leading to inefficiencies in the longer term.

Appendix B – References

5 Lessons Agile Teams Can Learn from Netflix. Retrieved from https://dzone.com/articles/5-lessons-agile-teams-can-learn-from-netflix

A Detailed Look at the Spotify Model for Scaling Agile. Retrieved from https://blog.gitscrum.com/a-detailed-look-at-the-spotify-model-for-scaling-agile/

A Holistic Approach to Scaling Agile at Salesforce. Retrieved from https://www.slideshare.net/sgreene/agile-2010-conference-a-holistic-approach-to-scaling-agile-at-salesforce

Adams, T. (2018). *Agile Leadership: A Leader's Guide to Orchestrating Agile Strategy, Product Quality, and IT Governance.* Apress.

Adkins, L. (2010). *Coaching Agile Teams: A Companion for ScrumMasters, Agile Coaches, and Project Managers in Transition.* Addison-Wesley Professional.

Agile Alliance. (n.d.). Actionable Metrics at Siemens Health Services. Retrieved from https://www.agilealliance.org/resources/experience-reports/actionable-metrics-siemens-health-services/

Agile Alliance. (n.d.). Agile Execution. Retrieved from https://www.agilealliance.org/agile101/

Agile Alliance. (n.d.). Agile Planning & Project Management. Retrieved from https://www.agilealliance.org/agile101/agile-basics/agile-planning-project-management/

Agile Alliance. (n.d.). Characteristics of Agile Organizations. Retrieved from https://www.agilealliance.org/characteristics-of-agile-organizations/

Agile Alliance. (n.d.). Embracing the Agile Mindset for Organizational Change. Retrieved from https://www.agilealliance.org/resources/experience-reports/embracing-agile-mindset-for-organizational-change/

Agile Alliance. (n.d.). How to Make the Whole Organization Agile. Retrieved from https://www.agilealliance.org/resources/videos/how-to-make-the-whole-organization-agile/

Agile Alliance. (n.d.). The Power of Three: The Journey of an Agile Leadership Team. Retrieved from https://www.agilealliance.org/resources/experience-reports/the-power-of-three-the-journey-of-an-agile-leadership-team/

Agile Alliance. (n.d.). What is Business Agility. Retrieved from https://www.agilealliance.org/agile101/

Agile Alliance. (n.d.). You Have to Say More There: Effective Communication in a Distributed Agile Team. Retrieved from https://www.agilealliance.org/resources/experience-reports/effective-communication-in-a-distributed-agile-team/

Agile Business Consortium. (n.d.). Retrieved from https://www.agilebusiness.org/

Agile Jottings. (2017). The 10 Core Values of Zappos. Retrieved from https://srinathramakrishnan.wordpress.com/2017/03/24/the-10-core-values-of-zappos/

All About Google Machine Learning and AI. Retrieved from https://intersog.com/blog/learn-about-google-machine-learning-and-ai/

Amabile, T. M. & Kramer, S. J. (2011). The Power of Small Wins. *Harvard Business Review*. Retrieved from https://hbr.org/2011/05/the-power-of-small-wins

Amazon. (n.d.). Leadership Principles. Retrieved from https://www.amazon.jobs/content/en/our-workplace/leadership-principles

Amazon Staff. (2022). What do Each of Amazon's Leadership Principles Really Mean? Retrieved from https://www.aboutamazon.co.uk/news/working-at-amazon/what-do-each-of-amazons-leadership-principles-really-mean

Amazon Web Services. (n.d.). Netflix on AWS. Retrieved from https://aws.amazon.com/solutions/case-studies/innovators/netflix/

Ambler, S. W. (2001). The Agile Manifesto: Understanding Its Principles and Values. *Agile Modeling*.

Anderson, D. J. (2010). *Kanban: Successful Evolutionary Change for Your Technology Business*. Blue Hole Press.

Appelo, J. (2011). *Management 3.0: Leading Agile Developers, Developing Agile Leaders*. Pearson Education.

Atlassian. (n.d.). Agile Methodologies: A Comprehensive Guide to Agile. Retrieved from https://www.atlassian.com/agile

Atlassian. (n.d.). Atlassian Team Playbook. Retrieved from https://www.atlassian.com/team-playbook

Atlassian. (n.d.). Health Monitor. Retrieved from https://www.atlassian.com/team-playbook/health-monitor

Atlassian. (n.d.). How to Scale Agile: 7 Tips from Agile Leaders. Retrieved from https://www.atlassian.com/agile/agile-at-scale

Atlassian. (n.d.). Scaling Agile @ Atlassian: A Retrospective. Retrieved from https://www.atlassian.com/agile/scaling-agile-atlassian-retrospective

Atlassian. (n.d.). Team Health Monitors for Building High-Performing Teams. Retrieved from https://www.atlassian.com/team-playbook/health-monitor

Atlassian. (n.d.). The Spotify Model for Scaling Agile. Retrieved from https://www.atlassian.com/agile/agile-at-scale/spotify

Atlassian. (n.d.). What is an Agile Team? Definition, Roles, Responsibilities. Retrieved from https://www.atlassian.com/agile/teams

Atlassian. (n.d.). What is Continuous Improvement and Which Tools are Needed. Retrieved from https://www.atlassian.com/agile/project-management/continuous-improvement

Atlassian. (n.d.). Work Life: Everything You Wanted to Know About the Health Monitor (But Were Afraid to Ask). Retrieved from https://www.atlassian.com/blog/inside-atlassian/about-the-team-health-monitor

Austin, R. D. (1996). *Measuring and Managing Performance in Organizations.* Dorset House Publishing.

AWS Executive Insights. (n.d.). High-performing Organization – the Amazon Two Pizza Team. Retrieved from https://aws.amazon.com/executive-insights/content/amazon-two-pizza-team/

Beck, K. (2004). *Extreme Programming Explained: Embrace Change* (2nd Edition). Addison-Wesley Professional.

Beck, K. et al. (2001). A Comparison of Agile Methodologies: Scrum, XP, and Lean. *IEEE Software.*

Beck, K., Beedle, M., Van Bennekum, A., Cockburn, A., Cunningham, W., Fowler, M., et al. (2001). Manifesto for Agile Software Development. Retrieved from http://agilemanifesto.org/

Benefield, G. (2008). *Rolling Out Agile in a Large Enterprise.* Proceedings of the Hawaii International Conference on System Sciences.

Binns, P. (2023). Around 12,500 Jobs at Risk as Wilko Goes into Administration. Retrieved from https://news.sky.com/story/around-12-000-jobs-at-risk-as-wilko-goes-into-administration-12937106

Blockchain Council. (n.d.). How is Amazon Using Blockchain to Increase Its Efficiency? Retrieved from https://www.blockchain-council.org/blockchain/how-is-amazon-using-blockchain-to-increase-its-efficiency/

BMW Group. (n.d.). BMW Group and Local Motors Team Up to Identify the Future of Class-leading Functions for Premium Vehicles in an Urban Environment. Retrieved from https://www.press.bmwgroup.com/global/article/detail/T0132124EN/bmw-group-and-local-motors-team-up-to-identify-the-future-of-class-leading-functions-for-premium-vehicles-in-an-urban-environment?language=en

Bock, L. (2015). *Work Rules!: Insights from Inside Google That Will Transform How You Live and Lead.* Twelve.

The Bridge. (n.d.). How to Build Agile Culture: An Uber Case Study. Retrieved from https://thebridge.social/how-to-build-agile-culture-an-uber-case/

Brittain, M. (n.d.). Etsy's Experimentation and Continuous Delivery Journey. Agile Alliance. Retrieved from https://www.agilealliance.org/resources/experience-reports/etsys-experimentation-and-continuous-delivery-journey/

Business.com. (n.d.). Blockchain: The Future of Business. Retrieved from https://www.business.com/articles/blockchain-future-of-business/

Business Agility Institute. (2020). Business Agility Report. Retrieved from https://businessagility.institute/learn/reports/

Business Insider India. (n.d.). Jeff Bezos' Philosophy for Amazon is that it's Always "Day 1" – Here's What that Means and Why it Works. Retrieved from https://www.businessinsider.in/strategy/news/jeff-bezos-philosophy-for-amazon-is-that-its-always-day-1-heres-what-that-means-and-why-it-works/articleshow/72459617.cms

Cegielski, C. G. & Hazen, B. T. (2016). Diffusion of Innovations Perspective for Assessing Future Directions in Agile Systems Development. *Journal of Systems and Software.*

Choudhury, P., Foroughi, C. & Larson, B. Z. (2021). Work-From-Anywhere: The Productivity Effects of Geographical Flexibility. *Strategic Management Journal.*

CIO. (n.d.). 5 Ways Amazon's Business Metrics Drive Success. Retrieved from https://www.cio.com/article/3429204/5-ways-amazon-s-business-metrics-drive-success.html

CIO. (n.d.). What is Holacracy and Why Does it Work for Zappos? Retrieved from https://www.cio.com/article/244722/what-is-holacracy-and-why-does-it-work-for-zappos.html

Cockburn, A. (2006). *Agile Software Development: The Cooperative Game*. Addison-Wesley Professional.

Code as Craft. (n.d.). Managing and Leading Globally Distributed Teams. Retrieved from https://www.etsy.com/uk/codeascraft/managing-and-leading-globally-distributed-teams?ref=codeascraft

Coffee, P. (2019). How Salesforce Became the World's #1 CRM. ZDNet. Retrieved from https://www.zdnet.com/article/how-salesforce-became-the-worlds-1-crm/

Cohen, D., Lindvall, M. & Costa, P. (2004). An Introduction to Agile Methods. *Advances in Computers*.

Cohn, M. (2004). *User Stories Applied: For Agile Software Development*. Addison-Wesley Signature Series.

Cohn, M. (2005). *Agile Estimating and Planning*. Prentice Hall.

Cohn, M. (2009). *Succeeding with Agile*. Pearson Education.

ConfEngine. (n.d.). Agile on the Edge – Case Study from Uber. Retrieved from https://confengine.com/conferences/agile-india-2021/proposal/15882/agile-on-the-edge-case-study-from-uber

Conner, D. R. (1993). *Managing at the Speed of Change: How Resilient Managers Succeed and Prosper Where Others Fail*. Random House Business.

Coyle, D. (2018). *The Culture Code: The Secrets of Highly Successful Groups*. Bantam Press.

Cusumano, M. & Wu, A. (2020). How Netflix Reinvented HR. *Harvard Business Review*. Retrieved from https://hbr.org/2020/01/how-netflix-reinvented-hr

DCM Learning. (n.d.). Top 8 Industries That Are Adopting Scrum Other Than Software. Retrieved from https://dcmlearning.ie/scrum-resources/top-8-industries-that-are-adopting-scrum-other-than-software.html

Deloitte. (n.d.). The Future of Business Agility: Remote Work and Digital Transformation. Retrieved from https://www2.deloitte.com/us/en/insights/economy/covid-19/remote-work-digital-transformation-business-agility.html

Deloitte US. (n.d.). DevOps and SRE: A Capability Model for these Complementary Roles. Retrieved from https://www2.deloitte.com/us/en/blog/deloitte-on-cloud-blog/2023/devops-SRE-capability-model-for-these-complementary-roles.html

Denning, S. (2018). *The Age of Agile: How Smart Companies Are Transforming the Way Work Gets Done*. AMACOM.

Denning, S. (13 August 2019). Understanding The Agile Mindset. *Forbes.* Retrieved from https://www.forbes.com/sites/stevedenning/2019/08/13/understanding-the-agile-mindset/

Derby, E. & Larsen, D. (2006). *Agile Retrospectives: Making Good Teams Great.* Pragmatic Bookshelf.

Desklib. (n.d.). Uber Case Study Analysis: Challenges, Solutions, and Recommendations. https://desklib.com/document/uber-case-study-analysis/

Diebold, P. et al. (2018). Challenges and Success Factors for Large-Scale Agile Transformations: A Systematic Literature Review. *Journal of Systems and Software.*

Digital.ai. (2020). 14th Annual State of Agile Report. Retrieved from https://www.digital.ai/14th-annual-state-of-agile-report

Digital.ai. (n.d.). Siemens Increases Productivity: Case Studies. Digital.ai. Retrieved from https://www.digital.ai/case-studies/siemens

Digital Works Group. (n.d.). Inside Amazon's Culture of Scaling, Agility and Innovation. Retrieved from https://digitalworksgroup.com/inside-amazons-culture-of-scaling-agility-and-innovation/

Dikert, K., Paasivaara, M. & Lassenius, C. (2016). Challenges and Success Factors for Large-Scale Agile Transformations: A Systematic Literature Review. *Journal of Systems and Software.* Retrieved from https://www.sciencedirect.com/science/article/pii/S0164121216000693

Doerr, J. (2018). *Measure What Matters: How Google, Bono, and the Gates Foundation Rock the World with OKRs.* Portfolio.

Duck, J. D. (1993). Managing Change: The Art of Balancing. *Harvard Business Review.* Retrieved from https://hbr.org/1993/11/managing-change-the-art-of-balancing

Dweck, C. (2006). *Mindset: The New Psychology of Success.* Ballantine Books.

Equal Experts. (n.d.). 7 Common Barriers to Agile Adoption – and How to Overcome Them. Retrieved from https://www.equalexperts.com/blog/our-thinking/7-common-barriers-agile-adoption-ways-overcome/

Etsy DevOps Case Study. (n.d.) The Secret to 50 Plus Deploys a Day. Retrieved from https://www.simform.com/blog/etsy-devops-case-study/

Fitzgerald, M., Kruschwitz, N., Bonnet, D. & Welch, M. (2014). Embracing Digital Technology: A New Strategic Imperative. *MIT Sloan Management Review.*

Forbes. (27 May 2020). 5 Ways Blockchain Will Transform the Future of Business Agility. Retrieved from https://www.forbes.com/sites/theyec/2020/05/27/5-ways-blockchain-will-transform-the-future-of-business-agility/

Forbes. (25 March 2021). AI and the Future of Business Agility. Retrieved from https://www.forbes.com/sites/cognitiveworld/2021/03/25/ai-and-the-future-of-business-agility/

Forbes Business Council. (1 May 2023). Building Agile Teams: 13 Tips to Foster Employee Adaptability. *Forbes.* Retrieved from https://www.forbes.com/sites/forbesbusinesscouncil/2023/05/01/building-agile-teams-13-tips-to-foster-employee-adaptability/

Forbes Technology Council. (2021). AI is the Future of Business: Here's How to Get Ahead. *Forbes.* Retrieved from https://www.forbes.com/sites/forbestechcouncil/2021/02/18/ai-is-the-future-of-business-heres-how-to-get-ahead/?sh=7bb9e53930b9

Forbes Tech Council. (2 December 2021). Tech Leaders Predict the Next Biggest Trends of 2022 and Beyond. Retrieved from https://www.forbes.com/sites/forbestechcouncil/2021/12/02/tech-leaders-predict-the-next-biggest-trends-of-2022-and-beyond/

Forsgren, N., Humble, J. & Kim, G. (2018). *Accelerate: The Science of Lean Software and DevOps.* IT Revolution Press.

Fowler, M. (2022). Introducing a Product Delivery Culture at Etsy. Retrieved from https://martinfowler.com/articles/bottlenecks-of-scaleups/etsy-product-delivery-culture.html

GeekWire. (2017). Jeff Bezos on Amazon's "Day 1" Philosophy. Retrieved from https://www.geekwire.com/2017/jeff-bezos-amazons-day-1-philosophy/

Google. (n.d.). Google's OKRs. Retrieved from https://rework.withgoogle.com/guides/set-goals-with-okrs/steps/introduction/

Gothelf, J. & Seiden, J. (2013). *Lean UX: Applying Lean Principles to Improve User Experience.* O'Reilly Media.

Grinter, R. E. et al. (2014). *Characteristics of High-Performing Agile Teams.* Agile Conference.

Hastings, R. & Meyer, E. (2020). *No Rules Rules: Netflix and the Culture of Reinvention.* Penguin Press.

HBR. (April 2013). How Google Uses People Analytics to Create a Great Workplace. Retrieved from https://hbr.org/2013/04/how-google-uses-data-to-build-a-better-worker

Heath, N. (2016). How Spotify's Agile Framework Has Evolved. *InfoQ*. Retrieved from https://www.infoq.com/news/2016/12/spotify-agile-framework/

Highsmith, J. (2009). *Agile Project Management: Creating Innovative Products.* Addison-Wesley Professional.

Hindel, B. & Tschopp, M. (n.d.). Scaling Agile @ Siemens Healthineers. Agile Alliance. Retrieved from https://www.agilealliance.org/resources/experience-reports/scaling-agile-siemens-healthineers/

Houser, J. S. (n.d.). Using Metrics to Drive Agility: Amazon's Journey. Agile Alliance. Retrieved from https://www.agilealliance.org/resources/experience-reports/using-metrics-to-drive-agility-amazons-journey/

Hsieh, T. (2010). *Delivering Happiness: A Path to Profits, Passion, and Purpose.* Grand Central Publishing.

Humble, J. & Farley, D. (2010). *Continuous Delivery: Reliable Software Releases through Build, Test, and Deployment Automation.* Addison-Wesley.

Hugos, M. H. (2009). *Business Agility: Sustainable Prosperity in a Relentlessly Competitive World.* Wiley.

IBM. (n.d.). Empowering Clients to Be Future-Ready with 5G and Edge Computing. Retrieved from https://www.ibm.com/blog/empowering-clients-to-be-future-ready-with-5g-and-edge-computing/

IBM. (n.d.). IBM Agile Planning. Retrieved from https://www.ibm.com/docs/en/engineering-lifecycle-management-suite/workflow-management/7.0.3?topic=management-agile-planning

Imaginovation Insider. (n.d.). How Cloud Adoption Can Improve Business Agility and Competitiveness. Retrieved from https://imaginovation.net/blog/cloud-adoption-improve-business-agility-competitiveness/

Inc. (n.d.) Google Spent 2 Years Studying 180 Teams. The Most Successful Ones Shared These 5 Traits. Retrieved from https://www.inc.com/michael-schneider/google-thought-they-knew-how-to-create-the-perfect.html

ING. (2017). Our Agile Way of Working. Retrieved from https://www.ing.jobs/Global/Careers/why-would-you/work-at-ing/our-culture/Our-agile-way-of-working.htm

IoT for All. (n.d.). AI and IoT: Transforming Business. Retrieved from https://www.iotforall.com/ai-and-iot-transforming-business

IT Revolution. (n.d.) Case Study: IBM DevOps Transformation. Retrieved from https://itrevolution.com/articles/case-study-ibm-radcliffe/

John Deere. (n.d.). Precision AG Technology. Retrieved from https://www.deere.com/en/technology-products/precision-ag-technology/

Kanellopoulos, C. (2014). The Principles of Agile Execution. *Agile Connection*.

Karnati, S. (2018). Measuring Business Agility: A Comprehensive Framework. *Agile India*.

Kersten, M. (2018). *Project to Product: How to Survive and Thrive in the Age of Digital Disruption with the Flow Framework*. IT Revolution Press.

Kim, G. (2016). Etsy, Sprouter and Conway's Law. IT Revolution. Retrieved from https://itrevolution.com/articles/etsy-sprouter-and-conways-law/

Knaster, R. & Leffingwell, D. (2020). *SAFe 5.0 Distilled: Achieving Business Agility with the Scaled Agile Framework*. Addison-Wesley Professional.

Kniberg, H. (2014). Spotify Engineering Culture (Part 1). Retrieved from https://engineering.atspotify.com/2014/03/spotify-engineering-culture-part-1/

Kniberg, H. (2017). Agile Transformation: Creating an Agile Culture. *InfoQ*.

Kniberg, H. & Ivarsson, A. (2012). Scaling Agile at Spotify with Tribes, Squads, Chapters & Guilds. *InfoQ*. Retrieved from https://www.infoq.com/articles/scaling-agile-spotify/

Kotter, J. P. (1995). Leading Change: Why Transformation Efforts Fail. *Harvard Business Review*. Retrieved from https://hbr.org/1995/05/leading-change-why-transformation-efforts-fail-2

Kotter, J. P. (2012). *Leading Change*. Harvard Business Review Press.

Larman, C. & Vodde, B. (2008). *Scaling Agile: A Guide for the Perplexed*. Addison-Wesley Professional.

Larman, C. & Vodde, B. (2016). *Large-Scale Scrum: More with LeSS*. Addison-Wesley Professional.

Larman, C. & Vodde, B. (2016). Scaling Agile: A Multi-dimensional Challenge. *Communications of the ACM*.

Lashinsky, A. (2017). *Wild Ride: Inside Uber's Quest for World Domination*. Portfolio.

Leading Sapiens. (n.d.). Amazon's 16 Leadership Principles: A Deep Dive. Retrieved from https://www.leadingsapiens.com/amazon-leadership-principles-deep-dive/

Leffingwell, D. (2007). *Scaling Software Agility: Best Practices for Large Enterprises*. Addison-Wesley.

Leffingwell, D. (2011). *Agile Software Requirements: Lean Requirements Practices for Teams, Programs, and the Enterprise.* Addison-Wesley Professional.

Lencioni, P. (2002). *The Five Dysfunctions of a Team: A Leadership Fable.* Jossey-Bass.

Liberty Mind. (n.d.). Zappos – The Culture Everyone Wants to Copy. Retrieved from https://libertymind.co.uk/zappos-the-culture-everyone-wants-to-copy/

Mamoli, S. & Mole, D. (2016). *Creating Great Teams: How Self-Selection Lets People Excel.* Pragmatic Bookshelf.

Marquet, L. D. (2013). *Turn the Ship Around!: A True Story of Turning Followers into Leaders.* Portfolio.

McKinsey. (n.d.). Enterprise Agility: Measuring the Business Impact. Retrieved from https://www.mckinsey.com/capabilities/people-and-organizational-performance/our-insights/enterprise-agility-buzz-or-business-impact

McKinsey & Company. (n.d.). Future of Work. Retrieved from https://www.mckinsey.com/featured-insights/future-of-work

McKinsey & Company. (n.d.). The Impact of Agility: How to Shape Your Organization to Compete. Retrieved from https://www.mckinsey.com/capabilities/people-and-organizational-performance/our-insights/the-impact-of-agility-how-to-shape-your-organization-to-compete

McKinsey & Company. (n.d.). ING's Agile Transformation. Retrieved from https://www.mckinsey.com/industries/financial-services/our-insights/ings-agile-transformation

McKinsey & Company. (n.d.). What Employees Are Saying About the Future of Remote Work. Retrieved from https://www.mckinsey.com/business-functions/organization/our-insights/what-employees-are-saying-about-the-future-of-remote-work

McKinsey Quarterly. (2019). Agile Transformation at Bosch: An Interview with Bosch CIO Elmar Pritsch. Retrieved from https://www.mckinsey.com/business-functions/mckinsey-digital/our-insights/agile-transformation-at-bosch-an-interview-with-bosch-cio-elmar-pritsch

Medium. (n.d.). Airbnb Overcoming Agile Challenges. Retrieved from https://medium.com/airbnb-engineering/how-airbnb-overcomes-the-challenges-of-scale-in-its-engineering-organization-2ff3a3fddabb

Medium. (n.d.). A Culture of Freedom and Responsibility: The Netflix "No Rules" Approach. Retrieved from https://medium.com/people-lab-research/a-culture-of-freedom-and-responsibility-powerful-by-netflix-s-patty-mccord-a623ee3d2d86

Microsoft Learn. (n.d.). Scaling Agile to Large Teams – Azure DevOps. Retrieved from https://learn.microsoft.com/en-us/devops/plan/scaling-agile

Microsoft. (n.d.). Best Practices for Agile Project Management. Retrieved from https://learn.microsoft.com/en-us/azure/devops/boards/best-practices-agile-project-management?view=azure-devops&tabs=agile-process

Microsoft. (n.d.). Microsoft Agile Methodology. Retrieved from https://learn.microsoft.com/en-us/devops/plan/what-is-agile

Minhas, W. et al. (2018). The Role of Leadership in Successful Agile Transformation: A Systematic Literature Review. *International Journal of Agile Systems and Management*.

Mobile Reality. (2023). Top 10 Fast-Growing Fintech Companies in the UK in 2023. Retrieved from https://themobilereality.com/blog/top-10-fast-growing-fintech-comapnies-in-the-uk-in-2023.

Moe, N. B., Dingsøyr, T. & Dybå, T. (2008). Understanding Self-Organizing Teams in Agile Software Development. 19th Australian Software Engineering Conference. Retrieved from https://ieeexplore.ieee.org/document/4413142

Overby, E., Bharadwaj, A. & Sambamurthy, V. (2006). Enterprise Agility and the Enabling Role of Information Technology. *European Journal of Information Systems*.

Overeem, B. (2015). Microsoft's Agile Transformation Journey. Retrieved from https://medium.com/@Barryovereem/microsofts-agile-transformation-journey-eade6c1768db

Palan, H. (n.d.). Agile at Uber: How We Do It. Agile Alliance. Retrieved from https://www.agilealliance.org/resources/experience-reports/agile-at-uber-how-we-do-it/

Patton, J. (2014). *User Story Mapping: Discover the Whole Story, Build the Right Product*. O'Reilly Media.

Pichler, R. (2016). Agile Planning: A Step-by-Step Guide. *InfoQ*.

Planview. (n.d.). Selling Agile to Executives: 8 Ways to Get Buy-in. Retrieved from https://blog.planview.com/selling-agile-to-executives-8-ways-to-get-buy-in/

Professional Development. (n.d.) Spotify. A Case Study in Successful Agile Culture. Retrieved from https://www.professionaldevelopment.ie/spotify-and-agile-a-case-study-on-agile-environments

ProjectManager.com. (n.d.). What is Agile? A Definition of Agile Project Management. Retrieved from https://www.projectmanager.com/agile-project-management

Prosci. (2003). ADKAR® Model. Retrieved from https://www.prosci.com/adkar/adkar-model

Rigby, D. K., Sutherland, J. & Noble, A. (2018). Agile at Scale. *Harvard Business Review*. Retrieved from https://hbr.org/2018/05/agile-at-scale

Rigby, D. K., Sutherland, J. & Takeuchi, H. (2016). Embracing Agile. *Harvard Business Review*. Retrieved from https://hbr.org/2016/05/embracing-agile

Rousseau, D. M. (2018). *Evidence-Based Management: How to Use Evidence to Make Better Organizational Decisions*. Kogan Page.

Salesforce. (n.d.). An Agile Case Study. Retrieved from https://resources.scrumalliance.org/Article/salesforce-an-agile-case-study

Salesforce. (n.d.). An Agile Case Study – Scrum Alliance. Retrieved from https://resources.scrumalliance.org/Article/salesforce-an-agile-case-study

Salesforce. (September 2016). Salesforce Agile Processes. Retrieved from https://www.salesforce.com/blog/2016/09/salesforce-agile-processes.html

Salesforce Trailhead. (n.d.). Learn Salesforce Agile Practices. Retrieved from https://trailhead.salesforce.com/content/learn/trails/learn-salesforce-agile-practices

Schmidt, E. & Rosenberg, J. (2014). *How Google Works*. Grand Central Publishing.

Schwaber, K. & Sutherland, J. (2017). The Scrum Guide. Retrieved from https://www.scrumguides.org/docs/scrumguide/v2017/2017-Scrum-Guide-US.pdf

Scrum Alliance. (n.d.). The Agile Leader: The Role of Leadership in Agile Software Development. Retrieved from https://www.scrumalliance.org/agile-leadership

Scrum.org. (n.d.). So, What is Organizational Agility? 2022 Update. Retrieved from https://www.scrum.org/resources/blog/so-what-organizational-agility-2022-update

Senge, P. (1990). *The Fifth Discipline: The Art and Practice of the Learning Organization*. Doubleday/Currency.

Serrador, P. & Pinto, J. K. (2015). Does Agile Work? – A Quantitative Analysis of Agile Project Success. *International Journal of Project Management*.

Shore, J. & Warden, S. (2007). *The Art of Agile Development*. O'Reilly Media.

Siemens. (n.d.). Seven Lessons Learned in Agile. Retrieved from https://resources. sw.siemens.com/en-US/white-paper-seven-lessons-agile

Siemens. (n.d.). Increase Efficiency with Agile Software Development. Retrieved from https://resources.sw.siemens.com/en-US/white-paper-achieving-agile-soft-ware-development-in-complex-environments

Siemens. (n.d.). Siemens Agile Methodology. Retrieved from https://www.plm. automation.siemens.com/global/en/our-story/agile-development.html

Simform. (n.d.). How Netflix Became a Master of DevOps? An Exclusive Case Study. Retrieved from https://www.simform.com/blog/netflix-devops-case-study/

Smartsheet. (n.d.). A Best Practices Guide to Agile Planning for Project Managers. Retrieved from https://www.smartsheet.com/best-practices-guide-agile-planning-project-managers

Spayd, M. & Madore, M. (2017). *Agile Transformation: Using the Integral Agile Transformation Framework to Think and Lead Differently*. Addison-Wesley Professional.

Spotify Engineering. (2021). Agile at Spotify. Retrieved from https://engineering. atspotify.com/2021/03/08/agile-at-spotify/

Spotify Labs. (27 March 2014). Spotify Engineering Culture Part 1. Retrieved from https://labs.spotify.com/2014/03/27/spotify-engineering-culture-part-1/

Squirrel, D. (n.d.). How We Scaled Agile at Airbnb. Agile Alliance. Retrieved from https://www.agilealliance.org/resources/experience-reports/how-we-scaled-agile-at-airbnb/

Stanton, D. M. & Fisher, D. L. (2021). The Future of Agile: How the Next Generation is Transforming the Workplace. *Agile 20 Reflect Festival*.

Steiber, A. & Alänge, S. (2013). A Corporate System for Continuous Innovation: The Case of Google Inc. *European Journal of Innovation Management*.

Stone, B. (2013). *The Everything Store: Jeff Bezos and the Age of Amazon*. Little, Brown and Company.

Sutherland, J. & Sutherland, J. J. (2014). *Scrum: The Art of Doing Twice the Work in Half the Time*. Crown Business.

Talukder, M. & Quazi, A. (2016). The Impact of Social Networking on Business Agility. *Procedia Economics and Finance*.

Van Lamsweerde, A. (2009). *Requirements Engineering: From System Goals to UML Models to Software Specifications*. Wiley.

VisionX. (n.d.). How to Use AI to Improve Agile Software Development Process? Retrieved from https://visionx.io/blog/agile-software-development-process/

Wavelength. (n.d.). Developing a Self-Managed Team at Zappos. https://wavelength.asana.com/zappos-self-managed-team/

Wired. (n.d.). Inside Airbnb's Innovation and Design Lab. Retrieved from https://www.wired.com/2017/03/inside-airbnbs-innovation-and-design-lab/

World Economic Forum. (2020). The Future of Jobs Report 2020. Retrieved from http://www3.weforum.org/docs/WEF_Future_of_Jobs_2020.pdf

Yohn, D. L. (2019). What You Can Learn from Netflix's Culture of Reinvention. *Forbes*. Retrieved from https://www.forbes.com/sites/deniselyohn/2019/02/20/what-you-can-learn-from-netflixs-culture-of-reinvention/

Zappos. (n.d.). Our 10 Core Values. Retrieved from https://www.zappos.com/about/what-we-live-by

Zumvie. (n.d.). History of Agile: What Can We Learn from Microsoft's Agile Transformation Journey? Retrieved from https://www.zumvie.com/history-of-agile-what-can-we-learn-from-microsoft-and-cisco/

Acknowledgements

None of this would have been possible without the help of my wife and best friend, Anneke. She read and reviewed every draft chapter and gave me much feedback that I accepted (most of the time). It is safe to say that if it had been the other way around, the feedback I would have shared would not have been so happily accepted. Listening to all the fantastic feedback Anneke provided throughout made this book a reality.

I also have to give a shout-out to my mother-in-law Penny, who reviewed the content more for spelling and grammar improvements than anything else but gained considerable insight into the domain of Business Agility. I hope you now understand more about what I care about daily.

Writing a book is a lot harder than I thought and more rewarding than I could ever have imagined. Russ Lewis, a great friend, expert Business Agilist, supporter and reviewer of my book-writing journey, told me that you never set out to write a book for others, you set out to write a book for yourself; this has become a cathartic exercise for me over the last few months. Thank you for all your amazing support throughout this experience. I really appreciate it.

Writing a book about much of what you have discovered in your professional career is surreal. To all the individuals I have had the opportunity to lead, to be led by successfully or to watch their leadership from afar, thank you for inspiring me to perform the job I love doing daily.

To all those managers or peers I have had in my career who failed in their leadership roles due to bureaucracy, micromanagement and command and control tendencies in not allowing Agile to succeed or getting rid of it, I wish you well in whatever you are doing now.

A big thanks goes to Brian Proffitt, who took a chance on me in 2016 and let me lead, coach and transform an underperforming technology department, only to see them make outcome improvements of 800%–900% in the first 12 months alone. Your guidance and mentorship helped shape me into the technology leader I am today.

To all the courageous people who have let me lead, coach, train and mentor them over many years, I am eternally grateful for the opportunity to do so and for the learning and feedback given.

A very special thanks to Neil Walker and T. C. Gill, not only for all your amazing feedback on draft copies of the book but also for being my partners in crime in launching the UK Chapter of the Business Agility Institute. The effort we have put in, being supported by the awesome pair of Evan Leybourne and Laura Powers on the journey, has made it all worthwhile.

To the "DaD boys", Mandeep, Ash and Afeez, thanks for being on the Agile journey twice with me over the years. I could not have achieved it all without you. Let's do it again sometime.

In thanking people who have helped shape my Agile career, I also have to give special thanks to Mark Lines and Scott Ambler, co-creators of Disciplined Agile. I first picked up their book in 2013, and its pragmatic guidance has helped shape my career and enhanced my leadership ability over the years. Being on stage along with Mark at Business Agility conferences, virtual seminars and online workshops have been real career highlights.

I have to say thank you to Dominic Hilleard, who, during the COVID-19 pandemic, gave such supportive advice over many phone calls, keeping me sane while I was looking for the next opportunity, such that I had the courage to start my own business and see it grow over the last few years. I remember all the supportive calls and where I took them as if it was yesterday – thanks, Dom.

Thank you to Peter Stojanovic, who gave me such positive and warm feedback after I asked him to read a couple of my blog posts, which ultimately became the basis of the first two chapters. Without that support, I am not sure how far I would have gone with this.

Just one example of his feedback: "Had a read of the two posts, and they're great reads. I can see why 'even' your mum understands them: you signpost the articles nicely, the pace is good, and sentences are short and simple."

Thank you to Avril Chester, who gave me such amazing feedback and information about book publishing, along with many great contacts. I appreciate the help you gave me when I was blocked. Thank you ever so much.

I have to thank Ashleigh Dueker for co-hosting the amazing Agility Leadership Network with me for a number of amazing years. The people we met on the journey were incredible.

Thanks to Sheetal Thaker for allowing me to co-host the Agile Xpertise Meetup Group, helping each other rediscover our Agile mojo during a couple of tough years.

Thank you also to Shellianne Duffin, who read an early draft for me and also gave me such detailed feedback too. I appreciate the effort you put in on this.

I also have to thank Paul Keaveny who suggested I share a talk I gave in January 2020 to every CEO in London. That talk was one of the catalysts in writing this book, so that I could get the message out to every CEO, and not just in London.

To Ian Mulvany and the amazing people at BMJ, Anthony Eskinazi and the amazing people at JustPark, Flemming Bengsten and the amazing people at Nimbla and Sinéad McHale and the amazing people at Satago, thank you for letting me lead the Agile charge. Thanks to all the fantastic people in these awesome organizations over the last few years on their ongoing Agile journey for supporting the change throughout. Your support, learning and feedback have made this book possible.

Finally, to all my friends and colleagues in both the CxO communities and the Agile communities who have been a part of my journey in getting to this point today. There are too many to name, but you know who you are and will forever have my eternal thanks.

About the Author

Giles is a seasoned senior technology executive, CEO of Agile Delta Consulting, a global Agile consulting and coaching business and an award-winning Agile expert passionate about empowering organizations to achieve their full potential through strategic planning, operational excellence and continuous improvement. With over 25 years' experience in the technology industry, Giles has been at the forefront of digital transformation initiatives, leading global cross-functional teams in successfully delivering innovative software solutions.

As a certified Agile practitioner, instructor, coach and keynote speaker at Agile conferences, Giles is well versed in Agile ways of working, enabling teams to optimize performance and embrace a culture of innovation. Adept at fostering talent development and mentorship, Giles is dedicated to nurturing and retaining top talent while guiding professionals to achieve their career aspirations.

Giles and several colleagues in the UK are currently working with the Business Agility Institute to set up the first Global BAI Chapter for the UK and will assume the role of President upon its launch. He is also the co-founder of the Agility Leadership Network, which hosts meetups on various Business Agility-based topics.

Previously, Giles served as a Disciplined Agile Consortium Advisory Council member for over two years before PMI acquired the rights to Disciplined Agile. Following this acquisition, he was asked to join the newly formed PMI Disciplined Agile Advisors Group in 2021. As an Ambassador for the UK for the "Agile 20 Reflect Festival" in February 2021, Giles celebrated 20 years of the Agile Manifesto by co-hosting one of the festival's largest individual events, with over 1,300 virtual attendees.

On a lighter note, amidst his professional accolades, Giles has garnered unique souvenirs throughout his Agile journey. Upon leaving a company in 2022, one such memento was a pizza-sized cookie affectionately emblazoned with "Best Agile Coach Ever!". Adding to this collection, he was gifted a promotional video documenting Agile practices' transformative success at one Fintech organization. In another venture, he was honoured with a T-shirt, symbolizing the continuing success of an Agile transformation. Jokingly, he often remarks, "Now I've got the

Book, the Film, and the T-shirt". Writing this book seemed a fitting endeavour to complete this trifecta.

Giles has held leadership roles at global technology companies throughout his career, driving growth and innovation while navigating complex stakeholder relationships with skill. His experience spans various industries, including finance, telecommunications, travel and healthcare. He has consistently demonstrated a keen ability to identify and manage potential risks, ensuring timely and appropriate mitigation strategies.

As a Fellow of the Chartered Management Institute (FCMI), the BCS, The Chartered Institute for IT (FBCS) and The Institution of Analysts & Programmers (FIAP), Giles is recognized as an esteemed professional in his field. He has presented at conferences and seminars internationally, sharing his insights and experiences with other industry professionals. He is known for his ability to articulate complex concepts in an accessible manner, making it easier for others to understand and adopt Agile principles in their organizations.

In *Clearly Agile: A Leadership Guide to Business Agility*, Giles draws on his wealth of experience and expertise, offering valuable guidance and practical advice for business leaders seeking to embrace Agile practices and create more nimble, responsive organizations. Giles aims to inspire and equip readers with the tools they need to navigate the challenges of our changing business environment and unlock the full potential of their organizations. Whether you are a seasoned executive, an aspiring leader or an Agile enthusiast, Giles' book promises to be an indispensable resource in your professional growth and success journey.

Index

Note: References in *italics* are to the Glossary, those in **bold** to tables.

A quick word from Practical Inspiration Publishing...

We hope you found this book both practical and inspiring – that's what we aim for with every book we publish.

We publish titles on topics ranging from leadership, entrepreneurship, HR and marketing to self-development and wellbeing.

Find details of all our books at: www.practicalinspiration.com

 Did you know...

We can offer discounts on bulk sales of all our titles – ideal if you want to use them for training purposes, corporate giveaways or simply because you feel these ideas deserve to be shared with your network.

We can even produce bespoke versions of our books, for example with your organization's logo and/or a tailored foreword.

To discuss further, contact us on info@practicalinspiration.com.

 Got an idea for a business book?

We may be able to help. Find out more about publishing in partnership with us at: bit.ly/PIpublishing.

Follow us on social media...

🐦 @PIPTalking

📷 @pip_talking

f @practicalinspiration

♪ @piptalking

in Practical Inspiration Publishing

Printed in the USA
CPSIA information can be obtained
at www.ICGtesting.com
JSHW011551010724
65693JS00008B/128

9 781788 605489